Early praise for *iOS 9 SDK Development*

I like this book. I like its approach to building something real in Swift. The result is an app that feels good and is useful. Along the way, you learn the basics of iOS development from an experienced pro. Highly recommended.

➤ **Eric J. Knapp**
Program Director, Mobile Applications Development, Madison College

iOS 9 SDK Development is the perfect book to get your feet wet with iOS. The authors introduce you to iOS by way of Swift, giving you cutting-edge skills at the perfect time. Whether you're new to programming or simply new to Apple platforms, this book will leave you ready to create your own amazing apps.

➤ **Jeff Kelley**
iOS developer at Detroit Labs and author of *Developing for Apple Watch, Second Edition*

This book neatly covers building apps with iOS 9 from the ground up, starting with the basic tools and the nuances of the Swift language, and then progressing through interface design. You'll see how to build interfaces that auto-resize cleanly to multiple screen sizes. There's more to building an app than just assembling the pieces and getting it to compile. With *iOS 9 SDK Development*, you'll also learn invaluable testing practices, and the right approach using the tools at your disposal to fix things when they go wrong. The chapters on closures are particularly well placed for people new to Swift. I'd recommend this book to anyone.

➤ **Kevin J. Garriott**
Director, Mobile Technology, Rockfish

Not many books cover both programming interfaces and deeper software engineering topics. It's refreshing to see both covered, expertly, in one book. Chris and Janie are masters at making technical content approachable. It's like having two of your best friends teaching you iOS.

➤ **Mark Dalrymple**
Author of *Advanced Mac OS X Programming: The Big Nerd Ranch Guide* and co-founder of CocoaHeads, the international Mac and iOS programming community

Whether you're new to iOS programming or just need some help getting up to speed on iOS and Swift, this is the perfect book for you. Chris and Janie take you on a well-thought-out and fun journey into iOS SDK development.

➤ **Dave Klein**
Founder of CocoaConf and author of *Grails: A Quick-Start Guide*

iOS 9 SDK Development

Creating iPhone and iPad Apps with Swift

Chris Adamson with Janie Clayton

The Pragmatic Bookshelf

Dallas, Texas • Raleigh, North Carolina

Many of the designations used by manufacturers and sellers to distinguish their products are claimed as trademarks. Where those designations appear in this book, and The Pragmatic Programmers, LLC was aware of a trademark claim, the designations have been printed in initial capital letters or in all capitals. The Pragmatic Starter Kit, The Pragmatic Programmer, Pragmatic Programming, Pragmatic Bookshelf, PragProg and the linking *g* device are trademarks of The Pragmatic Programmers, LLC.

Every precaution was taken in the preparation of this book. However, the publisher assumes no responsibility for errors or omissions, or for damages that may result from the use of information (including program listings) contained herein.

Our Pragmatic courses, workshops, and other products can help you and your team create better software and have more fun. For more information, as well as the latest Pragmatic titles, please visit us at *https://pragprog.com*.

The team that produced this book includes:

Rebecca Gulick (editor)
Potomac Indexing, LLC (index)
Liz Welch (copyedit)
Dave Thomas (layout)
Janet Furlow (producer)

For international rights, please contact *rights@pragprog.com*.

Printed in the United States of America.
ISBN-13: 978-1-68050-132-2
Printed on acid-free paper.
Book version: P1.0—March 2016

Contents

Part II — Creating the App

Part IV — Beyond the App

Acknowledgments

One of these years, we'll be able to do a book where the information stays good for longer than a year, right? If so, apparently it won't be about iOS. Once again, Apple's annual update of its mobile OS and tools has unleashed a torrent of changes. At this point, it's not even a question of leaving last year's book on the shelf for a while longer; last year's code *doesn't even compile anymore.*

So, for this book being in your hands or on your screen, thanks start with the Pragmatic Programmers. Working with the Prags themselves, Dave and Andy, and Susannah Pfalzer, recognized the need for the Prags introductory book on iOS to become an annual thing, if it's to be a viable title and serve as a prerequisite for other Prags iOS titles. Together, we worked out a plan that would make for a book with enough new content and revisions to be worthy of a new release, without killing the primary author by trying to get 300 pages out of him in five months (while holding down a day job). Of course, that still wouldn't have been possible without the support of editor Rebecca Gulick, who helped keep everything on track, caught lots of mistakes, and had a keen ear for when the prose needed to stop info-dumping and work more intuitively with the reader.

Thanks also go out to friends and colleagues in the Mac/iOS (and watchOS and tvOS...) development community, who helped out with questions, feedback, and encouragement on Twitter and IRL at conferences like WWDC and CocoaConf. Speaking of CocoaConf, thanks as always to Dave Klein and his family for putting on that traveling event, which is still my favorite way to meet fellow developers and catch up on the state of the art of iOS programming, outside of Apple's official channels.

Speaking of conferences, Janie spent most of the summer and fall putting together ambitious new talks for CocoaConf, 360iDev, and CocoaLove, so she was quite limited in what she could contribute to the book this time around. Still, we've incorporated all her work from the previous book, and updated it for iOS 9, and she did give us a new story sidebar about her continuing development as an iOS developer. It's been great to watch her career take off over the last few years, and if you see her speaking at a conference near you, be sure to go see her.

Once again, the Prags' "beta book" process allowed us to roll out a mostly complete book for early feedback as soon as Apple's NDA dropped, allowing us to make improvements and corrections while finishing up the last few chapters. The book's tech reviewers also gave us great feedback to build on: thanks to Jacob Chae, Kevin Garriott, Gábor László Hajba, Laura Hart, Carlos Lopez, Wil Moore III, Mario Tatis, and Stephen Wolff.

As always, thanks to family members who got used to the office door being closed and the headphones blocking everything out while I banged away in TextMate and Xcode (and sometimes banged on my desk because of the latter) for too many evenings and weekends.

Obligatory end-of-book music check: This time it was Metric, Joe Jackson, Dire Straits, Minami Kuribayashi, Yuki Kajiura, and Scandal (the one from Japan, not the one from the '80s). Current musical stats at http://www.last.fm/user/invalidname.

Preface

It's hard to remember a time without mobile apps. For a 10-year-old who uses an iPad to watch videos, play games, and draw pictures, apps have always been a part of his or her life. There are over a million and a half iOS apps out there, running on iPhones, iPads, iPod touches, and now Apple Watches. It's tempting to say that apps aren't novel, or that they're not a big deal anymore.

But that's like saying the web isn't a big deal. Of course it is. And for mobile users, the app often replaces the web. Apps are faster, more secure, more immediate, and more personal than any web page can be. When you use an app, you have a sense that it's *yours*, because everything it's doing is happening right there in your hands.

This immediacy is a big part of what makes writing iOS apps so compelling. It's also what makes it so different from other kinds of development. If you've done web development before, on the server or in the browser, some of it will seem familiar, and yet much will be quite different. Writing apps places different responsibilities on the developer, and gives you different opportunities.

In this book, we're going to jump into development for iOS, the leading mobile platform, atop which literally millions of apps have been written, installed and run on hundreds of millions of devices. Soon, yours can be one of them.

About This Edition

This is the fourth time Pragmatic Programmers has offered an introductory book for iOS developers. The previous entries were *iPhone SDK Development* in 2009 (covering iPhone OS 3), *iOS SDK Development* in 2012 (for iOS 6), and *iOS 8 SDK Development* in 2014 (for iOS 8).

Notice that instead of a two-to-three-year gap like the previous titles, the book you're holding is coming out just one year and one iOS version after the previous one. The motivation for this is that the platform has developed so quickly that the previous books were near-total rewrites of their predecessors, which took years to finish, yet quickly became dated with the release of a new version of the OS and its software development tools.

Also weighing on our minds is the fact that because of all of the changes in Swift 2.0, most of the code from the iOS 8 book doesn't even compile anymore.

So we're trying something different this year: a refresh, not a reboot. Instead of rewriting the whole book every three years, we're going to try to rewrite roughly a third of it every year. If this plan works, it means a perpetually up-to-date title for beginning iOS developers, whenever they happen to decide they're ready to give the platform a try.

For this year's edition, specifically, we targeted our handling of the Swift programming language. After a year in the wild (with both authors using it extensively or exclusively in their day jobs), the language is ready to be taken seriously and described in detail. So whereas our iOS 8 book treated Swift as a means to an end (namely, calling the various iOS frameworks), this year we put Swift front-and-center. The first three chapters are an entirely new introduction to the Swift language itself, working in coding "playgrounds" to get us ready to build real apps. The next two chapters after that were inspired by the previous book, but are radically rewritten and reorganized to ease the transition into full-on app development.

None of this should be inferred as saying the rest of the book is a copy-and-paste job. Every example in the book has been rewritten from scratch to take advantage of the Swift 2.0 programming language and its features. Many chapters also have entirely new sections to cover new iOS 9 features, such as automated UI testing (see *User Interface Testing*, on page 110) and stack views (see *Stack Views and the User Detail View Controller*, on page 192). Also, we have completely rewritten the final chapter, Chapter 17, *Publishing and Maintaining the App*, on page 289, to include Apple's TestFlight beta-testing service and the many changes to its developer Member Center and iTunes Connect sites.

So Here's the Plan

Our goal for this book is to create a plausibly realistic and useful app, to the point where we can take it through the process of publication on the App Store in the final chapter. To accomplish this, we will spend a few chapters playing around with the Swift language, and then create the app project and slowly build out its functionality. This approach is similar to real-world development, so much so that we'll take time partway through to reorganize our work for maintainability and code reuse. We'll also spend time on important non-code topics, like testing and debugging, which are crucial and sometimes overlooked parts of the development process.

With that in mind, here's where our journey will take us:

Expectations and Technical Requirements

The technical requirements for iOS development are pretty simple: the latest version of Xcode, and a Mac OS X computer that can run it. As of December 2015, that means Xcode 7.1 or later, and a Mac running OS X 10.10.5 ("Yosemite") or 10.11 ("El Capitan").

All code in this book uses the Swift programming language. Swift is a performant, practical language that Apple clearly intends to be the future of all development for its platforms. When it was open-sourced in late 2015, the "About Swift" page declared:

> The goal of the Swift project is to create the best available language for uses ranging from systems programming, to mobile and desktop apps, scaling up to cloud services. Most importantly, Swift is designed to make writing and maintaining correct programs easier for the developer.

On the same page, it says that Swift "is intended as a replacement for C-based languages (C, C++, and Objective-C)." That's not an unreasonable goal! Swift is a neat language that cleans out a lot of cruft from C and Objective-C, while also drawing inspiration from functional programming languages like Haskell.

We're sure you'll be able to pick it up quickly, provided you're a proficient programmer in at least one object-oriented language. That can be one of the many curly-brace descendants of C (C++, C#, or Java), or an OO scripting language like Ruby or Python.

Online Resources

This book isn't just about static words on a page or screen. It comes with a web page, https://www.pragprog.com/titles/adios3, where you can learn more and access useful resources:

- Download the complete source code for all the code examples in the book as ready-to-build Xcode projects.

- Participate in a discussion forum with other readers, fellow developers, and the authors.

- Help improve the book by reporting errata, such as content suggestions and typos.

If you're reading the ebook, you can also access the source file for any code listing by clicking on the gray-green rectangle before the listing.

As we build our sample projects in this book, we will often write simple code, only to rewrite it with more ambitious code later as our knowledge increases.

All the different versions would be hard to put in one source file. So in the downloadable book code, we often have multiple copies of each project, each representing a different stage of its development. The different stages use numbered folders, like PragmaticTweets-1-1, PragmaticTweets-2-1, and so on, with the first number representing the chapter number and the second being a revision within that chapter. These folder names also appear in the captions for each code example in the text. You can either code along for the entire book from scratch, or copy over one of these "stages" and pick up from there.

And Here We Go

With our expectations set and our goal in mind, let's head into our first task: getting our tools set up and learning just enough Swift to make our devices do neat stuff.

Part I

Coding in Swift

CHAPTER 1

Playing with Xcode

In this chapter, you'll get a taste of what iOS development is like. You'll set up the tools for creating iOS apps, flex your fingers by playing around with some code, and learn how to find your way in the development environment.

You'll start by simply playing around, and by the time you're done, you'll be ready to ship an app.

There is one must-have tool for iOS development: *Xcode*. This integrated development environment (IDE) will be where we do nearly all our work of developing, testing, and unleashing iOS apps. Xcode lets us build our apps, run them, debug them, and submit them to App Store. There's very little in this book that *won't* involve working in Xcode.

Tooling Up with Xcode

So let's get Xcode on our Macs. Yes, we did say "Mac." Xcode is a native application that is only available for Mac OS X. Typically, it is available for the current version of OS X, and (sometimes) one version back. For this book, we will be working with Xcode 7, running on El Capitan (Mac OS X 10.11) or Yosemite (Mac OS X 10.10).

We get Xcode from the Mac App Store, which is always available from the Apple menu in any application. Search for Xcode in the store, and click the Get button. Don't worry, it's free, but you will need to have an Apple ID to get apps from the store. Actually, you'll need an Apple ID for a bunch of other tasks later, so create an Apple ID now if you don't have one, either in the Mac App Store app or at https://appleid.apple.com.

Xcode is an *integrated development environment* (IDE), meaning it combines many of the tools we need to create apps:

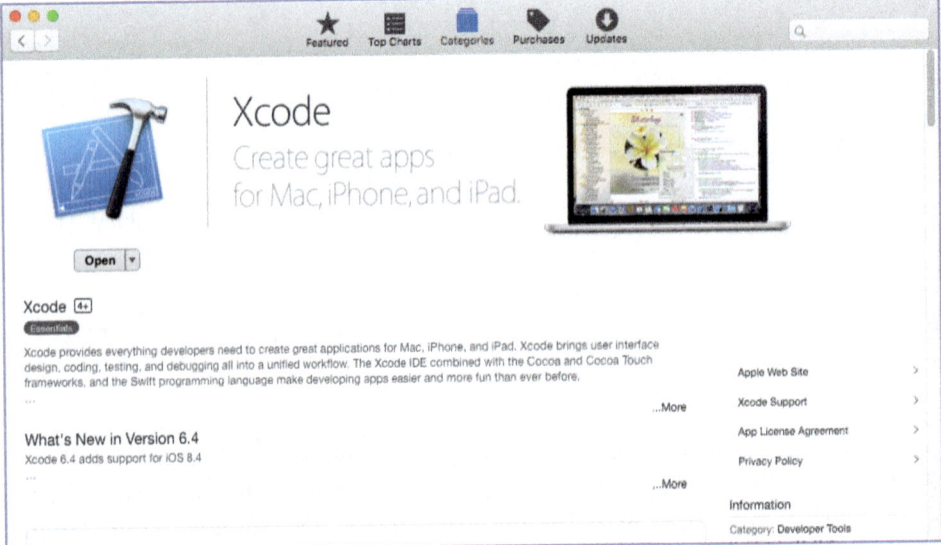

- A *text editor*, in which we write code

- *Interface Builder*, for creating user interfaces visually, rather than in code

- A *build system*, to convert our source code and user interface files into runnable apps

- A *Simulator*, allowing us to run our apps in a window on the Mac, which is sometimes more convenient than running on an actual device

- *Debugging tools*, which help us find and fix errors in our code

- *Profiling tools*, for finding performance bottlenecks at runtime

- *Testing tools*, to verify the correctness of our code and ensure that fixed bugs do not return

- A *documentation viewer*, containing the full developer documentation for the iOS, OS X, and watchOS SDKs

- *Organizational tools*, for preparing and archiving the apps we submit to the App Store

That's a lot of stuff to fit in one app! It might be overwhelming, but our first run of Xcode will offer a pretty gentle introduction. Launch Xcode from the Applications folder (you may want to put it in your Dock, too), and click OK if it asks to install additional components, which are the command-line executables that will build our projects for us. When we get to the first window, Xcode keeps things simple:

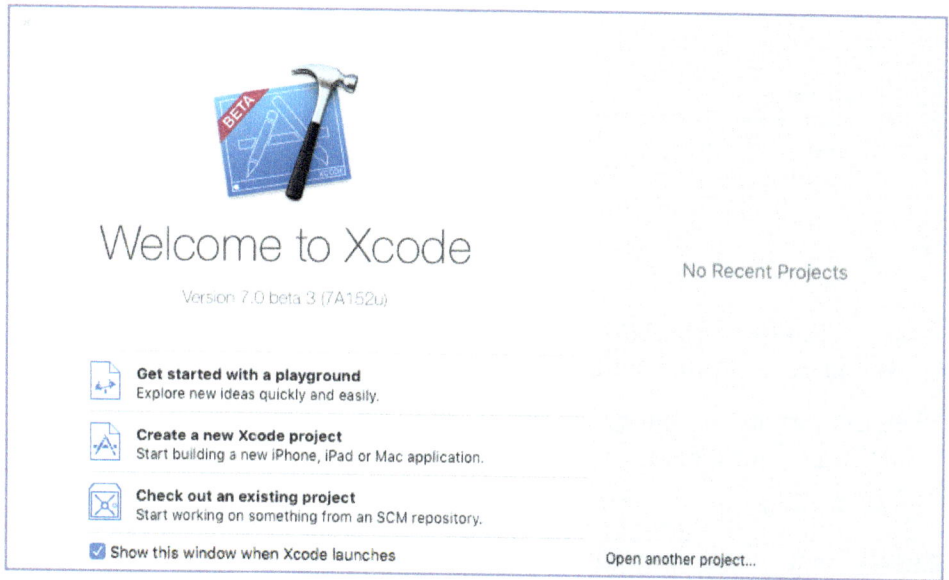

We start with three simple options: "Get started with a playground," "Create a new Xcode project," and "Check out an existing project." On the right, there's a blank space that says No Recent Projects as we start working in Xcode; this will fill in with a list of our Xcode creations.

For now, let's start off with a little directed play.

Messing Around in a Playground

We'll start getting a feel for programming for iOS in what Xcode calls a *playground*, so click the "Get started with a playground" button. This brings up a new window, with a sheet showing two options for the playground: a name (defaulting to My Playground) and a platform. Make sure the platform is set to iOS, accept the default name, and click Next. Now we have to choose a destination folder to store the playground file. Anything will do here—Desktop, Documents, whatever—so pick something and click Create.

This brings up a window like the following, with a toolbar and status pane at top, a source editor on the left, an empty pane on the right, and a time slider at the bottom that says "30 sec." For a moment, the status indicator will say Running MyPlayground..., and then the text "Hello, playground" will appear in the right pane, directly across from the source code line var str = "Hello, playground".

What's happening here is that the playground is an interactive environment for writing and running small snippets of code. Anything we type in will be immediately executed—as long as it's valid code—and the results shown on the right side. By default, there is a single line of code that creates a string

("Hello, playground") and assigns it to the variable str. The result of this assignment is also the return value, which is why it shows up in the results pane.

Well, two can play at that game, right? On a new line at the bottom, let's write something really simple:

```
var two = 1 + 1
```

After a moment, the number 2 appears in the results pane.

Great, now we can do some math. Let's add another line to use that result:

```
two = two * two
```

As we expect, the number 4 appears in the results pane.

That's all well and good, but it's not much better than we could achieve with a calculator, or even by punching mathematical expressions into the Spotlight search bar. Let's think of something a little more ambitious.

Getting Serious on the Playground

I know, let's write a streaming web radio application!

Don't panic; this isn't as scary as you think. We can get this running with shockingly little code. But let's do so in a new playground. Close the current playground window, and use File > New > Playground to create a new playground. Call it WebRadioPlayground. Keep the line that says import UIKit, but delete the var str = "Hello, playground" line, and replace it with the following:

playing/WebRadioPlayground.playground/Contents.swift

```
Line 1  import AVFoundation
     2  let url = NSURL(string: "http://armitunes.com:8010/listen.pls")
     3  let player = AVPlayer(URL: url!)
     4  player.play()
```

Nothing will happen just yet, but hang in there...

The code we've written is in a language called *Swift*, introduced by Apple in 2014 for iOS and OS X development. It's a flexible language that's well suited to various styles of programming, as we'll see throughout the book. Swift is also the *only* language we can use inside a playground. You can also use C, C++, or Objective-C to write apps, but we'll only use Swift in this book.

Line 1 tells the Swift compiler that we want to use *AV Foundation*, a programming framework that lets us bring audio and video features to our apps. On line 2, we create a URL for the station we want to play. Technically, this is an NSURL object, which we create by passing in a string.

Line 3 creates an AVPlayer, which is an object that can play various kinds of audio and video media. We create it with the url on the previous line, and the ! character is our assertion that the url is valid and not nil. This is actually a dangerous practice—we're not really in a position to know whether the URL is valid—and is something we will want to fix up a little later. Finally, on line 4, we tell the player to start playing.

Be Your Own DJ

You don't have to use our default URL, especially if you don't share our silly affection for anime theme songs. We just chose this URL because the http://armitunes.com site has been up for more than 10 years, so we felt it was a safe choice for this example.

Feel free to find a station you like in iTunes' Internet Radio section (but not the Radio section, which is only for Apple Music subscribers), and while it's playing, use Get Info (⌘I) to show its URL. Copy and paste this string in the storyboard. The AVPlayer class can handle the sort of HTTP-based audio streams seen in the Internet Radio section, so thousands of choices are available.

The results pane will show the URL string next to the line that creates the NSURL, and the lines involving the player will show AVPlayer and a big (64-bit) hexadecimal number (the player object's address in memory, which does us no good here). But nothing's actually playing, right?

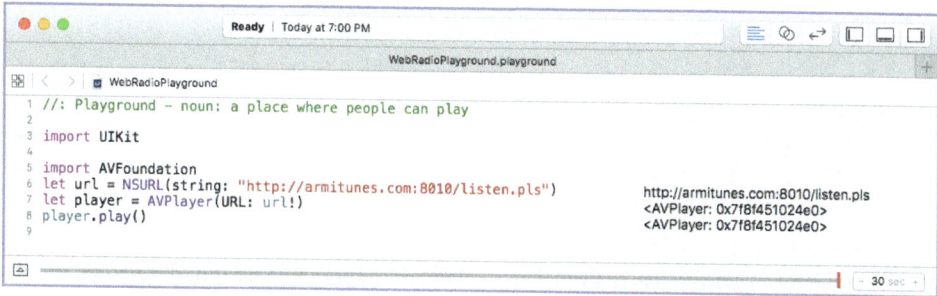

We need to do one special thing for this example. Swift is a language with built-in memory management that frees unused objects for us. Once we say player.play(), all the code in the playground has been executed, and Xcode assumes it's OK to clean everything up. Unfortunately, this results in the immediate destruction of the player object that we want to play our audio!

When we have a case where we want the contents of the playground to hang around after the initial execution finishes, we need to send a special command to Xcode to do so. Add the following to the end of the playground code:

playing/WebRadioPlayground.playground/Contents.swift

```
Line 1  import XCPlayground
     2  XCPlaygroundPage.currentPage.needsIndefiniteExecution = true
```

The import statement on line 1 tells the playground to load the functions and methods that let us interact with the playground execution itself, and the XCPlaygroundPage.currentPage.needsIndefiniteExecution call on line 2 gets the current page of the playground and tells it to keep executing indefinitely, instead of exiting (which would destroy the player variable).

Notice that as soon as you enter this last line and stop typing for a few seconds, you'll start hearing the web radio station playing (provided you have an Internet connection). Cool! Web radio with five lines of code!

Typing again causes the music to stop, until you let up on the keyboard. Basically, when the playground thinks you're done, it tries to build and run the code, and in this case, that means music starts playing again.

So that's our first little bit of code that does something cool. Now let's look at how we got it to work at all.

My First Computer (Chris)

Messing around in the Xcode Playground reminds me of how computers used to dump you into an interactive programming environment by default. My first computer was a Texas Instruments TI-99 4/A, bought by my father because the saleswoman at K-Mart was really persuasive, and maybe because it cost $400 when the Apple IIs we had at school were over $1,000 (*Plus ça change, plus c'est la même chose*).

When you turned it on, the menu gave you two choices by default: TI BASIC, or whatever cartridge (if any) was in the slot. With no cartridge, all it could do was BASIC. Back in those days, messing around with some flavor of BASIC was what every home computer did. For a while, the idea was that anyone could program—and would actually want to—and pretty much any student in our school at least knew enough to do 10 PRINT "SARA IS GREAT" 20 GOTO 10.

In the TV documentary *Triumph of the Nerds*, Steve Jobs once recalled that for every one person who wanted to hack on hardware in that era, there were another thousand who wanted to hack on software. And beyond Jobs's observation, it seems that for every one person who wanted to hack on software, another thousand just wanted to run the stuff, without necessarily knowing how it works. Inevitably, computers got away from writing programs as being the primary user experience, and coding eventually became a specialist skill and no longer accessible to the layperson, despite the occasional programming renaissance like Hypercard.

Having a playground is like going back to those summer nights of the 1980s, with mosquitos banging off the window screen (attracted by the glow of the TV that served as a monitor), a Styx cassette playing on the tape player that was used to load and save programs, and a blinking cursor inviting me to write some code…just to see what happens.

Digging Into Documentation

How did we know that an AVPlayer class exists, and that it can play an audio stream? Well, for now, your authors are happy to steer you in the right direction, but eventually you'll want to find features and functionality on your own, so let's see how that's done.

The documentation for the iOS Software Development Kit (SDK) is available within Xcode itself, in a handy documentation viewer. Use the menu item Window > Documentation and API Reference (⇧⌘0) to show it.

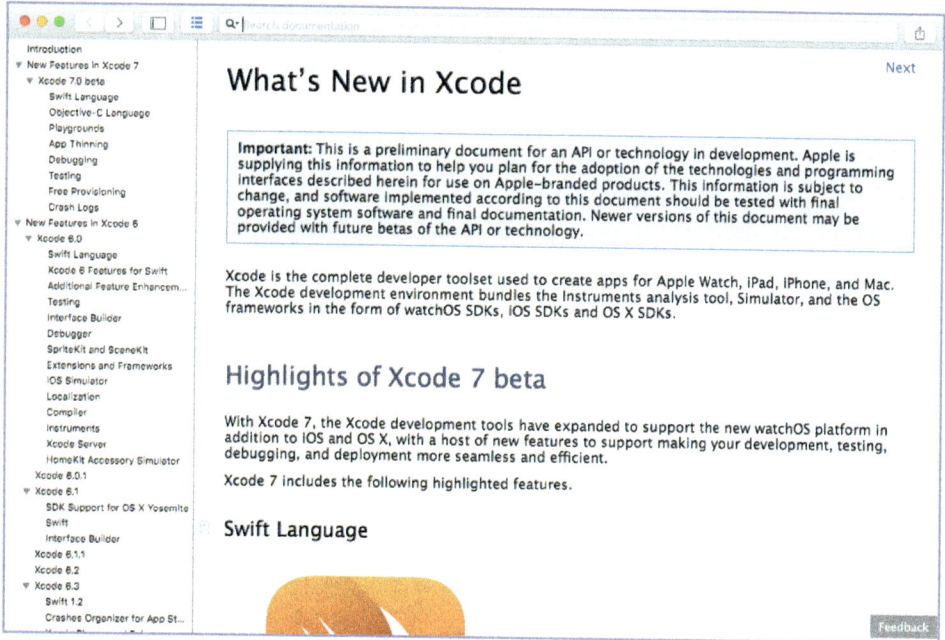

When opened for the first time, the documentation viewer shows a "What's New in Xcode" document, with an index of topics in a pane on the left. At the top, there's a toolbar, with forward and back buttons, two other buttons, and a search field.

The two buttons hide and show two panes on the left side. The leftmost one, disabled by default, shows or hides the Navigator for all documentation, whereas the second button shows a Table of Contents for the current document. Click the Navigator to show its top-level contents. We get a list of four top-level topics—iOS, OS X, watchOS, and Xcode—each with a disclosure indicator (the triangle spinner) that lets us drill down for more information. Expand the iOS topic to see what it has to offer.

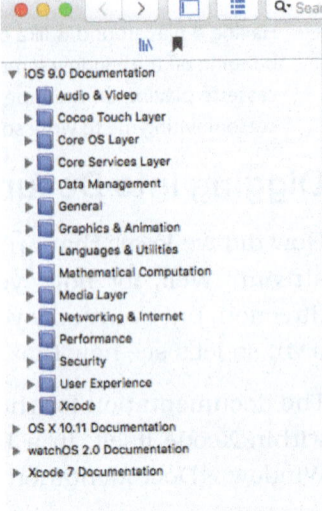

This top level is organized by topics, and the first is "Audio and Video." Perfect! That's just what we need. Expand that topic to see that it has three entries— Sample Code, Guides, and Reference—along with subfolders that are specific to audio and video. Open up Guides to find a document called Audio & Video Starting Point, and open that.

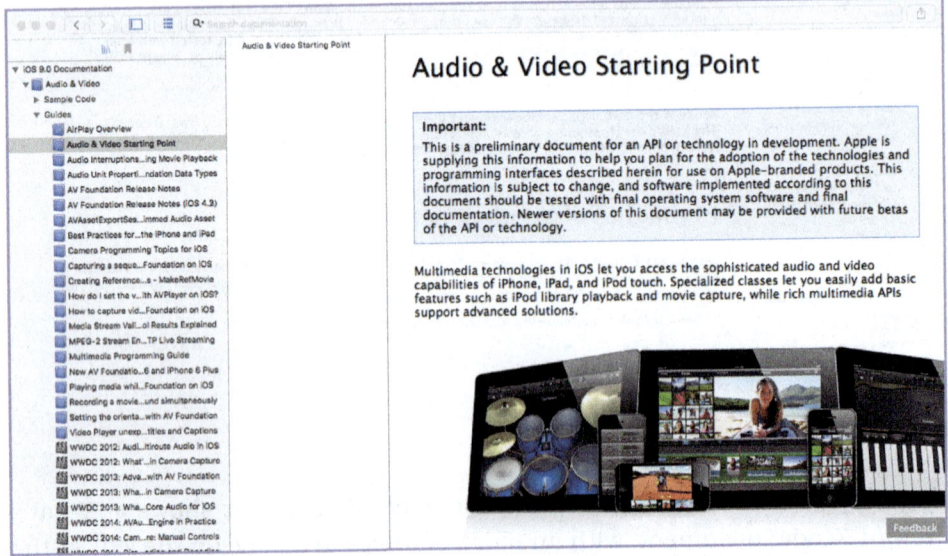

This document offers an overview of all the audio and video APIs available in the iOS SDK. It's got a lot to cover, because it turns out there are a bunch of them, with some overlap that's not always easy to figure out. But not too far down the first page, we find this useful gem:

To play streamed audio content, such as from a network connection, use an AVPlayer object as described in *Playback*. You can also play certain Internet audio files by using the MPMoviePlayerController class; for sample code that shows how, see MoviePlayer.

Excellent! Playing streamed audio content is just what we wanted! And notice that the text AVPlayer is in a blue monospaced font; that means it's a link. So, click the link to go to the AVPlayer documentation.

The content pane on the right contains a description of every method, property, constant, function, and so on in the AVPlayer class. On the left, the table of contents offers quick access to these contents by name, organized by functional topic (Creating a Player, Managing Playback, and so on).

If we look under Creating a Player, we find initWithURL, and the Swift syntax for creating an AVPlayer from a URL. It just says init(URL URL: NSURL), with the NSURL formatted as a link. So now we know that to create an AVPlayer to play our audio, we just need to create an NSURL object. And if we scroll down, we'll find the play() method that started our stream.

Searching Documentation

Now if we were working backward like this, we'd say to ourselves: "OK, to get an AVPlayer, we need to have an NSURL, so how do we do that?" Obviously, it would be easy to just click the NSURL link here, but let's learn how to do a search, too. Click in the search bar at the top, and type URL. The results of the search will immediately appear in a sheet beneath the search bar, as shown in the screenshot on page 12.

There are a bunch of different kinds of hits. The NSURL class we want is at the top, denoted by a "C" icon to indicate it's a class. There are other results, like properties called url in various classes, and some guides on how to work with URLs in different APIs. But let's select that first result and go to the NSURL page. This documentation page is organized by topic, just like the last one, and under Creating an NSURL Object, we can find the initializer that takes a string.

So, by browsing, searching, and working backward, we can find the two classes we needed to create our streaming audio playground. We'll have more to say about the language itself in the next few chapters, but whenever we need functionality that we believe the SDK provides, we now know we can just bring up the documentation viewer and look for it.

Getting Local Documentation

All the documentation we're browsing is looked up from Apple's servers, so we're out of luck if we want to do some coding on an airplane or deep in the forest where there's no Wi-Fi (and, yes, the authors have done both of these things!). It's really helpful to have documentation installed right on our computer, but it requires signing in with Apple and doing a one-time download.

Open up Xcode's preferences with Xcode > Preferences, and select the Downloads tab. This shows optional pieces that can be downloaded into our local copy of Xcode. These include different versions of the iOS Simulator application (which we'll be using a little later) and documentation.

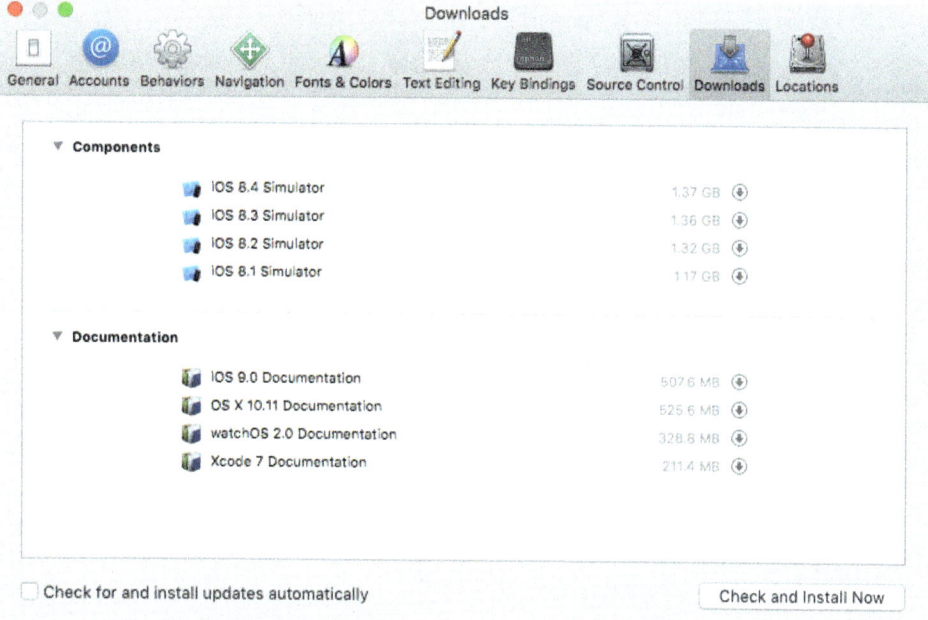

We want the iOS 9 SDK documentation, so click the arrow next to that. This is where things are going to get a little sticky.

If this is your first time using Xcode, you'll see an alert sheet slide out saying that you have to authenticate with Apple in order to download documentation. There's a free level of participation, but it means some extra steps, so let's see what's involved.

Click the Open Accounts button in the alert to switch to the Accounts tab of Xcode preferences. The left pane of this tab organizes three kinds of accounts you can be logged into with Xcode: Apple IDs for development, source code repositories, and Servers for certain advanced tasks. The list is initially blank; we add to it with the plus (+) button at the bottom left.

What we need to add is an Apple ID, which you should already have, since it's what you used to download Xcode from the Mac App Store. Click the plus button to add an Apple ID, and then enter the email and password for your Apple ID account. Assuming authentication succeeds, your Apple ID will be added to the list.

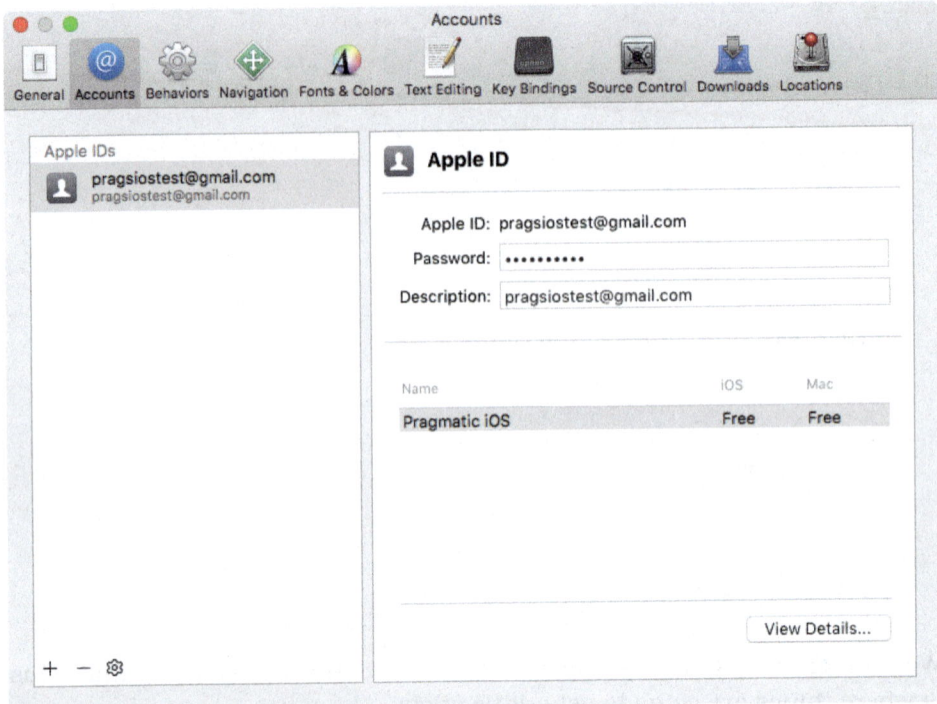

Notice that the detail pane fills in with the Apple ID email and password, and a table shows the account as now having a free-level membership to the iOS and Mac developer programs. The reason this is a table is that it's possible to join other development teams—for example, if you join a company or take on freelance work for an organization with its own development account—and those memberships and their privileges will be listed here.

With a free membership, we can develop apps on our own as much as we like, and even run them on our own devices. To submit to the App Store, we'll need to upgrade to a paid membership, something you'll see much later, in Chapter 17, *Publishing and Maintaining the App*, on page 289.

For the time being, our concern is downloading documentation. Now that you have a basic developer membership, switch back to the Downloads tab, and click the arrow on the iOS 9 documentation line. Now the documentation set should download to your Mac, and you'll find the documentation viewer loads faster and works offline.

What We've Learned

In this chapter, we've tooled up for our journey into iOS 9 development and gotten a tiny taste of how it works. We downloaded and installed Xcode 7, which is what we'll use to create our apps.

Since we'll be writing our apps with the Swift programming language, we created a playground to try out some simple Swift code in an interactive sandbox, which lets us type in a little code and see what happens. The playground gives us access to most of the things we could do with the iOS SDK, from crunching numbers to playing web radio. And with so much to play with in the SDK, we looked at how the documentation viewer lets us browse or search the documentation for classes, methods, and functions that we can call. And, finally, we downloaded a local copy of the iOS 9 documentation, so we'll be able to keep coding even without Wi-Fi.

Our next step will be to get a real grip on the Swift programming language so we can start building more sophisticated behavior.

CHAPTER 2

Starting with Swift

Playgrounds let us play around with iOS development, but it's not really obvious what we can do with them yet. When we browse the documentation, we can see there are thousands of classes and tens of thousands of methods and functions we can call. But how do we do that? It kind of feels like we opened up the box for a model kit and we now have a thousand plastic pieces to put together but no instructions and no glue.

In this chapter, we're going to start learning the Swift programming language, which will let us create our applications by giving us a way to call into the iOS SDK, and a way to compose our app's internal logic. We'll spend the entire chapter in playground mode, which will allow us to try things out, see what does and doesn't work, and quickly learn from our mistakes.

The Swift Programming Language

Swift is a programming language developed internally at Apple and released to the public in 2014 for use in developing iOS and OS X apps. In 2015, Apple made major updates to the language, upping its version number to 2.0. This is the version of the language supported by Xcode 7, and the version we'll be using throughout this book. Apple is also open-sourcing the language, and, while it's a work in progress, this may eventually lead to opportunities for Swift developers beyond the Apple ecosystem.

Swift is defined by several essential traits. Swift is:

- *Compiled*, meaning that our source code is converted into bytecode at build time, rather than being interpreted at runtime, as with scripting languages like JavaScript and Ruby.

- *Strongly Typed*, meaning that objects we work with are clearly identified as strings, integers, floats, and so on. These types are *static*, meaning they can't change once they're assigned. Swift also provides *type inference*, so we don't have to explicitly indicate a type when the compiler can unambiguously figure it out.

- *Automatically Reference Counted*, meaning that objects allocated from memory keep track of how many incoming references they have, and their memory is freed up once there are zero references to them (since they're useless at this point, as no other objects now know about them). This is subtly different from the *garbage collection* system popular in many languages. The difference is that a garbage collector periodically goes out looking for unreferenced objects; Swift's *Automatic Reference Counting* (ARC) keeps constant track of references and frees objects immediately when they have zero references.

- *Name-spaced*, like many modern languages, but, importantly, not like Swift's predecessor, Objective-C. Name-spacing allows us to avoid collisions when multiple parts of our code (our app, frameworks we import, etc.) use the same name for different things. We can safely use a generic name like MyThing, because it's understood to be part of a *module* with a unique name like com.mycompany.myapp, so it won't be confused with com.othercompany.otherapp's MyThing (although we should still come up with better names than "MyThing"!)

Perhaps most importantly, Swift is a deeply *pragmatic* language, with a unique mission: providing a more modern and expressive way to code than Objective-C offered, while retaining compatibility with over 20 years of existing Apple frameworks and system code. The iOS SDK is written mostly in Objective-C, but parts of it are in C or even C++, and many different idioms are used in the various frameworks and libraries. Swift has to make it easy and natural to call all of it. As we'll see, Swift makes some accommodations to the past, because a more linguistically clean alternative that would require rewriting the iOS frameworks would be a non-starter.

In this book, we are covering Swift 2.0, which is supported by Xcode 7. Earlier versions of the language were supported by Xcode 6. Swift and Xcode versioning moves in lock-step, meaning you can't write Swift 1.2 syntax in Xcode 7, nor can you write Swift 2.0 in any version of Xcode 6. Fortunately, the compiled code is forward- and backward-compatible, so Swift 1.2 code written in Xcode 6 will run on iOS 9, and Swift 2.0 code written in Xcode 7 will run on iOS 8 (provided that the app as a whole is marked as being backward-compatible with iOS 8). For simplicity, we are focusing only on current versions in this book: Swift 2.0, Xcode 7, and iOS 9.

Using Variables and Constants

Let's start writing some code and get a feel for how Swift works. Start a new playground (File > New > Playground), and call it NumbersPlayground. Delete the first line that creates the string (var str = "Hello, playground"), but leave the import UIKit. The import statement pulls in iOS frameworks we almost always want to use, so we will always leave that as the first line of our playgrounds.

Computers were originally built for math, so let's start with some simple numbers. Type the following:

startingswift/NumbersPlayground.playground/Contents.swift
```
let foo = 1
```

The right pane shows a 1. This is nice and simple: we've created foo and assigned it the value 1, which is what's shown in the results pane.

So far, so good. Now let's do some math. Like many languages, Swift has a += operator to add and assign, so let's try that.

startingswift/NumbersPlayground.playground/Contents.swift
```
foo += 1
```

Problem! It doesn't give us a 2! Instead, we get a red bar that says

```
Left side of mutating operator isn't mutable: 'foo' is a 'let' constant.
```

There's also a red circle in the left gutter next to our new line of code. Red means "error" in Xcode, so that's bad. On the other hand, the circle icon means "instant fix," so that's good! Click the icon to see the problem and its solution:

Clicking the error icon shows us a two-line pop-up menu. The first restates the error, and any subsequent lines give us instant-fix options. The error is that let creates a *constant*, a value that can't change. Once we set foo to 1, we can never change it again. If we do want foo to change, it needs to be a *variable*. That's what the second line is offering: click it and the declaration changes from let to var, and now we can perform all the math on foo that we like.

Constants versus variables might seem like a semantic difference: some languages like C make variables the default and constants uncommon, while JavaScript doesn't have constants at all. In Swift, using constants is preferred when you know that a value should not or cannot change. This allows the compiler to make certain performance optimizations for constants. We always have to choose between marking things as constants or variables, and this is on purpose; as we'll see again and again, many of Swift's design choices are built on the idea of the developer being explicit about his or her intentions.

Counting with Numeric Types

Let's play with some more math. We'll create another variable:

```
var bar = 0
```

That looks good, and since it's a variable, we can change its value:

```
bar = 0.5
```

Oh, no! We get another error, and this time without an instant fix. Worse yet, the description is unhelpful: "Cannot assign a value of type 'Double' to a value of type 'Int'."

So what's the deal? Can Swift seriously not convert between floating-point numbers and integers? Actually, Swift can, but our variable bar cannot. The problem is that we never specified what the type of bar is, so the Swift compiler made its best guess. Replace the second bar = 0.5 line with the following:

```
bar.dynamicType
```

The dynamicType property allows us to see what type a value has. In the right pane, we see that the type evaluates to Int.type. That makes sense: since the original value was 0, Swift took a guess and assumed we would want an integer, not a floating-point type. This inferring of types is called, appropriately, *type inference.*

We could tell Swift to use a floating-point type by using 0.0 as the initial value; try that and you'll see the dynamicType becomes Double.type. But if we want a given type, we can and should just declare it that way. Change the declaration like this:

```
var bar : Double = 0
```

Now Swift doesn't need to infer anything: we've explicitly declared that we want bar to be a Double, meaning a double-precision floating-point type.

There's also a lower-precision floating-point type, Float, and a Boolean type Bool. In some languages, such as C, you can cast between integers, floats, doubles, and Bools, and the worst that will happen is that the compiler will warn you about loss of precision. Swift forbids this altogether, even if you wouldn't be losing anything. Try this:

```
startingswift/NumbersPlayground.playground/Contents.swift
let myInt = 1
let myDouble : Double = myInt
```

This pops up an error saying "'Int' is not convertible to 'Double'." To create myDouble, we need to tell Swift to create a new Double:

```
startingswift/NumbersPlayground.playground/Contents.swift
let myInt = 1
let myDouble = Double(myInt)
```

The second line here uses Double's *initializer* to create a new Double, using the value passed in as a parameter.

Swift's numeric types work with the usual arithmetic operators popular in other languages: +, -, *, /, and %. The last one, the *modulo* or "remainder" operator, works not just on Int but also Float and Double, which isn't always true of other languages. On the other hand, thanks to strong typing, Bools aren't just numeric values, and thus *none* of these mathematic operators work with Boolean values. And that's a good thing because what would "false divided by true" mean, anyway? Instead, we use the usual Boolean operators ! (NOT), && (logical AND), and || (logical OR).

Storing Text in Strings

Strings—blocks of textual data—are another essential data type supported in nearly all programming languages, and Swift's are really great. Let's start a new playground to try them out: create the playground with File > New > Playground, and call it StringsPlayground.

Of course, right off the bat, the playground template creates a string for us with var str = "Hello, playground", which evaluates as Hello, playground in the results pane.

Since str is defined with the var keyword, it's a variable, so let's change it up a bit. Type the following:

```
startingswift/StringsPlayground.playground/Contents.swift
str = str + "!!"
```

This evaluates as Hello, playground!!, and proves that we can combine strings with the + operator.

Swift strings are fully Unicode compliant, meaning they can contain any Unicode character, including all the various written languages and symbols supported by iOS. Let's add some of those characters now. Xcode offers quick access to Unicode characters with the menu item Edit > Emoji & Symbols (^⌘space). The popover, shown in the following figure, allows quick selection of groups of emojis and other characters like "technical symbols" and "pictographs." Scroll to the top to find a search field to look up characters by name, and a button to switch to the full-size character input window.

Let's see if we can add an emoji character to our string. Write the following code, and when you need to insert the emoji inside the quotes, bring up the symbols window, find an emoji character, and double-click it to insert it into the source code:

```
str += "🏃"
```

As you'll see in the results pane, this appends the emoji to the end of the string. And it turns out Swift's support for Unicode isn't just for strings; Unicode is fully supported throughout Swift source code as well. That means we can do something really silly, like this:

```
var 🏃 = str
```

This creates a variable whose name is actually the running person emoji, and the assignment operator (=) sets its value to the current value of str, so we see the same value as before in the results pane.

Aside from the + operator, we can also build up strings through a substitution technique. Whenever the sequence \() is found in a string in source code, the contents of the parentheses are evaluated and substituted into the string. The contents could be variables, mathematical expressions, or other strings, as in the following screenshot:

```
let book = "📘"                                              "📘"

let phone = " 📱"                                            " 📱"

let sentence = "This is a \(book) about \(phone) apps."    "This is a 📘 about 📱 apps."
```

Now what about the contents of a string? In some languages, such as C, a string is just an array of characters. That's largely true of Swift, subject to some technical details. Swift strings are really smart about Unicode, and sometimes multiple characters can be combined into one. Consider what happens when we combine Unicode's "combining accent character" (Unicode code point 301) with the letter "e," just as if we had typed ⌥e and then e:

startingswift/StringsPlayground.playground/Contents.swift
```
let accentedE = "e" + "\u{301}"
```

This evaluates to the single character "é." Two characters go in, and one comes out.

When we do want to pull out the contents of a string, we can use its characters property to let us treat the string contents as an array, one of the collection types we'll be talking about in the next section. This lets us count the number of user-readable characters, and for kicks, we'll substitute that number into a larger string:

startingswift/StringsPlayground.playground/Contents.swift
```
"Sentence has \(sentence.characters.count) characters"
```

This evaluates to "Sentence has 25 characters" in the right pane.

The contents of the characters array are of a type called Character, which represents a single human-readable character. Using our Unicode string from before, we can find the location in the string of the "book" emoji by representing it as a Character, and then using the array's indexOf() to find it in the characters array.

```
let bookChar : Character = "📘"
"book is at index \(sentence.characters.indexOf(bookChar)) in sentence"
```

Once we write this, we see the result "book is at index Optional(10) in sentence". The 10 is right, but the Optional() is weird, right? We're going to discover what's up with that a little later.

Packaging Data in Collections

With numeric types and strings, one thing we'll frequently want to do is to put them into *collections*. Nearly all languages have multiple ways of putting items into groups so we can then organize and perform operations on the entire group. Swift provides three main types of collections: arrays, sets, and dictionaries.

To start playing with these, start a new playground called CollectionsPlayground, and delete the line that creates the "Hello, playground!" string.

Arrays

For many of us, the most frequently used collection is the *array*. Arrays contain multiple items and maintain the ordering of those items. They also allow for the same item to appear multiple times in the array.

We'll start with an array of strings that lists our favorite iPhone models. Declare an array as follows, and immediately check its dynamicType:

```
startingswift/CollectionsPlayground.playground/Contents.swift
var models = ["iPhone 5", "iPhone 5s", "iPhone 6s"]
models.dynamicType
```

We can create an array by just putting its contents, comma-separated, inside square brackets. We can see from the results pane that this evaluates to these three strings, and the dynamicType is inferred to be Array<String>, meaning an Array of Strings.

Now let's add an item at the front of the array:

```
startingswift/CollectionsPlayground.playground/Contents.swift
models.insert("iPhone 6s Plus", atIndex: 0)
```

Our array now has four strings. Keep in mind, however, that we can add *only* Strings because that's the type of the array. If we wanted to be able to add other types, like any of the numeric types, we would have had to originally declare that models accepts any type of object, which we would write as var models : Array<AnyObject>. There's also a simpler syntax for array type declarations: [AnyObject].

As our array grows, it likely won't fit on one line of the results pane. Fortunately, there's a way to see the whole thing. Mouse over the the last line in the results pane, and two icons will appear on the far right: Quick Look and Preview.

["iPhone 6s Plus", "iPhone 5", "iPhone 5s", "iPhone... ⊙◯

Click the rightmost button, Preview, to see the results shown directly below the line of code that produced them.

```
models.insert("iPhone 6s Plus", atIndex: 0)                    ["iPhone 6s Plus", "iPhone 5", "iPhone 5... ◉
    [0] "iPhone 6s Plus"
    [1] "iPhone 5"
    [2] "iPhone 5s"
    [3] "iPhone 6s"
```

The Quick Look button tries to do a similar presentation in a popover window rather than presenting the results in our source pane. In this case, the array members are too wide to fit in the popover, so it's not that useful this time.

Now let's dig into our array. To access a member of an array by its index, we can use the square-brace syntax familiar from C, Java, and many other languages:

startingswift/CollectionsPlayground.playground/Contents.swift
```
let firstItem = models[0]
```

The evaluation pane shows that firstItem has been set to the value "iPhone 6s Plus", which we inserted a few lines back.

Since we can insert, we can, of course, remove items as well, either with removeAtIndex() or removeLast(). To see the shortened array in the results pane, we type models by itself on the next line.

startingswift/CollectionsPlayground.playground/Contents.swift
```
models.removeLast()
models
```

Keep in mind that all of these mutating operations are possible only because models was originally declared with the var keyword. If we'd used let, Swift would infer we wanted the array to be constant and would have created an immutable array.

Swift arrays have a few other neat tricks that make it easy to combine and split arrays, provided their types are compatible. Try this:

startingswift/CollectionsPlayground.playground/Contents.swift
```
Line 1  let iPhones = ["iPhone 5", "iPhone 5s", "iPhone 6s", "iPhone 6s Plus"]
     2  let iPads = ["iPad Air 2", "iPad mini"]
     3  models = iPhones
     4  models.appendContentsOf(iPads)
     5  models.insertContentsOf(["iPod touch"], at: 4)
```

In this section of code, lines 1 and 2 create immutable arrays called iPhones and iPads, respectively. Line 3 assigns our models array to now be the contents of iPhones. Then, on line 4, we use the appendContentsOf() function to append the contents of the iPads array to the models array. If we don't want to add items at the end, we can use the insertContentsOf() function to insert an array at a given index. On line 5, we insert a one-element array of iPod touch models at index 4, putting it between the iPhones and iPads. As we can see in the evaluation pane, our array now has seven items.

Sets

Arrays are a bread-and-butter collection, but for certain tasks, *sets* make more sense. A set has no sense of order and does not allow duplicate items. Sets are useful for when you want to simply know whether or not a given item is part of a collection, and you don't care if it's "before" or "after" other members of the collection.

Let's kick off an empty set and start adding stuff to it.

startingswift/CollectionsPlayground.playground/Contents.swift
```
Line 1  var set = Set<String>()
     2  set.insert("iPhone 6s")
     3  set.insert("iPhone 6s")
```

Line 1 shows the recipe for creating an empty collection of any type. We have to declare the type (because there are no objects to infer it from), so we use the type Set<String>, and then empty parentheses to call the initializer for that type.

On line 2 we add the string "iPhone 6s", and on line 3, we do it again. Look at the results pane: after the second insert(), the set still only has one member. That's because a given item can appear only once in a Set; we don't care how many of something are in the set, just whether that thing is in or out.

Where sets really shine is their operators for determining membership between members of multiple sets. Let's create two sets to play with:

startingswift/CollectionsPlayground.playground/Contents.swift
```
var iPhoneSet : Set = ["iPhone 6s"]
var iPadSet : Set = ["iPad Air 2", "iPad mini", "iPad Pro"]
```

Notice that as a convenience we can create a Set from an Array. In this example, ["iPhone 6s"] is one array, and ["iPad Air 2", "iPad mini", "iPad Pro"] is another. We have to declare the Set type (because otherwise the square-brace syntax would imply an Array), but the type of the contents (Strings) can be inferred.

If we were interested in what members are in both sets, that's a one-line call:

startingswift/CollectionsPlayground.playground/Contents.swift
```
iPhoneSet.intersect(iPadSet)
```

The results pane shows us that no items are members of both sets. Let's change that. The iPhone 6s Plus feels nearly as big as an iPad mini, so let's add it to both sets and try another call to intersect().

startingswift/CollectionsPlayground.playground/Contents.swift
```
iPadSet.insert("iPhone 6s Plus")
iPhoneSet.insert("iPhone 6s Plus")
iPhoneSet.intersect(iPadSet)
```

Now the results pane shows us the one item in both sets, "iPhone 6s Plus". Notice that the returned collection is also a Set.

If you studied set theory in high school, you'll recall that an intersection is the items that are in both sets and that the union is all the members of both sets. Swift gives that to us, too:

startingswift/CollectionsPlayground.playground/Contents.swift
```
iPhoneSet.union(iPadSet)
```

This gives us everything from both sets. Notice that "iPhone 6s Plus" appears only once, despite being present in both sets. After all, the return type is a Set, and any object can appear only once in a set.

Dictionaries

Swift's third major collection type is *dictionaries*. A dictionary is a collection that maps *keys* to *values*, which gives you a way to quickly look up a given value in the future, provided you have the corresponding key.

Let's create a dictionary that lets us look up iOS device sizes by model name:

startingswift/CollectionsPlayground.playground/Contents.swift
```
let sizeInMm = [
  "iPhone 6s": 138.1,
  "iPhone 6s Plus" : 158.1,
  "iPad Air 2" : 240.0,
  "iPad Pro" : 305.7]
sizeInMm.dynamicType
```

As we can see in the results pane, this creates a dictionary with four key-value pairs, and the type of this collection is inferred to be Dictionary<String, Double>, meaning the keys are Strings and the values are Doubles.

To access a value, we put the key in square braces, like this:

```
sizeInMm["iPhone 6s"]
sizeInMm["iPad mini"]
```

The results pane shows that we got back 138.1 for the "iPhone 6s" key and nil for the "iPad mini" key, which makes sense because sizeInMM doesn't have that key.

Dictionaries are good for fast lookups of single items, although it's also possible to walk through the whole collection. To do that, though, we're going to need ways to have our code loop through the collection. So let's move on to that.

Looping and Branching: Control Flow

Control flow refers to how we specify the order of how our Swift instructions are executed, or in a bigger picture, what parts of our code are to be run and under what conditions. In Swift, as in other languages, this is mostly implemented as conditionals and loops. Conditionals are statements that do or don't execute code based on whether certain conditions are true or false at the time they're evaluated. Loops build on conditionals by running some part of the code 0 or more times based on the conditions we provide.

Swift's tools for control flow are probably very familiar to most developers, since many languages have if, for, while, and so forth. We'll try them out now, so start a new playground called ControlFlowPlayground.

for Loops

Control flow also goes hand-in-hand with collections, which is why we're reaching it now: once you have a collection of items, it's natural to want to go through the collection and run some code on each item. We'll start with going through an array with for.

```
startingswift/ControlFlowPlayground.playground/Contents.swift
Line 1  let models = ["iPhone 6s", "iPhone 6s Plus", "iPad Air 2",
     2      "iPad mini", "iPad Pro"]
     3  for model in models {
     4      NSLog ("model: \(model)")
     5  }
```

On lines 1–2, we create the models array, consisting of five strings. Line 3 is the *for-in* loop syntax, which says we want to go through every member of the models collection, and each time through, the item we're working with will be represented with the local variable model.

The results pane doesn't show us anything about what happened each time through the loop. To see that we're actually doing something each time, we use the NSLog() function on line 4 to write a message to the debug log. The output from NSLog() isn't shown by default; bring it up with View > Debug Area > Activate Console (⇧⌘C), or the middle button on the pane-switcher on the toolbar: ▯ ▭ ▯

Once the console pane is revealed, you should see the output of this loop:

```
model: iPhone 6s
model: iPhone 6s Plus
model: iPad Air 2
model: iPad mini
model: iPad Pro
```

If it's useful to have the index of members of the collection, we can do a loop that counts the members of the collection numerically, like this:

startingswift/ControlFlowPlayground.playground/Contents.swift
```
for i in 0 ..< models.count {
  NSLog ("model by index: \(models[i])")
}
```

This style of for loop creates a variable for the index (i in this case), and counts through a range of values. We create this with the *range operator:* ..<, which counts from the starting value (0) to one less than the ending value (models.count, the length of the array). If we wanted to include the ending value, we would use the range operator ... instead.

What if it would be convenient to have both the index and a local variable inside the loop? Sure, we could do let model = models[i] as the first line inside the loop, and then use that. However, Swift gives a much more elegant alternative, albeit one we'll have to wait to discover in the next chapter.

if-else Statements

We often want to execute some statements only if certain conditions are true, and while the if statement is unfashionable in some coding circles, it's familiar to nearly every programmer. Swift's are simple enough, with one or two unique wrinkles. Let's try an if statement that pulls a value out of a dictionary:

startingswift/ControlFlowPlayground.playground/Contents.swift
```
Line 1  let sizeInMm = [
   -      "iPhone 6s": 138.1,
   -      "iPhone 6s Plus" : 158.1,
   -      "iPad Air 2" : 240.0,
   5      "iPad Pro" : 305.7]
   -
   -   let model = "iPhone 6s"
   -   if sizeInMm[model] != nil {
   -     NSLog ("size of \(model) is \(sizeInMm[model])")
  10   } else {
   -     NSLog ("couldn't find \(model)")
   -   }
```

After creating the sizeInMm dictionary, we define the model key we are interested in, and then try to get its matching value from the dictionary. If the value is not nil, we execute the NSLog() on line 9, and otherwise the NSLog() on 11. Change the value of model to different values to see each block of the if-else log its message to the console.

The one truly interesting thing to say here is that the curly braces in Swift if-else statements are *required*, even if only a single line is to be executed in either case. This is different from the single-line behavior of C and Java, and eliminates easy-to-miss bugs caused by the inconsistent syntax of making the curly braces optional.

goto fail;

When Apple first announced that if statements in Swift would always require curly braces, a lot of us cheered and snarked that Apple had learned its lesson. Because just a few months earlier, missing curly braces hurt them badly.

In early 2014, Apple quietly updated its SSL implementation—used for any secure networking on iOS or OS X—and security researchers found that the earlier versions had a critical bug.

One part of the code needed to carry out a series of checks before calling an all-important sslRawVerify() method. It basically looked something like this:

```
Line 1  if ((err = FirstFunction()) != 0)
   2        goto fail;
   3    if ((err = SecondFunction()) != 0)
   4        goto fail;
   5        goto fail;
   6    if ((err = ThirdFunction()) != 0)
   7        goto fail;
   8
   9    err = sslRawVerify(...)
```

Without curly braces, a true if statement in C will execute one statement. So the if statement on line 3 executes line 4 if the SecondFunction() test fails, which means we're in an error state and call goto fail;, which means we never call sslRawVerify(). And that's fine; that's what's supposed to happen.

The problem is that, despite the indentation, line 5 is *always* called, regardless of what happened in the if statement. It looks like it's part of the if, but it's not, and the result is that sslRawVerify() is never called, because line 5 always makes us goto fail;.

It's a simple mistake, and lots of people missed it, but the loose syntax of C led to a critical security hole. It's no wonder that when they designed Swift, Apple required curly braces on all if statements, to make sure this kind of bug was no longer possible!

Swift also offers a guard statement that is sort of like the opposite of if: it doesn't have a curly-brace clause for the true case, just an else for when the condition is not true. We typically use these for early exits when we don't want to run many lines of code if the condition isn't met, and we don't want to have to nest important code deeply in if-else indentation. Typically, guard statements perform early returns to bail out of code we don't want to run, and we can't do that kind of early return in a playground, so we'll have to wait until we're writing a real app to get our guard on.

switch Statements

The last kind of control flow technique we need to be aware of is switch. The switch keyword lets us test a variable against several possible values, and execute different code in each case. Let's write a simple example:

```
startingswift/ControlFlowPlayground.playground/Contents.swift
switch model {
  case "iPhone 6s Plus":
    NSLog ("That's what I want")
  case "iPhone 7":
    NSLog ("Have they even released that?")
  default:
    NSLog ("Not my thing")
}
```

This switch will log "That's what I want" if model is "iPhone 6s Plus", or "Have they even released that?" if it's "iPhone 7", or "Not my thing" in all other cases.

If you're familiar with C's switch, you'll be pleasantly surprised by one feature here: Swift's switch works on Strings (or any type that can be evaluated with ==, actually), and not just on numeric types. Another improvement from other languages is that a matched case *doesn't* fall through to the ones after it; in C, you would have to put a break at the end of the first case, or the code would execute the second case and the default as well.

One thing to be aware of is that switch statements must be *exhaustive*, meaning they must cover every possible value of the item being tested. Often, we use default as a catchall for this.

The switch statement gets heavily used in Swift because it's the perfect way to deal with enumerations, which you'll learn about in the next chapter.

Maybe It's There, Maybe It Isn't: Optionals

A few times so far we've seen our log messages include the term "optional," a behavior we've put off explaining until now. But it's time to deal with it, because optionals are one of Swift's defining features. Create a new playground called OptionalsPlayground and delete the "Hello, playground" line, as usual.

We'll start by adding the sizeInMm dictionary from a few sections back, since that's something that started giving us this "optional" stuff.

startingswift/OptionsPlayground.playground/Contents.swift
```
let sizeInMm = [
  "iPhone 6s": 138.1,
  "iPhone 6s Plus" : 158.1,
  "iPad Air 2" : 240.0]
```

Looking at this, we can see that sizeInMm["iPhone 6s"] should evaluate to 138.1, which is a Double, meaning a double-precision floating-point number.

Well, that's great, but what if we evaluate sizeInMm["iPhone 7"], a key not in the dictionary. If our return value is a Double, what's the right value for its size? 0? -1? Some huge positive or negative value that we just interpret as a "no-value"?

Swift has a better answer for this: *optionals*. An optional is a type that represents two different things: whether there's a value at all and, if so, what the value actually is.

It turns out that dictionaries always return optionals for their values, as we can see by inspecting the dynamicType of the value we get back:

startingswift/OptionsPlayground.playground/Contents.swift
```
let size6 = sizeInMm["iPhone 6s"]
size6.dynamicType
```

In the results pane, this shows size6 as 138.1 and the dynamicType as Optional<Double>.Type.

Now let's try the same thing with a nonexistent value, like the size of the fictional iPhone 7:

startingswift/OptionsPlayground.playground/Contents.swift
```
let size7 = sizeInMm["iPhone 7"]
size7.dynamicType
```

This shows us a size of nil and the dynamicType of Optional<Double>.Type. It's the same type as before, a Double optional, only this time there isn't a value.

Unwrapping Optionals

As you might imagine, we're frequently going to be concerned with whether an optional value is nil, and when it's not, we often want to get to the value itself. We do this through a process called *unwrapping*. To "unwrap" a Double optional like the values in our dictionary means to take an Optional<Double> and turn it into just a normal Double.

One way to unwrap is to use the *force-unwrap operator*, which is the ! character. Try it out on size6:

startingswift/OptionalsPlayground.playground/Contents.swift
```
size6!.dynamicType
```

This force-unwraps size6 to be a non-optional type, and then gets its dynamicType. The results pane shows the dynamicType as Double. Huzzah! We got our Double out from inside the optional!

Not so fast. Try the same thing with size7:

startingswift/OptionalsPlayground.playground/Contents.swift
```
size7!.dynamicType
```

Ack! The results pane says "Error," and there's a red band with a bunch of scary text about EXC_BAD_INSTRUCTION.

```
 30  size7!.dynamicType
 31          Execution was interrupted, reason: EXC_BAD_INSTRUCTION (code=EXC_I386_INVOP, subcode=0x0).
```

This is pretty bad: our code has *crashed* inside the playground. And the reason for that is something we need to remember: *unwrapping nil values crashes our code!* size7 is nil, we said to unwrap it with the ! operator—bang, we're dead. Let's delete that line so it doesn't give us any more trouble!

Now we need to figure out what we're going to do to not crash anymore. One option would be to always test optionals against nil, and only unwrap if they're non-nil. That works, but it gets ugly. Nest a few if foo != nil blocks, and soon you've got what Swift developers call the "pyramid of doom" from all that indentation.

Unwrapping Optionals with if let

Fortunately, there's a way out of this mess. We can combine let and if to create an expression that says "if you can assign this to a non-optional value, then give it the following name." Here's what that looks like:

startingswift/OptionalsPlayground.playground/Contents.swift
```
if let size = size6 {
  size.dynamicType
}

if let size = size7 {
  size.dynamicType
}
```

Once we finish typing this, notice that the first if let block shows Double.Type for the type in the results pane, meaning that size is a normal Double inside the block and not an optional. But the second block of code doesn't show anything, because its if let fails (because size7 is nil, so size is not assigned).

The if let keyword gets used a lot, so it has a few tricks that will help us write more concise code. The first is that we can combine several if lets on a single line, comma-separated:

startingswift/OptionalsPlayground.playground/Contents.swift
```
if let size6 = size6, size7 = size7 {
  size6.dynamicType
  size7.dynamicType
}
```

There are two things to notice here. First, each assignment in an if let creates a variable name that's only visible inside the scope of the curly braces. Often, it makes sense to just use the same name that a variable has outside the if let. So, in this case, if let size6 = size6 is *not* a meaningless tautology; instead, it looks at the right side (the optional size6) and says "if that's not nil, create an unwrapped variable *also* called size6 inside the curly-brace scope." At first it may look weird, but it's a convention that comes easily to Swift programmers and is better than having to come up with different variable names for use only inside the if let block.

Second, there's nothing in the results pane, because not all of the if let assignments succeeded. Since size7 is nil, we can't unwrap it, and the if let fails.

One other trick we use a lot is testing a value that we've just unwrapped, as part of the if let. For example, what if we want to run some code on an optional Double only if it's non-nil *and* its value is greater than some constant. We could use an if let followed by a if size6 > 100.0, but nesting ifs is going to give us that "pyramid of doom" we spoke of before. Instead, we can do this:

startingswift/OptionalsPlayground.playground/Contents.swift
```
if let size6 = size6 where size6 > 100.0 {
    size6
}
```

The where clause on an if let allows us to perform logic with the unwrapped size6 Double while still on the if let line. This makes it clear that *everything* on the if let line has to pass for us to get into the curly-brace block.

It may seem like a lot of work to deal with optionals, but the concept ends up being powerful: we can use a single variable to both hold a value and to say "nothing to see here" if there isn't a value. In some languages, we'd either have to use two variables for that, or a magical flag value that we just agree to treat as a "no value" value. And programming history has shown that approach can cause a lot of unexpected problems.

What We've Learned

Optionals are tricky subject to get your head around, so it's probably a good time to take a break and take stock of what we've learned so far.

This chapter has been all about working with the essential data types in Swift. We started with the numeric types—integers, floating-point numbers, and Booleans—and strings. We saw how to combine strings with the basic concatenation operator (+) and pattern substitution, and how to access their contents. Also, we went a little nuts with the Unicode support in Swift strings, but it'll pay off if we ever want to support multiple languages, or lots of emoji.

We also played around with the different types of collections—arrays, sets, and dictionaries—and what each is particularly good for. Then we looked at Swift's control flow operators, so we could use loops to go through the contents of collections.

Finally, since dictionaries may or may not give us a value for a given key, we started working with Swift optionals, to see how they represent the presence or absence of a value, and how to get to the value.

These are the building blocks we'll use to build full-blown iOS apps. In the next chapter, you'll see how to combine them into more sophisticated data structures, how to create functions to work with them, and how to do so with style and aplomb.

CHAPTER 3

Swift with Style

In the previous chapter, we explored the basics of Swift: the type system, control flow, optionals, and so on. And, assuming Swift isn't your first programming language, you've probably guessed the next step is combining these simple pieces together into more complex, more capable, and more interesting constructs. While that is what we're going to do, it's not as straightforward as you might think.

Swift is a remarkably flexible language, one that takes its inspiration from a number of different sources. It's true to both the object-oriented nature of Objective-C and to new ideas about design, elegance, and maintainability in functional programming languages. You can write Swift like Objective-C, like C, like Java, or even like Haskell, and it will still work.

Since there's no one right way to write Swift, we will be making choices about how we want to organize our code. In this chapter, we're going to look at what Swift offers us for building bigger data structures, and how our choices will affect the evolution of our apps as we write and rewrite them. If the one hammer in your toolbox when you started this book was the good ol' class, let's discover what we can do by taking lightweight types like structures and enumerations and extending them with custom functionality.

Creating Classes

Many programmers—professionals and students, hobbyists and cowboy coders—have grown up in the mind-set of *object-oriented programming*. As Janie once said on the NSBrief podcast, "I didn't think I was learning object-oriented programming. I thought I was learning programming...like that was the only way to do it."

And it's not like anyone's wrong to learn OO! It's the dominant paradigm for a good reason: it has proven over the decades to be a good way to write applications. Whole languages are built around the concepts of OO: it's nigh-impossible to break out of the OO paradigm in Java, and Objective-C has OO in its very name, after all!

So let's see how Swift supports object-oriented programming. The heart and soul of OO is to create *classes*, collections of common behavior from which we will create individual instances called *objects*. We'll begin by creating a new playground called ClassesPlayground, and deleting the "Hello, playground" line as usual.

In the last chapter's collections examples, we used arrays, sets, and dictionaries to represent various models of iOS devices. But it's not easy or elegant to collect much more than a name that way, and there are lots of things we want in an iOS device model. So we will create a class to represent iOS devices.

We'll start by tracking a device's model name and its physical dimensions: width and height. Type the following into the playground:

```
stylishswift/ClassesPlayground.playground/Contents.swift
class IOSDevice {
        var name : String
        var screenHeight : Double
        var screenWidth : Double
}
```

In Swift, we declare a class with the class keyword, followed by the class name. If we were subclassing some other class, we would have a colon and the name of the superclass, like class MyClass : MySuperclass, but we don't need that for this simple class.

Next, we have *properties*, the variables or constants associated with an object instance. In this case, we are creating three variables: name, screenHeight, and screenWidth.

There's just one problem: this code produces an error. We need to start thinking about how our properties work.

Properties

The error flag tells us "Class IOSDevice has no initializers," and the red-circle instant-fix icon offers three problems and solutions. The problem for each is that there is no initial value for these properties. Before accepting the instant fix, let's consider what the problem is.

The properties we have defined are not optionals, so, by definition, they must have values. The tricky implication of that is that they must *always* have values. The value can change, but it can't be absent: that's what optionals are for.

We have a couple of options. We could accept the instant-fix suggestions and assign default values for each. That would give us declarations like

```
var name : String = ""
var screenHeight : Double = 0.0
var screenWidth : Double = 0.0
```

That's one solution, as long as we're OK with the default values. But here they don't quite make sense because we probably never want an iOS device with an empty string for a name.

Plan B: we can make everything optionals. To do this, we append the optional type ? to the properties.

```
var name : String?
var screenHeight : Double?
var screenWidth : Double?
```

Again, no more error, so that's good. Problem now is that any code that wants to access these properties has to do the if let dance from the last chapter to safely unwrap the optionals. And again, do we ever want the device name to be nil? That seems kind of useless.

Fortunately, we have another alternative: Swift's rule is that all properties must be initialized *by the end of every initializer*. So we can write an *initializer* to take initial values for these properties, and since that will be the only way to create an IOSDevice, we can know that these values will always be populated.

So rewrite the class like this:

```
stylishswift/ClassesPlayground.playground/Contents.swift
class IOSDevice {
    var name : String
    var screenHeight : Double
    var screenWidth : Double

    init (name: String, screenHeight: Double, screenWidth: Double) {
      self.name = name
      self.screenHeight = screenHeight
      self.screenWidth = screenWidth
    }
}
```

The initializer runs from lines 6 to 10. The first line is the important one, as it starts with init and then takes a name and type for each of the parameters to be provided to the initializer code. In the initializer itself, we just use the self keyword to assign the properties to these arguments.

To create an instance of IOSDevice, we call the initializer by the name of the class, and provide these arguments by name. Create the constant iPhone6 after the class's closing brace, as follows (note that a line break has been added to suit the book's formatting; it's OK to write this all on one line).

stylishswift/ClassesPlayground.playground/Contents.swift
```
let iPhone6 = IOSDevice(name: "iPhone 6",
  screenHeight: 138.1, screenWidth: 67.0)
```

Congratulations! You've instantiated your first custom object, as the "IOSDevice" in the results pane indicates. Notice that the names of the arguments to the initializer are used as labels in actually calling the initializer. This helps us keep track of which argument is which, something that can be a problem in other languages when you call things that have lots of arguments.

Computed Properties

The three properties we've added to our class are *stored properties*, meaning that Swift creates the in-memory storage for the String and the two Doubles. We access these properties on an instance with dot syntax, like iPhone6.name.

Swift also has another kind of property, the *computed property*, which is a property that doesn't need storage because it can be produced by other means.

Right now we have a screenWidth and a screenHeight. Obviously, it would be easy to get the screen's area by just multiplying those two together. Instead of making the caller do that math, we can have IOSDevice expose it as a computed property. Back inside the class's curly braces—just after the other variables and before the init() is the customary place for it—add the following:

stylishswift/ClassesPlayground.playground/Contents.swift
```
var screenArea : Double {
  get {
    return screenWidth * screenHeight
  }
}
```

Back at the bottom of the file, after creating the iPhone6 constant, fetch the computed property by calling it with the same dot syntax as with a stored property:

```
iPhone6.screenArea
```

The results pane shows the computed area, 9,252.7 (or possibly 9252.699...).

With only a get block, the screenArea is a read-only computed property. We could also provide a set, but that doesn't really make sense in this case.

It's also possible for stored properties to run arbitrary code; instead of computing values, we can give stored properties willSet and didSet blocks to run immediately before or after setting the property's value. We'll use this approach later on in the book.

Methods

Speaking of running arbitrary code, one other thing we expect classes to do is to let us, you know, *do stuff*. In object-oriented languages, classes have *methods* that instruct the class to perform some function. Of course, Swift makes this straightforward.

Let's take our web radio player from the first chapter and add that to our IOSDevice. After all, real iOS devices are used for playing music all the time, right? We'll start by adding the import statement to bring in the audio-video APIs, and the special code we used to let the playground keep playing. Add the following at the top of the file, below the existing import UIKit line:

stylishswift/ClassesPlayground.playground/Contents.swift
```
import AVFoundation
import XCPlayground
XCPlaygroundPage.currentPage.needsIndefiniteExecution = true
```

We need our IOSDevice to have an AVPlayer we can start and stop, so add that as a property after the existing name, screenHeight, and screenWidth:

stylishswift/ClassesPlayground.playground/Contents.swift
```
private var audioPlayer : AVPlayer?
```

Notice that this property is an optional type, AVPlayer?, since it will be nil until it is needed.

Now, let's add a method to the class. We do this with the func keyword, followed by the method name, a list of arguments, and a return type. Add this playAudio() method somewhere inside the class's curly braces, ideally after the init's closing brace, since we usually write our initializers first and our methods next.

stylishswift/ClassesPlayground.playground/Contents.swift
```
func playAudioWithURL(url: NSURL) -> Void {
  audioPlayer = AVPlayer(URL: url)
  audioPlayer!.play()
}
```

Like the init, the parentheses contain the parameters to the method and their types. By convention, we often imply the first parameter type in the name of the method. This is because when we call the method, we do *not* label the first parameter, but we do use labels for any other parameters. For example, if playAudioWithURL() also took a rate argument, we would call it like playAudioWith-URL(someURL, rate: 1.0). Compared to some languages, the labeled parameters may seem chatty or verbose, but, in practice, they make the code more readable by exposing what each value is there for.

After the parameters, the return type is indicated by the -> arrow. In this case, the method returns nothing, so we return Void. (In fact, when we return Void we can omit the arrow and the return.) The rest of the method is the two lines of code we used in the first chapter to create the AVPlayer and start playing.

Now let's call it and start playing music. Put the following at the bottom of the file, after where we create the iPhone6 instance.

stylishswift/ClassesPlayground.playground/Contents.swift
```
if let url = NSURL(string: "http://armitunes.com:8010/listen.pls") {
  iPhone6.playAudioWithURL(url)
}
```

The first line attempts to create an NSURL out of the provided string. We use an if let because, if our string is garbage, what we get back from the initializer could be nil. This is because the NSURL provides a *failable initializer*, one that reserves the right to return nil instead of a new object. It's denoted this way in the documentation with the keyword init?, where the ? clues us in to the fact that optionals are in play.

Wrapping this in an if let means that we will only enter the curly-braced region if the initialization succeeds and assigns the value to the local variable url. This is the proper practice for failable initializers and gets around the bad practice we used in the first chapter when we just force-unwrapped the NSURL? optional with the ! operator.

And once we're safely inside the if let, we call the playAudioWithURL() method that we just wrote, and the music starts playing. If we wanted to write a proper stopAudio() method, that would look like this:

stylishswift/ClassesPlayground.playground/Contents.swift
```
func stopAudio() -> Void {
  if let audioPlayer = audioPlayer {
    audioPlayer.pause()
  }
  audioPlayer = nil
}
```

Again, we use an if let to safely unwrap the audioPlayer optional, and only if that succeeds do we pause() it. Then we can set audioPlayer back to nil.

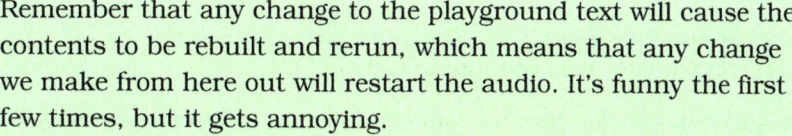

Turn That Music Down

Remember that any change to the playground text will cause the contents to be rebuilt and rerun, which means that any change we make from here out will restart the audio. It's funny the first few times, but it gets annoying.

If you want to turn it off, just comment out the call to playAudioWith-URL(). Swift uses the same comment syntax as all C-derived languages (Objective-C, C#, Java, etc.). That means you can either put // on the start of a line to turn it into a comment, or surround a whole range of lines with a starting /* and a closing */.

Protocols

Swift classes are *single-inheritance*, in that a given class can have only a single superclass. We can't declare that IOSDevice is a subclass of two different classes and inherit the behaviors of both. (In practice, that kind of thing gets messy!) Actually, IOSDevice isn't currently declared as the subclass of anything, so it's just a generic top-level class.

In many languages, we can get common behavior across multiple classes by providing a list of methods that all of them are expected to implement. In Java and C#, for example, the interface keyword performs this function. In Swift, we have *protocols*, and types that provide implementations for methods defined in a protocol are said to "conform to" the protocol. In Swift, protocols aren't limited to methods: they can also specify that a given property is to be made available.

Let's try it out to do something useful. At the bottom of the file where we create the iPhone6, and then again on the line that plays the music, the evaluation pane on the right just says IOSDevice. That's because those lines evaluate to just the iPhone6 object, but the playground doesn't know what it can tell us about the object other than its class. We can do better than that.

Swift defines a protocol called CustomStringConvertible that lets any type declare how it is to be represented as a String. Playgrounds use this for the evaluation pane, as does NSLog() when using the \() substitution syntax, like in NSLog ("I just bought this: \(iPhone6)"). To implement CustomStringConvertible, we just need to provide a property called description, whose type is a String.

To implement the protocol, we first have to change our class definition. In Swift, the class keyword is followed by a colon, the superclass that our class subclasses (if any), and then a comma-separated list of protocols we implement. So rewrite the class definition like this:

stylishswift/ClassesPlayground.playground/Contents.swift
```
class IOSDevice : CustomStringConvertible {
```

As soon as we do this, we will start seeing an error message. That's OK, because the error is that we don't yet conform to the protocol, since we haven't provided a suitable description. Let's do so now, as a computed property. Put this right before or after our other computed property, the screenArea:

stylishswift/ClassesPlayground.playground/Contents.swift
```
var description: String {
  return "\(name), \(screenHeight) x \(screenWidth)"
}
```

This method just uses string substitution to show the device name and its dimensions. As soon as we finish writing this, the evaluation pane starts using this description instead of the bare class name:

```
let iPhone6 = IOSDevice(name: "iPhone 6", screenHeight: 138.1, screenWidth:      iPhone 6, 138.1 x 67.0
    67.0)
```

There are many other protocols we'll be implementing throughout the book. Some, like CustomStringConvertible, come from the Swift language itself, but most are from UIKit and the other iOS frameworks we'll be working with.

Returning Tuples

So far, we've taken a thorough tour of what Swift offers for object-oriented development. In a lot of languages, that would be enough. But in Swift, it's only half the story.

Swift is great for object-oriented programming, but it also allows for more of a *functional programming* style. In functional programming, there's an emphasis on passing data around, instead of maintaining state in classes and mutating it all the time.

One significant trait of functional programming is that it's better to pass *values* to and from functions, rather than *references*. If we have an object of some class, and two parts of our code can modify its data at the same time, it can lead to confusing bugs. In functions, we generally want to pass the data itself, not a containing object. In other words, we prefer *pass-by-value* to *pass-by-reference*.

One thing that makes this difficult is the fact that functions can take many parameters, but they can typically only return one thing. Sometimes, it's natural to want to return multiple values from a function, and in some languages the options to do so are either to define a new type solely to hold those multiple values, or to use some kind of collection.

In Swift, we have *tuples*, which are just simple lists of values. One way to think of it is that just as a function or method can take a list of values wrapped in a pair of parentheses, a tuple lets us *return* a list of values wrapped in a pair of parentheses.

Let's give our existing IOSDevice class a computed property that returns a tuple of the screenHeight and screenWidth. Up with the other computed properties, type the following code:

```
stylishswift/ClassesPlayground.playground/Contents.swift
var screenHeightAndWidth : (height: Double, width: Double) {
  get {
    return (screenHeight, screenWidth)
  }
}
```

This is a lot like our other computed properties, but the type of the variable is in parentheses, which makes it a tuple. Inside the tuple definition, we identify each member by a name (which is not required) and a type. So, this tuple has two members, named height and width. Then we just use parentheses in our return line to package these values into a tuple.

To use the tuple, just access it like any other variable. Outside the class, after creating the iPhone6 variable, pull out the values like this:

```
stylishswift/ClassesPlayground.playground/Contents.swift
iPhone6.screenHeightAndWidth
iPhone6.screenHeightAndWidth.height
iPhone6.screenHeightAndWidth.0
```

For the first line, the evaluation pane shows all the values of the tuple, as (.0 138.1, .1 67). We can then access a value inside the tuple either by the name, like height, or its index in the tuple, like .0. Both of these evaluate to 138.1.

One place that tuples really shine is in counting over collections. In the last chapter, we said that iterating over a collection meant going either by index or by object. Tuples let us have our cake and eat it too. That's because Swift defines an enumerate() function that returns members of a collection as tuples of each member and its index. This lets us do a for-in loop where we have access to both the member and the index inside the loop.

To try it out, we'll need a few new IOSDevice instances and a collection. Add the following at the bottom of the playground:

stylishswift/ClassesPlayground.playground/Contents.swift

```
let iPhone6Plus = IOSDevice(name: "iPhone 6 Plus",
  screenHeight: 158.1, screenWidth: 77.8)
let iPhone5s = IOSDevice (name: "iPhone 5s",
  screenHeight: 123.8, screenWidth: 58.6)
let iPhones = [iPhone5s, iPhone6, iPhone6Plus]
```

This creates an array of three IOSDevice objects. If you like, check them out in the results pane with the QuickLook or Show Result button on the line that creates the iPhones array. Now we'll use enumerate() to count over them with a tuple:

stylishswift/ClassesPlayground.playground/Contents.swift

```
for (index, phone) in iPhones.enumerate() {
  NSLog ("\(index): \(phone)")
}
```

Inside the for loop, we now have access to the index and the phone object each time, so we can easily log them out with NSLog(). In the console (View > Debug Area > Show Debug Area, or ⇧⌘Y), we can see the output that shows each:

```
ClassesPlayground[2947:1037546] 0: iPhone 5s, 123.8 x 58.6
ClassesPlayground[2947:1037546] 1: iPhone 6, 138.1 x 67.0
ClassesPlayground[2947:1037546] 2: iPhone 6 Plus, 158.1 x 77.8
```

What's an Object, Anyway?

I (Janie), like many people, learned programming in the age of Imperative Programming. Java has been around for twenty years and many people learned programming with Java. A lot of us don't know anything except the object-oriented way of doing things. To many of us, this is what programming is.

It doesn't have to be.

One reason I am so vocal in my defense of Swift is because this realization has completely changed my reality. I used to think there was only one way of doing things. Well, I won't say that. There was one right way of doing things and then there was the "Dear god, what is this person thinking by having this property controlled in four different places?!" way of doing things.

Being exposed to Swift and seeing that you don't have to put everything in a class has been a revelatory experience for me. It is forcing me to reevaluate everything I know about programming.

I never thought about what an object was before; there was no point because everything was an object. Now I am trying to get a better understanding of what an object actually is. I wrote a blog about the difference between structs and classes, and at the time I really didn't understand why you would want to use a struct instead of a class if they essentially do the same things. I now understand that you want to try to use structs when possible because they aren't objects. Objects come with a lot of overhead. They let you do some more powerful things like subclassing through polymorphism, but you don't always need to do those things. Looking at how powerful the enums are that Brad Larson (my boss and mentor) uses in his code, I am fascinated by how confined my own view was when I thought everything had to be an object and exist in a class.

So, yes, I once did ask what an object is. I know most programmers worth their salt can tell you the definition of what an object is, but I don't think many of them stop to think about why we use them and if they are the best way of doing things. Or if they bother to wonder if objects are the only way of doing things.

Building Lightweight Structures

If we want to get away from object-oriented programming and try something different, we have to free ourselves of classes. In the next few sections, we'll do just that, and see that we're not losing anything in the transition.

To make a clean start, close this playground and create a new playground called StructsPlayground.

Let's think about the IOSDevice that we created as a class: it had some simple properties for the device name and dimensions, and some methods that operated on those properties. If it mostly serves as a container for data, if we don't care about inheritance, and if the data is small and not difficult to copy around in memory, then it's the kind of thing that functional programmers would tell us doesn't need to be a class.

So what's the alternative? In Swift, we have *structures*, which are lighter containers for properties. Let's remake IOSDevice as a struct to see how they work. Delete the default "Hello playground" line and define the IODevice structure as follows:

stylishswift/StructsPlayground.playground/Contents.swift
```
struct IOSDevice {
  var name : String
  var screenHeight : Double
  var screenWidth : Double
}
```

This is a lot like the beginning of our old class: it's just the property names and their types. One thing has changed, though: we can define these properties as non-optional types, and we don't get an error message about how "IOSDevice has no initializers." That's because the struct gets an initializer for free: just pass in all the values, labeled by their property names in the structure. That means we can create an iPhone6 like this:

stylishswift/StructsPlayground.playground/Contents.swift
```
let iPhone6 = IOSDevice(name: "iPhone 6", screenHeight: 138.1,
  screenWidth: 67.0)
```

This shows an IOSDevice in the results pane, which means we've successfully created an instance of the IOSDevice structure. That was easy!

"But," the critic says, "you can't really *do* anything with it, can you?" Well, sure.

If this were C, our next step would probably be to write some global functions that work with this struct, either taking it as a parameter or returning it as a result. And the difference would be that the functions would receive copies of all the members of the structure, not just a reference to an object in memory (that some other part of the code might also be using, unbeknownst to us).

But still, Swift can do a lot better than just making us write a bunch of global functions.

Extensions

Swift gives us the ability to attach code to arbitrary types: structures, classes, enumerations, and even numeric types. The bits of code are called *extensions*, and they're delightfully powerful. Let's use them to beef up our IOSDevice.

To extend a type, we just write extension and the type we are extending, and then in curly braces we put code for methods or computed properties. This goes *outside* the struct's curly braces. So we can give the IOSDevice structure the screenArea computed property that the class had like this:

```
stylishswift/StructsPlayground.playground/Contents.swift
extension IOSDevice {
  var screenArea : Double {
    get {
      return screenWidth * screenHeight
    }
  }
}
```

Now just call that with iPhone6.screenArea on a new line, and we'll see 9,252.7 (or perhaps 9252.699...) in the results pane.

The fact that we write the code an extension outside the type's definition implies something very powerful: *we can provide extensions for anything.* We're not limited to extending the abilities of our own classes and structures; we can extend classes in UIKit, basic types in Swift, basically any named type. As a rather absurd example, we can add methods to Swift's Int type:

```
stylishswift/StructsPlayground.playground/Contents.swift
extension Int {
  func addOne() -> Int {
    return self + 1
  }
}
```

And then we would call this with 41.addOne() to get 42.

Joe asks:

Why Is the Keyword func When It's Not Really a Function?

The keyword func is so named because Swift does indeed have honest-to-goodness functions: executable segments of code that take parameters and can return a value, but that aren't attached to an instance of anything. We've been using these already: the NSLog() function is a global function that we've used to log messages to the Xcode console pane.

Defining a function is just like creating a method, just outside the scope of a class. Putting it inside the class makes it a method. Really, Swift methods are like a special case of functions: being inside a class, they pick up the stuff inside the class and are able to access its properties and other methods.

In fact, both functions and methods are a special case of the even more general-purpose concept of "closures," but we'll hold off talking about them until Chapter 8, *Managing Time with Closures*, on page 141.

Extensions and Protocols

We don't have to put all our code to extend a given type into one extension block; it's OK to use several. This is helpful when we split up our code more purposefully. For example, let's get back our nice description string to log the name and dimensions of an IOSDevice. When we were writing a class, we implemented the CustomStringConvertible protocol. With a struct, we just provide another extension that conforms to the protocol.

```
stylishswift/StructsPlayground.playground/Contents.swift
extension IOSDevice : CustomStringConvertible {
  var description: String {
    return "\(name), \(screenHeight) x \(screenWidth)"
  }
}
```

Notice that for a read-only computed property, we can omit the get {...} and just provide the code to compute the property in curly braces right after the variable declaration.

Once you write this extension, the IOSDevice gets a nicer representation in the results pane, just like before.

In fact, extensions can be used to extend protocols themselves: an extension can declare new functions, methods, and properties to implement, and can even provide default implementations. Used in this way, it's called a *protocol extension*, and gives us another way to provide object-oriented traits like abstraction and extensibility to simpler types, without classes.

Listing Possibilities with Enumerations

Structures are familiar to old C programmers, and they were available in Objective-C but were so limited that they were often ignored in favor of classes. Swift extensions tilt the balance back toward structs, as it does with another old C type: *enumerations*. The enum is a type that enumerates all its possible values. Its nice for times when you want to know there are a small number of valid values for something, like the suits of playing cards, positions in a team sport, and so forth.

Start a new playground called EnumsPlayground, and delete the "Hello playground" line. We're going to use this playground to rethink our IOSDevice.

So far, whether class or struct, we've assumed our IOSDevice is a touchscreen device like an iPhone, iPad, or iPod touch. But that's not necessarily so, is it? The Apple TV is technically an iOS device, and we currently have no way to account for its lack of a screen, short of turning screenHeight and screenWidth into optionals (which will be a hassle for callers), or using 0.0 flag values, which would just be ugly. Surely, we can do better.

Swift's enumerations give us an elegant solution to this problem. We can define a ScreenType enumeration to indicate what kind of screen the device has. Currently that would be "Retina" or "none," and we can extend it if, say, the iPhone 9 employs a pop-up hologram or something.

Define our ScreenType enumeration like this:

```
stylishswift/EnumsPlayground.playground/Contents.swift
enum ScreenType {
  case None
  case Retina (screenHeight: Double, screenWidth: Double)
}
```

The different values for the enumeration are marked off as separate cases, kind of like a switch statement. What's really interesting here is the Retina case. The two Doubles in parentheses are called *associated values*, and only exist when a given ScreenType is Retina. The None case has no associated values, and some other case might have completely different associated values; maybe a hypothetical case CrystalBall would have a radius: Double for its associated value.

Now let's create a new struct that can use this enum to represent its display, or lack thereof:

stylishswift/EnumsPlayground.playground/Contents.swift
```
struct IOSDevice {
  var name : String
  var screenType : ScreenType
}
```

That's easy enough; the enum acts like a new type, just like a String or Int. Now let's create some instances of this:

stylishswift/EnumsPlayground.playground/Contents.swift
```
Line 1  let iPhone6 = IOSDevice(name: "iPhone 6",
     2    screenType: ScreenType.Retina(screenHeight: 138.1, screenWidth: 67.0))
     3  let appleTV3rdGen = IOSDevice(name: "Apple TV (3rd Gen)",
     4    screenType: ScreenType.None)
```

Notice that just like with the struct, we automatically pick up the syntax for populating the associated values of the ScreenType.Retina case; we just label and provide a value for each one, comma-separated, in parentheses (see line 2).

Concise Swift

Swift likes concision, and many things that are redundant can be omitted. For example, the screenType variable in these initializers can only be of type ScreenType, so it's legal to omit the type and just write the value with the leading dot character. So we could create the appleTV3rdGen like this:

stylishswift/EnumsPlayground.playground/Contents.swift
```
let appleTV3rdGen = IOSDevice(name: "Apple TV (3rd Gen)",
  screenType: .None)
```

As opportunities for omitting syntax occur throughout the book, we'll generally spell it out the long way first, mention what can be left out, and use the concise version from then on.

Using Associated Values in Enumerations

As before, the results pane evaluates the two instances of our new structure as just IOSDevice, because we no longer have a CustomStringConvertible implementation to provide a pretty string for them. We can provide one with an extension, and in the process we'll see how to use the associated values we provided for the screenHeight and screenWidth.

When we work with enumerations, we almost always need to use a switch statement to pick apart the possible cases. switch and enum go together perfectly, since they make it clear that we are walking through each possible value of the enum with case statements. In fact, Swift requires that the switch be exhaustive, meaning that it handles every possible case of the enum. There are only two in ScreenType, so it's easy here; with lots of cases, we could use default at the end of the switch to deal with otherwise-unhandled cases.

So to implement the description method, we need to return a string. It will include the name of the device and, only if it has a .Retina screen type, the dimensions of the screen. Here's how we can do that with a switch:

```
stylishswift/EnumsPlayground.playground/Contents.swift
extension IOSDevice : CustomStringConvertible {
    var description : String {
        var screenDescription: String
        switch screenType {
        case .None:
            screenDescription = "No screen"
        case .Retina (let screenHeight, let screenWidth):
            screenDescription = "Retina screen " +
                "\(screenHeight) x \(screenWidth)"
        }
        return "\(name): \(screenDescription)"
    }
}
```

We begin on line 1 with an extension that says we are going to make IOSDevice conform to CustomStringConvertible. This means defining a description computed variable of type String.

Our description should provide a different string based on whether or not we have a screen. We declare the screenDescription on line 3. Notice that this is not an optional, yet we haven't provided a value for it; Swift lets us get away with this if it can tell that we are providing a value in any case before the value is read. We start the switch on line 4, and the .None case that starts on line 5 is easy: we can just set screenDescription to "No Screen".

The interesting part is on line 7, which starts the .Retina case. We use the let keyword in parentheses to receive the associated values as local variables. If we didn't care about one or more of these values, we could use the underscore character _ instead of let and the local variable name to say "I don't need this value." But in this case, we want both the screenHeight and screenWidth as local variables, so we can build a screenDescription that shows the dimensions.

Once this is written, the playground will immediately rebuild and rerun our playground, and the IOSDevice, now that it conforms to CustomStringConvertible, will pretty-print nice descriptions for our two devices in the evaluation pane:

```
let iPhone6 = IOSDevice(name: "iPhone 6",
  screenType: ScreenType.Retina(screenHeight: 138.1, screenWidth: 67.0))
let appleTV3rdGen = IOSDevice(name: "Apple TV (3rd Gen)",
  screenType: ScreenType.None)
```

iPhone 6: Retina screen 138.1 x 67.0

Apple TV (3rd Gen): No screen

Swift's So Functional!

So, between structs, enums, protocols, and especially extensions, we can replicate most of the power of object-oriented programming, without needing to use classes and the usual practices of maintaining and mutating state. Swift isn't the most pure functional programming language by a long shot, but functional programming (FP) fans have found much to like in it.

Keep in mind that most of the iOS frameworks are very object-oriented in nature—they were written for use with Objective-C after all—so much of the code we write will be of an OO style by necessity. Having said that, when we see an option to do things with a lighter touch, we'll try to do so.

Optionals Are Enumerations!

Here's a nifty little implementation detail that sometimes turns out to be useful: optionals are actually enumerations! An optional type is an enum with two cases, called .None and .Some. The .None case is where the optional is nil, whereas .Some has an associated value: the unwrapped value of the optional.

Some developers use this as a means of performing logic on the optional, particularly if we want to do something in the nil case. Rather than doing an if let and then testing the value against some other logic, we can put the logic in a switch like this:

```
stylishswift/EnumsPlayground.playground/Contents.swift
let optionalString : String? = "iPhone6"
switch optionalString {
case .None:
  NSLog ("nil!")
case .Some(let value):
  NSLog ("some! \(value)")
}
```

Handling Errors the Swift 2.0 Way

One thing we haven't considered is what to do when things go wrong. So far, our only defensive tactic has been the cautious use of if let to avoid crashing when we unwrap optionals that turn out to be nil. But there's more to robust coding practices than that.

Swift 2.0 introduces a new error-handling paradigm that is supported by many of the iOS frameworks. It will be familiar to readers who've seen try-catch-style semantics in other languages, but its differences are important to understand: these aren't your father's java.lang.Exceptions.

In Swift 2.0, methods (including initializers) can indicate that they signal errors by including the throws keyword. To call code that may throw, we need to do two things:

1. Wrap all related code in a do-catch block, where the catch will pull out and handle any thrown object.

2. Explicitly put the keyword try immediately before each method or initializer that can throw. Of course the compiler could figure it out for us; this is meant as a means of annotating the code by explicitly calling attention to parts of the code that can produce errors.

Let's try an example. The iOS frameworks have a number of APIs that throw errors in Swift. In many cases, these were implemented in Objective-C with an "in-out" system where a caller would provide a pointer to an NSError object. The caller would send in nil for this pointer, and check its value after the method returned. If it was now a pointer to an NSError, it meant that an error had occurred. All such "in-out" APIs are converted automatically to the throws idiom in Swift, so don't let the documentation scare you when you see all those Objective-C asterisks (**NSError always freaked us out).

As an example, there's a class called NSData that wraps an in-memory data buffer of any size. It can be populated with the contents of any NSURL with the init(contentsOfURL:options:) method, *but*...it's marked with throws, which means if we use it, we have to deal with a possible error. And that makes sense, of course: what should it do if your URL is nonsense or if there's a network error? Throwing an error describing the problem at least gives us a chance of recovering or telling the user what happend.

Start a new playground called ErrorHandlingPlayground, and delete the "Hello, playground" line. It's been a long chapter, so we'll make this short:

stylishswift/ErrorHandlingPlayground.playground/Contents.swift

```
Line 1  if let myURL = NSURL(string: "http://pragprog.com") {
     2    do {
     3      let myData = try NSData (contentsOfURL: myURL, options: [])
     4      let myString = NSString(data: myData, encoding: NSUTF8StringEncoding)
     5    } catch let error as NSError {
     6      NSLog ("NSError: \(error)")
     7    } catch {
     8      NSLog ("No idea what happened there")
     9    }
    10  }
```

Line 3 tries to create the NSData from the provided myURL. This initializer throws, so the initializer itself needs to have the try keyword right before it; when a method or function throws, the try will be at the beginning of the line.

If we successfully download the NSData, we use it on line 4, where it's used to create an NSString, iOS's older string class that can be initialized from raw data. (Don't worry: if we needed to turn it into a Swift String, the types are freely interchangeable.) This line needs to be inside the do-catch only because it needs to have the myData in scope.

So, when this works, we'll see the NSData and NSString represented over in the result area: the data will be clusters of hexadecimal digits, and the string will be the raw HTML.

Now let's get ourselves into the error handling. We'll do that by mangling the URL string. A simple way to do this is to change the URL scheme from http to some nonsense like foo. Do this, and the evaluation pane will go blank. Instead, down in the debug console, we'll see an error message:

```
ErrorHandlingPlayground[6258:1941577] NSError: Error Domain=
  NSCocoaErrorDomain Code=256 "The file couldn't be opened."
  UserInfo={NSURL=foo://pragprog.com}
```

This is coming from the block on line 5 that catches thrown NSErrors. The later catch on line 7 catches anything, although nothing in our code is declared as throwing something other than NSError, so it will never be reached and is shown only for demonstration.

So, in a nutshell, that's Swift error-handling: if something declares that it throws, wrap the call in a do-catch, decorate all calls that can throw with try, and then catch whatever was thrown, using the let as construct to pick apart the type that was thrown.

Oh, and let's please be sure to do more to recover than just logging an error to the Xcode console. In real life, we would want to tell the user what happened, or maybe automatically retry, or *something*.

What We've Learned

You came into this chapter knowing about strings, numeric types, control flow, and collections—the building blocks of a Swift application—but not enough to combine them together in interesting ways. In this chapter, we've gotten into the concepts of how to organize these types and their logic into meaningful and capable abstractions that can serve as the structure of an app.

We started in the comfort zone of object-oriented programming, building classes with properties and methods that would be perfectly recognizable to a Java 1.0 programmer from 1995. But, aware that toting around a bunch of state isn't always how we want to do things in the 21st century, we looked at Swift's functional programming–inspired alternatives for structuring our data. By using extensions and protocols, we can take simple enumerations and structures and make them as compelling as full-blown classes.

We've been able to do all this in the Xcode playground, which gives us a fine place to try out our Swift code. Now it's time to pick up our toys and move into developing actual iOS apps. In the next chapter, you're going to learn how to build actual iOS user interfaces and start building our real app.

Part II

Creating the App

CHAPTER 4

Building User Interfaces

We've had three chapters to play around with Swift. Now we're going to come at iOS development from a completely different angle: developing the user interface.

We'll kick things off with a little secret about iOS development, something it inherited from Mac development: *Create the user interface first.* This is totally backward for a lot of seasoned developers. A lot of us think through an application's requirements and immediately start thinking of our data models and strategies and...*nuh-uh.* Build the UI first. Build what users are going to see, what they're going to interact with, and start to understand how they'll experience it. Then figure out how the heck you're going to do that.

That philosophy is reflected in the tools provided for iOS development. If we built the user interface by writing code, it would be natural to code the functionality and then put buttons and views on top of it. Instead, the iOS SDK provides distinct tools for building the UI graphically and for coding its functionality. The tools let us see our interface first, and then make it work.

In this chapter, we're going to start building an app that will carry us through to submitting to the App Store, which we do in the final chapter. And since iOS apps start with the user interface, that's *all* we're going to do in this chapter: we'll familiarize ourselves with the tools for building UIs, and in the next chapter we'll start connecting it to code.

Our First Project

Our project for the rest of the book is a simple Twitter client, which will allow the user to post messages to Twitter, view his or her timeline, and drill down for more details on a tweet or the person who posted it. This lets us develop features that are genuinely valuable to real users, and exposes us to practical concerns about getting data from the Internet and presenting it in the iOS user interface. Not to mention, Twitter clients are among the most-used and most-loved iOS apps, and have been a hotbed of UI innovation: the familiar "pull to refresh" gesture first appeared in "Tweetie," which later became the official Twitter app for iOS.

As we develop the app, you can use your existing Twitter account or, if you don't have one or would prefer to use a separate account for development work, create a new Twitter account at http://twitter.com. While working on the book, we've used a test account, @pragsiostest, which we'll use for screenshots.

To begin work on a new app, we need to create a project using the menu sequence File > New > Project (⇧⌘N). There's also a button on the Xcode greeting window for starting a project, so that's another way to do it.

When we create a new project, a window opens, and out slides a sheet that asks us what kind of project we want to create. This project template sheet, shown here, has a list on the left side of project categories divided into iOS and Mac OS X, watchOS, and "Other" sections. Since we're building an iOS application, we'll select Application from the iOS section and then look at the choices in the main part of the frame. We can click each to see a general description of what kind of app to start on. For our first example, we'll select Single View Application.

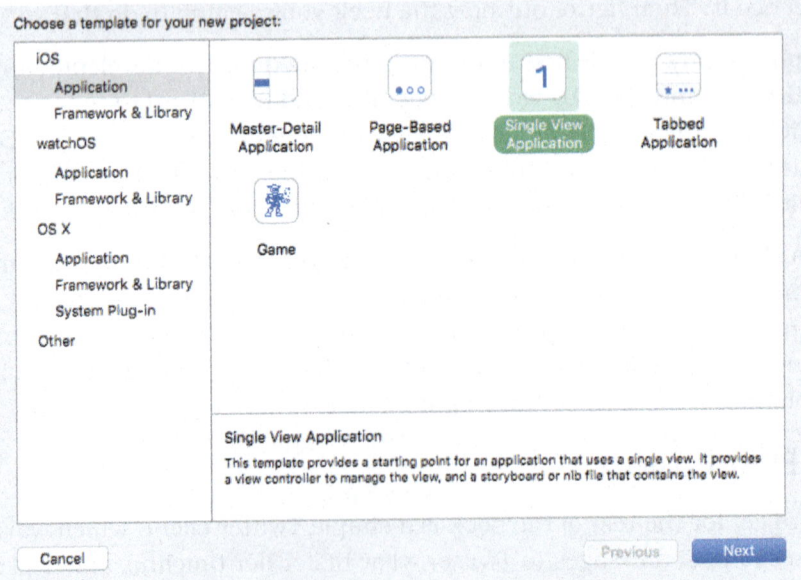

After we click Next, the sheet then asks us for details specific to the project, as shown in the following figure. Some of these change based on the project type; in general, this is where we need to provide names and other identifiers to the app, indicate which device formats (iPhone and/or iPad) it's for, and so on. For our first app, here's how we should fill out the form:

Choose options for your new project:

Product Name:	PragmaticTweets
Organization Name:	Pragmatic Programmers, LLC
Organization Identifier:	com.pragprog.yourhandle
Bundle Identifier:	com.pragprog.yourhandle.PragmaticTweets
Language:	Swift
Devices:	Universal

☐ Use Core Data
☑ Include Unit Tests
☑ Include UI Tests

Cancel   Previous   Next

- *Product Name*—A name for the product with no spaces or other punctuation. Our product will be called PragmaticTweets here.

- *Organization Name*—This can be a company, organization, or personal name, which will be used for the copyright statement automatically put at the top of every source file.

- *Organization Identifier*—This is a reverse-DNS style stub that will uniquely identify our app in the App Store, so if someone else submits a PragmaticTweets, the two apps won't be mistaken for each other because they'll each have a unique *Bundle Identifier*, which is the auto-generated fourth line of the form. If you have your own domain, you can use it for the company identifier; otherwise, just invert your email address, such as in com.company.yourhandle.

- *Language*—There are two choices for this pop-up menu: *Swift* and *Objective-C*. We've covered Swift for the last three chapters, so let's choose that here.

- *Devices*—This determines whether the template should set us up with an app that's meant to run on an iPhone (and iPod touch) or iPad or be a "universal" app with a different layout for each. Not all templates offer all three options. With the variety of iOS devices currently available, Apple is pushing hard for developers to build universal apps that run and look good on a variety of screen sizes, all four sizes of iPhone and two of iPad, so select Universal here.

- *Check boxes*—Do not select Use Core Data, which is a data persistence framework that is beyond the scope of this book. When we're done, feel free to move on to Marcus Zarra's excellent book *Core Data (2nd edition): Data Storage and Management for iOS, OS X, and iCloud.*[1] Go ahead and check both Include Unit Tests and Include UI Tests. These will make it easier to expose our app to automated testing, which we'll do in Chapter 6, *Testing the App*, on page 97.

After clicking Next, we choose a location on the filesystem for our project. There's also an option for creating a local Git source code repository for our files. Source control is beyond the scope of this book, but in short: if you want a local history of all your changes, select it. If you don't need it, or (better yet!) if you plan to check your code into an external source control system like GitHub later on, leave it unselected. Once we specify where the project will be saved, Xcode copies over some starter files for our project and reveals them in its main window.

The Xcode Window

Xcode 7 provides a single window for a project. This window provides our view into nearly everything we'll do with a project: editing code and user interfaces, adjusting settings for how the project is built and run, employing debugging tools, and viewing logged output.

The window is split into five areas, although some of them can be hidden with menu commands and/or toolbar buttons. These areas are shown in an "exploded" view in the figure on page 63.

The window is split up as follows:

Toolbar

The toolbar at the top of the window offers the most basic controls for building projects and working with the rest of the workspace. The leftmost buttons, Run and Stop, start and stop build-and-run cycles. Next are two borderless buttons collectively known as the scheme selector, which chooses which "target" to run (currently PragmaticTweets) and in what environment (a simulated "iPhone 6," or the name of an actual iOS device

---

1. https://pragprog.com/book/mzcd2/core-data

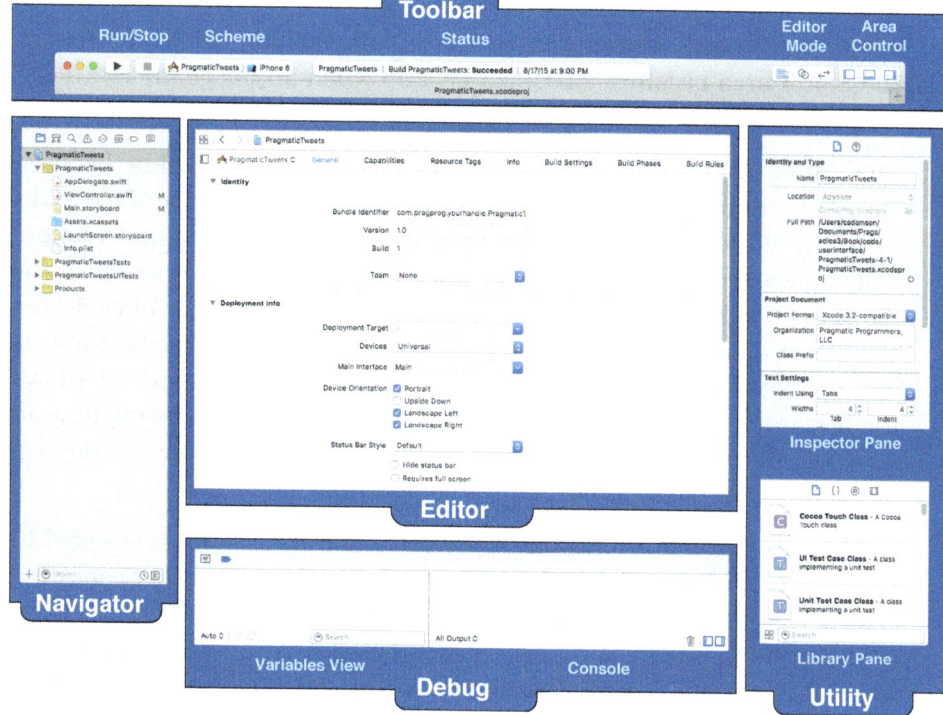

connected to the Mac). Next comes an iTunes-like status display that shows the most recent build and/or run results, including a count of warnings and errors generated by a continual background analysis of the code. Further right, the Editor Mode buttons let us switch between three different kinds of editors, which we'll describe shortly. Finally, three View buttons allow us to show or hide the Navigator, Debug, and Utility areas. These areas perform the following roles:

Navigator Area

The left pane (which may be hidden if the leftmost View button in the toolbar is unselected) offers high-level browsing of our project's contents. It has a mini-toolbar to switch between eight different navigators. The File Navigator (⌘1) shows the project's source and resource files and is therefore the most important and commonly used of the seven. Other navigators let us perform searches (⌘3), inspect build warnings and errors, inspect runtime threads and breakpoints, and more.

Editor Area

The main part of the window is the Editor area. This view cannot be hidden. Its contents are set by selecting a file in the Navigator area, and the form the editor takes depends on the file being edited—when a source file is selected, we see a typical source code editor, when a GUI file is selected, the Editor area becomes a GUI editor, and when an image file like a GIF or JPEG is selected, the Editor area displays the image.

The Editor Mode buttons in the toolbar switch the editor pane between three modes: standard, which is the default editor for the type of file that's selected; assistant, which shows related files side by side; and version, which uses source control to show current and historical versions of the file side by side, a "blame" mode that shows the committer of each line of code, or a log of commit comments alongside the code. The Editor area also contains a *jump bar*, a breadcrumb-style strip at the top that shows the hierarchy of the thing being edited; for a source file, this might read "project, group, file, method." Each member of the jump bar is a pop-up menu that navigates to related or recent points of interest.

By default, a new project comes up with its top-level settings selected in the Navigator area, which means that the Editor area defaults to showing settings for things like the app version number, the targeted SDK version and device families, and so on. There may also be a scary-looking "No matching provisioning profiles found" warning, which just means we're not set up to run our app on a real device yet; we'll deal with that in Chapter 17, *Publishing and Maintaining the App*, on page 289.

Utility Area

The right side of the window is a utility area that provides detailed viewing and editing of specific selections in the Editor area. Depending on the file being edited, the toolbar atop this area can show different tools in its Inspector pane. Basic information about a selected file and quick help on the current selection are always available. For GUI files, there are inspectors to work with individual UI objects' class identities (⌥⌘3), their settable attributes (⌥⌘4), their size and layout (⌥⌘5), and their connections to source code (⌥⌘6). We'll be using all of these shortly. At the bottom of the Utility area, a library pane gives us click-and-drag access to common code snippets, UI objects, and more.

Debug Area

The bottom of the window, below the Editor area and between the Navigator and Utility areas, is a view for debugging information when an app is running. Its tiny toolbar has a segmented button that lets us switch between the debugging-oriented *variables view* that allows us to inspect memory when stopped on a breakpoint, a textual *console view* of logging output from the application, or a split view of both. We'll make use of the right-side console view in a little bit, whereas the left-side variables view will be our focus in a later chapter.

So that's how Xcode presents our initial project to us, but what can we do? Well, there's a nice big Run button, and it's not like it's disabled. Let's try running the app. Make sure the scheme is some flavor of iPhone from the iOS Simulator section (and not iPad or the name of an actual device); in Xcode 7, our choices range from the iPhone 4s to the iPhone 6 Plus. Click the Run button. The status area will shade in with a progress bar that fills up as it builds all the files and bundles them into an app, and when it's done, it will launch the iOS Simulator. The Simulator is another OS X application, which looks and behaves more or less like a real iPhone or iPad. When our app runs in the Simulator, the main screen disappears and is replaced by a big white box that fills the Simulator screen.

Building Our User Interface

That white box in the Simulator is our app. It's not much, but then again, we haven't done anything yet, so let's start building it. Press Stop in Xcode to stop the simulated app, and then take a look at the project in Xcode.

If the File Navigator isn't already showing on the left side of the project window, bring it up with ⌘1. The File Navigator uses a tree-style hierarchy with a blue Xcode document at the top, representing the project itself as the root. Under this are files and folders. The folder icons are *groups* that collect related files, such as the views and logic classes for one part of the app; groups don't usually represent actual directories on the filesystem. We can expand all the groups to see the contents of the project, like this:

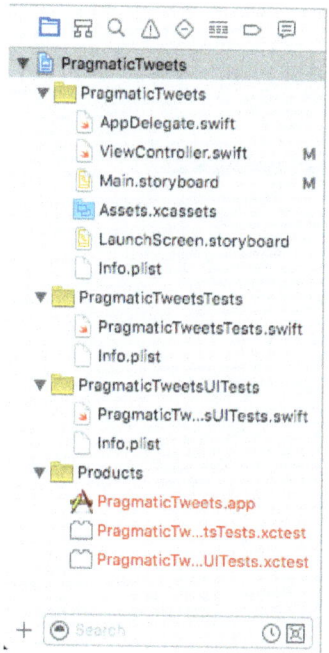

Different project templates will set us up with different files. For the view-based app, we get two source code files in the PragmaticTweets group, along with a Main.storyboard, a LaunchScreen.storyboard, and an Assets.xcassets. These are the files we'll be editing. There are also a few helper files like Info.plist, but we won't need to edit them directly. The PragmaticTweetsTests and group is where we will write unit tests to validate our code, something we'll do in Chapter 6, *Testing the App*, on page 97. Ditto for PragmaticTweetsUITests, which can test the purely UI parts of our app. Finally, the Products group shows the files our build will create: in this case, PragmaticTweets.app for the app, plus PragmaticTweetsTests.xctest and PragmaticTweetsUITests.xctest for the runnable unit tests. Files shown in red indicate they haven't been built yet; PragmaticTweets.app is red in the figure because, although we've run it in the Simulator, we haven't built it for the actual device yet.

We said at the outset that iOS development starts with the user interface. By focusing on what the user sees and how they interact with it, we keep our focus on the user experience and not on the data models and logic behind the scenes. We typically build our user interfaces visually and store them in *storyboards*. The project has one such file, Main.storyboard, so let's click it.

Storyboards

When we click on Main.storyboard, the Editor area switches to a graphical view called *Interface Builder*, or IB for short. In iOS, IB works with user interface documents called *storyboards*. Just like in movie-making, where a storyboard is a process used to plan out a sequence of shots in a movie or TV show, the storyboard of an iOS app shows the progression through the different views the app will present. The initial storyboard looks like the following figure.

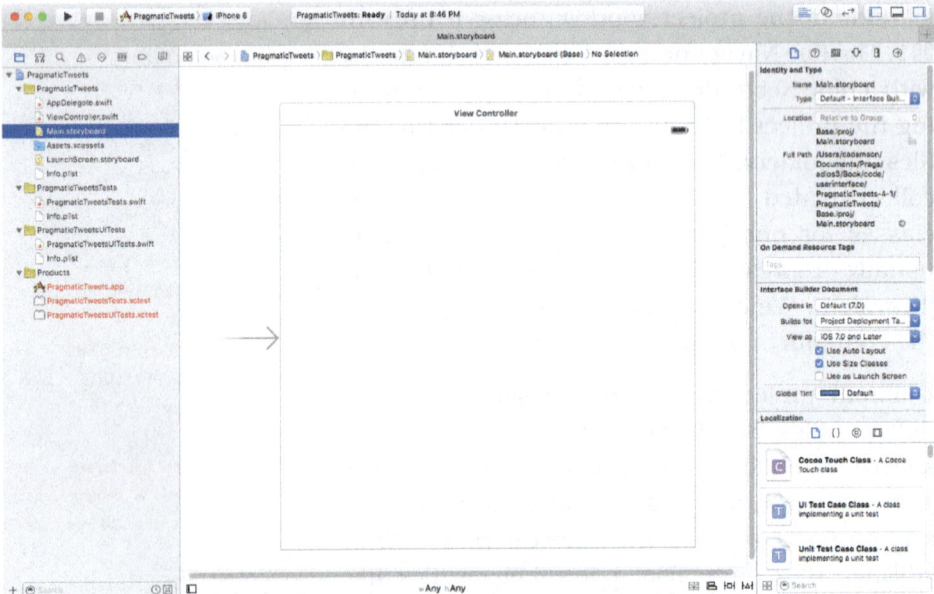

Our app uses a single view, so we follow the right-pointing arrow (which indicates where the app starts) into a square that represents the visible area of the screen. This is our app's one view; if we were building a navigation-style app, there would be one view rectangle for each screen of the navigation. Click the view to show a header box with three icons. These are *proxy objects* that represent objects that will work with the view at runtime: a *view controller* that contains logic to respond to events and update the view; a *first responder* that represents the ability to handle events; and an *exit segue*, used for when we back out of views in navigation apps (something we'll visit in a later chapter).

At the bottom left of the Editor area, IB shows a little view disclosure button. Click this to show and hide the scene list (shown here), which shows each "scene" of the storyboard and its contents as a tree structure. Currently, our one scene has the proxy objects discussed earlier, and inside the view controller, we find two layout objects and a "view." This view is

the big square in the UI; as we add UI elements like buttons and labels, the scene's tree list will show them as children of this view.

But wait a minute!, you might say, *iPhones aren't square, and neither are iPads!* Quite right. What we're seeing in our startup view is Apple pushing developers to "think different" about device sizes. At the bottom of the IB pane, a label indicates our current layout as "w: Any h: Any." This is actually a button that allows us to try our user interface layouts in different sizes and orientations. Click the label to show the sizing popover, which looks like the one in the figure.

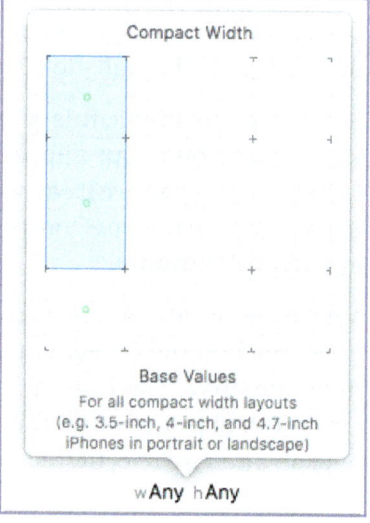

As we mouse over the grid of boxes in this popover, we can switch the height and width previews between Compact, Any, and Regular, and the popover titles will give us a hint of the class of sizes we're previewing, like "iPhone in landscape orientation." Click on the box to change the preview to see the main view change to this size and shape. Once we start laying out some contents for the view, this is how we will preview how they'll be laid out on different device sizes, and when we rotate from portrait to landscape, or vice versa. However, when we're not previewing and actually building the UI, this should be set to Any:Any.

Adding Buttons

So let's start adding some UI elements to our view. We'll begin by adding a button to send a tweet telling the world that our first app is running. To add components to our storyboard, use the toolbar to show the Utility area on the right (if it's not already showing), and find the Library pane at the bottom right. There's a mini-toolbar here that should default to showing user interface objects; if not, click the little icon of a square in a circle (or press ^⌥⌘3). The bottom of the pane has a button to toggle between list and icon views for the objects, and a search filter to find objects by name. Scroll down through this pane to find the icon that just says Button; we can tap once on any of the objects to get its name, class, and description to appear in a popover. Drag the button from the Object library into the iPhone-sized view in IB. This will create a plain button.

It leaves a lot to the imagination, huh? Without the edge and background decorations of earlier versions of iOS, it doesn't necessarily look like a button at all. It could easily be mistaken for a text label.

The recent look of iOS, introduced back in iOS 7, has three stated themes: *deference, clarity,* and *depth.* The first of these, deference, means that the UI appearance focuses attention on our content rather than competing with a bunch of pseudo-realistic effects.

So maybe our problem is a lack of content. iOS expects us to tell the user what's going on in our app, and we're not holding up our end of the deal yet. Let's fix that. First, we'll say what the button does. Double-click on the button to change its name to Send Tweet. Now it says what it does, but it still doesn't exactly feel button-y.

Maybe we can fix that by contrasting the blue text of the button with a plain label. Back in the Object library at the lower right, find the Label object, and drag one above the button. Change its text to "I finished the first project." Drag both objects so that they're centered in the view; a dashed blue line will appear when we're centered, and the drag will snap to this position. The view should now look like the figure.

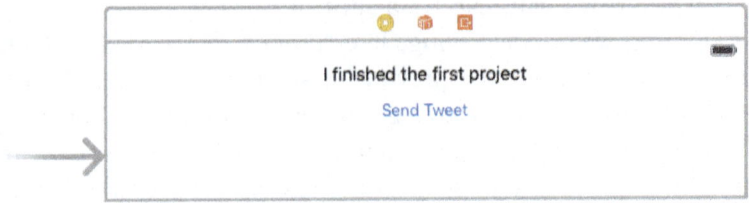

Go ahead and click the Run button to run this app again in the iOS Simulator. We should just see the label and the button, right? Sure, but there's a problem.

When we run the app in the Simulator, we typically start in portrait orientation. And right now, that's going to be a problem, because our label and button are not centered in portrait; in fact, they're cut off on the right edge, as seen in the following figure. Rotate to landscape with Rotate Left and Rotate Right items in the Hardware menu (⌘← and ⌘→, respectively), and it looks a little better, but it's still clearly not centered on tall models like the iPhone 5. What happened?

The problem is that we've been designing against a hypothetical square shape, and we never explicitly said these labels were supposed to be centered. What's happened instead is that they've kept a constant distance from the top and left sides of their parent view. In a way, it makes sense: iOS doesn't know what matters to us: a constant distance from the top or bottom, or being centered, or some other relationship entirely.

Stop the Simulator, go back to Xcode, and select the label. On the right side of the workspace, show the *Size Inspector*, by clicking the little ruler icon (or pressing ⌥⌘5). This inspector tells us about the size and location of elements in our UI. There's a section called Constraints, which currently reads:

> The selected views have no constraints. At build time explicit left, top, width, and height constraints will be generated for the view.

Autolayout

In iOS, our UI elements are placed onscreen with an *autolayout* system that lets you determine where objects should go and how big they should be based on *constraints* that we set on them. This allows our interfaces to adapt to being rotated between portrait and landscape, and to handle the differing screen sizes of the 3.5-inch models (original iPhone through iPhone 4s), 4-inch models (iPhone 5, 5c, and 5s), the 4.7-inch iPhone 6, and 5.5-inch iPhone 6 Plus. Constraints allow us to express what matters to us—the size of components, their alignment with or distance from other components, and so forth—and to let other factors vary as needed. In this example, we want our label and button to be horizontally centered, and we don't care what the resulting *x* and *y* coordinate values are.

⊞ ⊟ ⊢⊣ ⊦⊣ Interface Builder puts a floating set of buttons at the bottom right of the pane to give us access to autolayout features. These buttons display a popover or pop-up menu when tapped.

⊞ *Stack button*: This button embeds one or more selected views into a "stack view," a container for other views (and something we'll explore in a later chapter).

⊟ *Align popover*: This lets us create constraints that align a view's edges or horizontal or vertical center with another view, or horizontally or vertically center it within its containing view (its *superview*).

⊢⊣ *Pin popover*: This lets us create constraints that specify a fixed value for spacing from one or more edges to another view (possibly the superview), and/or a fixed width or height.

⊦⊣ *Resolve menu*: The options here will adjust a view position or size so it matches its constraints, or do the opposite and create constraints based on its current position and size. We can also clear all constraints and start over with this menu.

So what we need to do is to just tell our label and button to be centered. Click the label, and then click the Alignment button. This shows the popover in the figure.

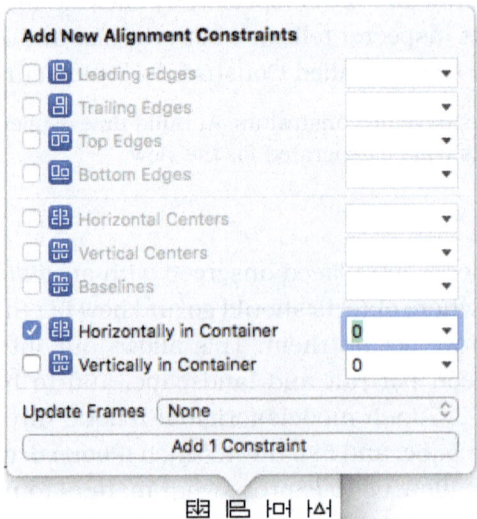

Click the check box next to Horizontal Center in Container. This will change the button at the bottom of the popover to say Add 1 Constraint. Click this

Storyboard Zooming

If you need to zoom in or out of a storyboard…well, we hope you have a laptop. With a trackpad, we can pinch zoom in and out to show more of the storyboard. Without a trackpad, there are zoom menu items available via a Control-click in the Editor area, or the menu item Editor > Canvas > Zoom.

button to dismiss the popover (note that if we tap outside the popover instead of tapping the button, the popover will dismiss *without* creating the constraint).

This causes an orange line to appear down the middle of the view, and an orange box around it, when the label is selected. In Interface Builder, orange is a warning color, meaning *there aren't enough constraints*. The label is *under-constrained* because, although we've provided a horizontal constraint, we haven't provided a vertical constraint, meaning autolayout can't know for sure how high or low on the screen to place the label.

Since we're happy with what the label looks like in Interface Builder, let's just tell it to keep this same distance from the top of the container view. We do that by *pinning* its distance from the top. With the label selected, click the Pin button to show the popover seen here.

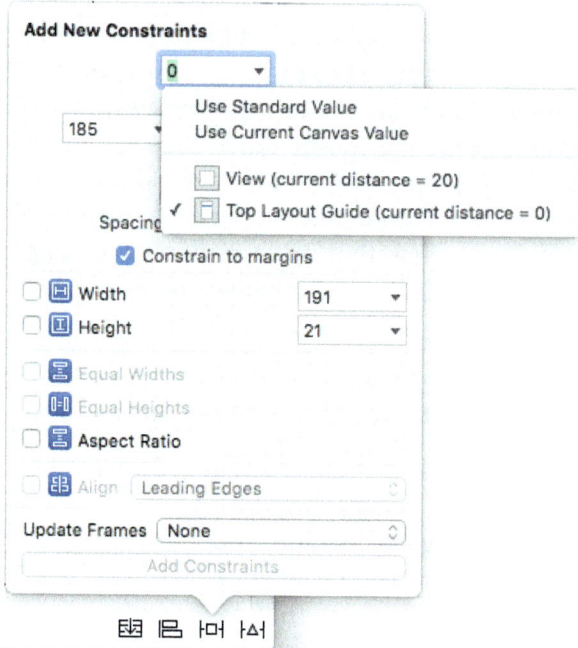

The pinning popover lets us lock down values such as width and height or distances from containers or other views, or force sides of multiple components to stay aligned. The top section is called "Spacing to nearest neighbor," and if we click the top pop-up menu in this part, we can select the value Top Layout Guide, meaning we want to lock the distance between the top of our label and the area at the top of the screen reserved for the status bar (where the battery level, signal strength, clock, and other indicators appear), or any other menus at the top of the screen (like the navigation bar we'll introduce much later). When we select this menu item, the "brace" graphic under the menu becomes solid, and the button in the popover again says Add 1 Constraint. Click this button to add the new constraint.

One other thing to watch for is orange markers indicating that an object is not in its correct position. Typically, these warnings will also show a size or distance number in a little bubble. When you see this, you can correct the problem by selecting the object, going to the resolve pop-up menu at the lower right, and choosing Update Frame. The only problem is that if the object is out of position *and* underconstrained, the update could send it all the way to one edge of the view, or radically change its size. If this happens, just undo (⌘Z), and think about what other constraints you might need.

Size-Specific Constraints

 When creating constraints, it's important that the sizing bar at the bottom of the pane is in "w:Any h:Any" mode. Although this creates somewhat unrealistic square views, the danger is that constraints created with any other sizes set for width or height *will only apply for those sizes.* If we set width to Compact to preview the appearance of an iPhone in portrait and add a constraint like horizontal centering, that will only apply for compact width, so there will be *no* constraint for landscape, or on an iPad, since those aren't cases of compact width.

We learned this one the hard way, when one of our buttons went flying offscreen on the iPad. We'll talk about the underlying size concepts later, in a later chapter.

Now when we select the label, Interface Builder shows the centering line as blue, and adds a blue brace from the top of the label up to the status bar area. Blue means that we  have enough constraints to not be ambiguous to autolayout, as shown in the following figure. Try running it again, and rotate the Simulator. The label stays horizontally centered and maintains a constant distance from the top, while the button continues to be uncentered in landscape orientation.

We can repeat the same steps to fix the button. First, select the button, click the Alignment button, choose Horizontal Center in Container, and click Add 1 Constraint. This again gives us the orange line to tell us we're not quite done. Now click the Pin button, and show the menu for the top spacing. This time we have a choice: we can pin either the distance to the Top Layout Guide as before, or the distance from the top of the button to the label. This is the power of constraints: we get to indicate what matters to us. Do we care about the button's distance to the top, or its relation to the label? In this case, the label helps explain what the button does, so it makes more sense to keep them together and pin the distance from the button to the label, rather than the button to the top. So, select "Label - I finished the ..." and click Add 1 Constraint. This gives us blue guides in Interface Builder, indicating that all is well, including a blue brace between the button and the label.

Run the app again and both our components are centered regardless of orientation, as seen in the Simulator screenshots. We can also change the device type between 3.5-inch and 4-inch iPhone models in the scheme selector to see the effect of the larger screen; it doesn't matter much now because our buttons' vertical positions are measured from the top of the screen, but it would be a big deal if we had anything pinned to the bottom, since we'd be losing a half inch of space in the middle as we go from an iPhone 5 to an older iPhone.

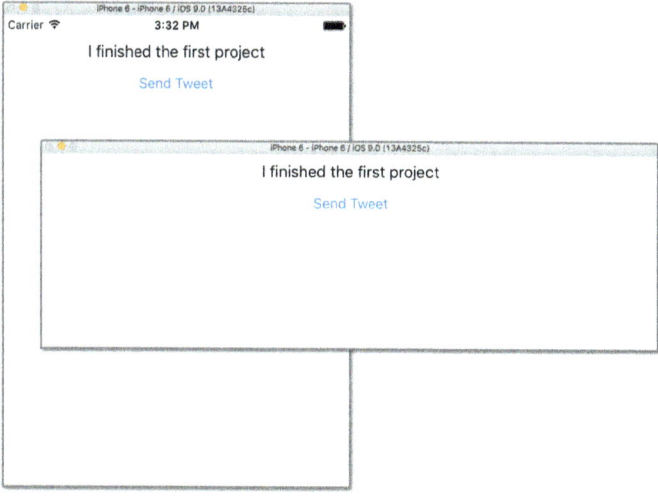

Now imagine if we had to explicitly set each object's position and size in code: it would be a nightmare! With autolayout, we get to describe size, shape, and position with constraints, whereas if we build our UI in code, we would be doing a bunch of math to set the position and size, using logic like "subtract the label's width from the superview's width and then indent half of that space to center up." For complex layouts on devices with different sizes and shapes, all of which can be rotated at any time, autolayout ends up being both easier and more dependable.

As layouts get more complex, autolayout has advanced features that we can use to help resolve complex situations. Each constraint has a priority value, so if we get into a case where conflicting constraints create an ambiguity, the autolayout system can compare priorities as a tie-breaker. It's also possible to create constraints in code, so if we did have to create an arbitrary number of views at runtime, we could still use autolayout on them and not resort to doing our own math to position them. It's a sophisticated system, but for starters, it's enough to just do the pinning and aligning supported by the storyboard UI.

What We've Learned

In this chapter, we've gotten out of the playground and into real app development. We created a new project in Xcode and looked at how its various parts are organized in the Xcode window.

Next, we turned our attention to the user interface, since the best practice for iOS development is to start with the UI and then build out the logic and behavior behind it. Our UI is absolutely barebones at this point, but even this is enough to make us come to grips with the differing sizes and shapes of iOS devices, and what happens when the user rotates the iPad or iPhone. To deal with this, we applied autolayout constraints to our UI elements, so they put themselves in sensible places depending on how much room they have to work with.

This chapter was a short diversion from our adventures in Swift in the first three chapters, and now it's time to bring it all together. In the next chapter, we will connect the UI we've built in this chapter to new code we'll write, to make our buttons and other UI elements do their thing.

CHAPTER 5

Connecting the UI to Code

You've learned how to build user interfaces with storyboards and Interface Builder, and, before that, you used playgrounds to learn the ins and outs of the Swift programming language. But from where you stand right now, these two things have nothing to do with each other: you can't write code in a storyboard, and you can't drag and customize buttons and labels in a playground.

Obviously, there has to be some way to bring your two skill sets together, so you can bring a user interface to life and have your code do more than just produce log messages.

This chapter will let you close the loop by bringing these two worlds together: you'll connect user interface to code, so buttons can react to taps and your code can update what's on the screen.

It's all about connections.

Making Connections

So, how do we get the Send Tweet button tap to do something? After all, we've been creating the user interface in the Main.storyboard file, but it doesn't look like there's any place in this editor to start writing code.

In iOS, we use Interface Builder *connections* to tie the user interface to our code. Using Xcode, we can create two kinds of connections:

- An *outlet* connects a variable or property in code to an object in a storyboard. This lets us read and write the object's properties, like reading the value of a slider or setting the initial contents of a text field.

- An *action* connects an event generated by a storyboard object to a method in our code. This lets us respond to a button being tapped or a slider's value changing.

What we need here is an action connecting the button tap in the UI to a method in our code, which we'll write in a little bit. To create either kind of connection, we need to declare an IBOutlet or IBAction in our code, and then create the connection with Interface Builder. Fortunately, IB makes this pretty easy by giving us a way to combine the steps.

With the storyboard showing in the Editor area, go to the toolbar and click the Assistant Editor button (it looks like two linked circles). This brings up a side-by-side view with the storyboard on the left and a source file on the right. If there's not enough horizontal room on the screen to see things clearly, use the toolbar to hide the Utility area.

The pane on the right has a jump bar at the top to show which file is in the pane. After a pair of forward/back buttons, there's a button that determines how the file for this pane is selected: Manual, Automatic, Top Level Objects, and so forth. Set this to Automatic and the contents of the file ViewController.swift should appear in the right pane. We'll have more to say about why ViewController.swift is the file we need in the next few chapters, but for now, let's take the name at face value: this is the class that controls the view.

Xcode's template prepopulates ViewController.swift with trivial implementations of two methods: viewDidLoad() and didReceiveMemoryWarning(). We'll be adding a new method to this class.

Creating the action is pretty easy. Control-click on the button in Interface Builder, and Control-drag a line over into the source code, anywhere between the set of curly braces that begin with class ViewController : UIViewController and end at the bottom of the file, and not within the curly braces of an existing method. Don't worry; a blue drop indicator and the tooltip "Insert Outlet, Action, or Outlet Collection" will appear only when we mouse over a valid drop zone. A good place to target is the line right before the final curly brace:

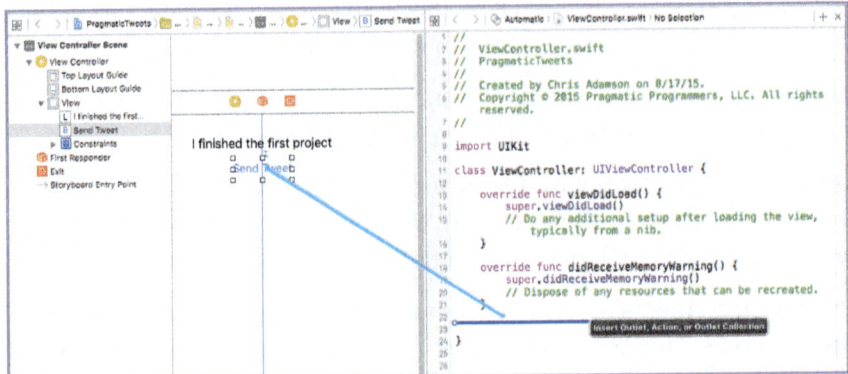

When we release the mouse in the source file, a popover asks us for the details needed to finish the method declaration. On the first line, change the Connection from Outlet to Action. This is important—for a button tap, we want a connection that goes from UI to code, and that's what an action is.

We need to give the method a name, so type handleTweetButtonTapped in the Name field. Next, the Type field determines what kind of object will be passed to the method as an argument identifying the source of the action. The default, AnyObject, represents any kind of object and works well enough, but we can save ourselves some typing later by switching it to UIButton so we know that the object calling us is a button. For the Event and Arguments fields we can take the default values. Click the Connect button to create the connection.

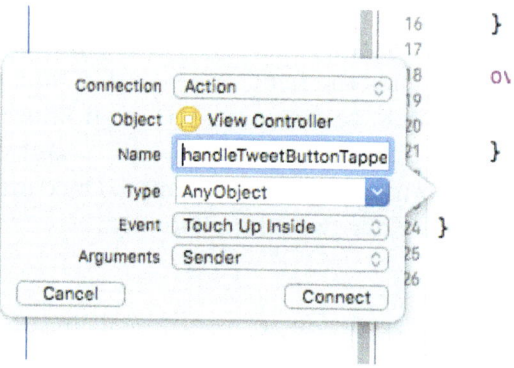

We're done with the Assistant Editor. Click the Standard Editor button in the toolbar to return to one-pane mode. Select ViewController.swift in the Navigator area amd you'll see that Xcode has stubbed out a method signature for us:

```
connecting/PragmaticTweets-5-1/PragmaticTweets/ViewController.swift
@IBAction func handleTweetButtonTapped(sender: UIButton) {
}
```

Xcode has also made a change to the storyboard, but it's not as easy to see. Switch to Main.storyboard and bring the Utility area back, if it's hidden. Click on the button to select it. Then, in the Utility toolbar, click the little circle with the arrow (or press ⌥⌘6) to bring up the *Connections Inspector*. This pane shows all the connections for an object in Interface Builder: all the outlets from code to the object, and all actions sent by the object into the code. In this case, one connection appears in the Sent Events section, from Touch Up Inside to View Controller handleTweetButtonTapped. This connection, shown in the figure that follows, is editable here. If we wanted to disconnect it, we could click the little "x" button, and then reconnect to a different IBAction method by dragging from the circle on the right to the View Controller icon in the scene.

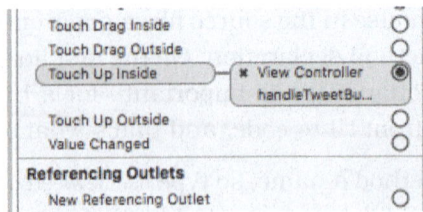

Honestly, we don't break and remake connections very often, but if a connection ever gets inadvertently broken (for example, by renaming the method in the source file), looking in the Connections Inspector is a good approach for diagnosing and fixing the problem.

Coding the Action

Now that we've added a button to our view and wired it up, we can run the app again. The app now has the Send Tweet button, and we can even tap it, but it doesn't do anything. In fact, we don't even know if we've made our connections correctly. One thing we can do as a sanity check is to log a message to make sure our code is really running. Once that's verified, we can move on to implementing our tweet functionality.

Logging

Back in Chapter 2, we learned about the NSLog() function for logging timestamped messages to the Xcode console. We can use that in our action to just log a message every time the button is tapped, and thereby verify that the connections are working. Select ViewController.swift in the File Navigator (⌘1) to edit its source code and rewrite handleTweetButtonTapped() like this:

connecting/PragmaticTweets-5-1/PragmaticTweets/ViewController.swift
```
@IBAction func handleTweetButtonTapped(sender: UIButton) {
  NSLog("handleTweetButtonTapped")
}
```

Run the app again, and tap the button. Back in Xcode, the Debug area automatically appears at the bottom of the window once a log or error message is generated, as seen in the following figure. Every time the button is tapped, another line is written to the log and shown in the Debug area. If the Debug area slides in but looks empty, check the two rightmost buttons at the bottom of the Debug area, next to the trashcan icon; the left one enables a variables view (populated only when the app is stopped on a breakpoint), and the right (which we want to be visible) is the console view where log messages appear. Another way to force the console view to appear is to press ⇧⌘C.

```
22
○ 23   @IBAction func handleTweetButtonTapped(sender: AnyObject) {
  24      NSLog("handleTweetButtonTapped")
  25   }
  26 }
```

```
▽  ▶  ‖  △  ⤒  ⤓  ◻  ◁  ▣ PragmaticTweets
                                2015-08-22 20:22:07.861 PragmaticTweets[3278:2034808] handleTweetButtonTapped
                                2015-08-22 20:22:08.314 PragmaticTweets[3278:2034808] handleTweetButtonTapped
                                2015-08-22 20:22:09.270 PragmaticTweets[3278:2034808] handleTweetButtonTapped

Auto ◊   ◌  ⓘ  ⊛ Search        All Output ◊                                        🗑  ▯ ◻◻
```

So now we have a button that is connected to our code, enough to log a message that indicates the button tap is being handled. The next step is to add some tweeting!

Showing a Tweet Composer

To send a tweet, we need something in the iOS SDK to at least let us get out to the network. As it turns out, iOS is far more generous than that. Bring up the documentation viewer with the menu item Window > Documentation and API Reference (⇧⌘0). In the search field, type social framework. Locate the result for Social Framework Reference and choose that.

The Social framework lets apps connect to social networks like Twitter and Facebook easily. There are just three classes listed, one of which is SLComposeViewController. Click that, and read its documentation:

> The SLComposeViewController class presents a view to the user to compose a post for supported social networking services.

Hey, that sounds perfect! When the user taps Send Tweet, we'll just show the SLComposeViewController, and let it do all the work of composing and sending a tweet.

In ViewController.swift, rewrite the handleTweetButtonTapped() method as follows:

connecting/PragmaticTweets-5-2/PragmaticTweets/ViewController.swift

```
Line 1  @IBAction func handleTweetButtonTapped(sender: UIButton) {
     -    if SLComposeViewController.isAvailableForServiceType(SLServiceTypeTwitter){
     -      let tweetVC = SLComposeViewController(forServiceType:
     -        SLServiceTypeTwitter)
     5      tweetVC.setInitialText(
     -      "I just finished the first project in iOS 9 SDK Development. #pragsios9")
     -      self.presentViewController(tweetVC, animated: true, completion: nil)
     -    } else {
     -      NSLog("Can't send tweet")
    10    }
     -  }
```

Getting in Trouble on Purpose

You will probably see some little error icons appear in the left gutter while typing this code. Sometimes these go away, as Xcode figures out that an incomplete line that wouldn't be valid code is in fact legitimate once it's completed. In this case, however, we're going to get in trouble on purpose, as will be explained and resolved shortly.

To start with, on line 2 we ask the SLComposeViewController class if it's even possible to send tweets: it might not be if a given social network isn't set up to post.

If we can send tweets, then we initialize a new SLComposeViewController on line 3, and we assign it to the variable tweetVC.

On lines 5–6, we set the initial text of the tweet to "I just finished the first project in iOS 9 SDK Development. #pragsios9" by calling the setInitialText() method on tweetVC.

This is all we need to do to prepare the tweet, so on line 7, we show the tweet composer by telling self (our own ViewController) to presentViewController() with the newly created and configured tweetVC, setting the animated parameter to true, which makes the tweet view "fly in." The third parameter, completion, specifies code to execute once the view comes up; we don't need that, so we send nil.

Finally, if isAvailableForServiceType() returned false, the else block on lines 8–10 logs a debugging message that we can't send tweets. As our skills improve, we'll want to actually show the user a message in failure cases like this.

And that's it. We did all the work in IB to create the button and have it call this method when tapped, so we should be able to just build and tweet at this point, right? Let's try running the app. Click the Run button and see what happens.

Disaster—the project doesn't build anymore! Instead, we get a bunch of error messages in red displayed alongside our code, as seen in the following figure. Worse, depending on the width of the window, the errors are likely truncated. What are we supposed to do?

```
22
23    @IBAction func handleTweetButtonTapped(sender: AnyObject) {
24        if SLComposeViewController.isAvailableForServiceType(SLServiceTypeTwitter){    ⓘ Use of unresolved identifier 'SLComposeViewController'
25            let tweetVC = SLComposeViewController(forServiceType: SLServiceTypeTwitter)    ⓘ Use of unresolved identifier 'SLServiceTypeTwitter'
26            tweetVC.setInitialText(
27                "I just finished the first project in iOS 9 SDK Development. #pragsios9")
28            presentViewController(tweetVC, animated: true, completion: nil)
29        } else {
30            NSLog("Can't send tweet")
31        }
32    }
```

Broken Builds

Let's get a more detailed look at what's going on. Visit the Report Navigator using the rightmost button in the Navigator area toolbar, or just type ⌘8. This replaces the list of files with a list of our builds and runs, with the most recent at the top. Click the top Build, and the Content area shows a build log, as seen in the next figure. By default, the selected filter in this view is All Issues, and aside from a possible warning about CODE_SIGN_ENTITLEMENTS (which you'll see as long as you aren't set up to build for actual iOS devices), most of the actual errors are Use of undeclared identifier 'SLComposeViewController' and Use of undeclared identifier 'SLServiceTypeTwitter', which in turn cause the later errors.

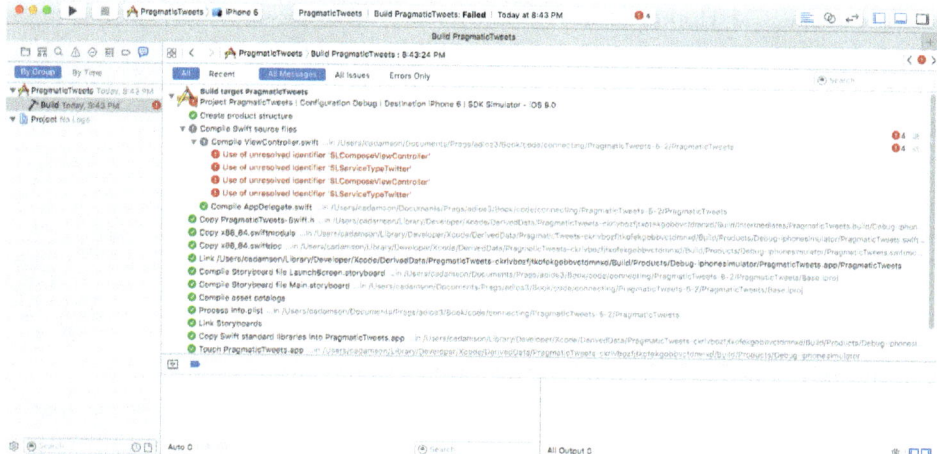

This error means that the compiler doesn't know we're using the Social framework, and therefore it doesn't recognize the SLComposeViewController. Xcode project templates only set us up to use the most common frameworks: Foundation, Core Graphics, UIKit, and XCTest. Anything else has to be added manually. So to tell the compiler about the Social framework, add the following line near the top of ViewController.swift, after the import UIKit line:

connecting/PragmaticTweets-5-2/PragmaticTweets/ViewController.swift
```
import Social
```

The import directive tells the compiler to pull in another framework. This tells the compiler and the linker about our dependency on the Social framework. Once we add the import Social declaration, the red error icons on the side of our code disappear. This is a good sign, so let's try running again.

Tweeting at Last

This time the build completes without errors, and the app will launch in the Simulator. Try clicking the button; either the Xcode log will say Can't send tweet, or the Simulator will show an error alert saying that no Twitter accounts have been configured, with buttons offering to take you to Settings or to cancel.

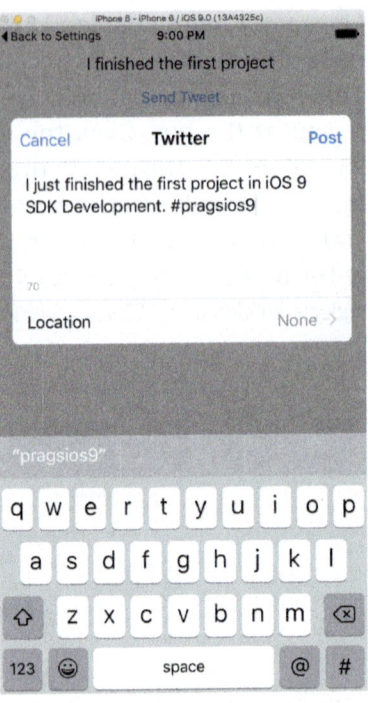

To fix this, we use the Simulator as we would a real iPhone: tap the Settings button in the alert, or use the Home button (menu item Hardware > Home or keyboard shortcut ⇧⌘H) to switch out of the app and launch the Settings app. In the Twitter settings, configure a Twitter account with a valid Twitter username and password. With username and password entered, tap the Sign In button. Once the check marks appear to indicate the credentials have been accepted, use the Home button menu item again and switch back to PragmaticTweets. This time when you tap the button, the tweet composer should come up, like the one pictured. Edit the text if desired and then click Post. Go visit your Twitter page on the web with a browser—for style points, go ahead and use Safari in the Simulator—to see your brand-new tweet, posted for all the world to enjoy and admire.

The iOS Programming Stack

Now we're rolling: we can visually create automatically resizing GUIs in the storyboard, connect them to methods and properties in the view controller class that owns the view, and write code in Swift to do stuff. Life is good.

Except that we're still taking a lot on faith when it comes to actually calling stuff in our code. We can search the documentation for cool-looking methods all day, but first we should make sure we understand where all these classes are coming from and how they're organized.

The iOS SDK divides its functionality into a set of frameworks. We saw this in the last section when we used import Social to add Social.framework to the frameworks used by the project. Conceptually, we can divide the SDK's frameworks into four layers:

Cocoa Touch Layer

> The top-level abstractions over applications and their UIs (UIKit) and integration with system-provided UI features like mapping (MapKit), and Notification Center

Media Layer

> Graphics, sound, and video frameworks

Core Services

> Frameworks for essential, non-UI functionality, like filesystem access, in-app purchase (StoreKit), health-tracking device integration (HealthKit), and so on

Core OS

> Low-level frameworks and libraries needed by the upper layers, including the BSD libraries that are the core of iOS and Mac OS X

In this book, we will spend most of our time working with the frameworks that are included by default in the Xcode project templates: Foundation and UIKit.

Building Views with UIKit

The UIKit framework provides the building blocks of touch-based applications for iOS. That means it's responsible both for the concept of what an app *is* and how it interacts with the rest of the system, as well as for providing a suite of user interface views. Every user interface control we add to the app comes from UIKit, as well as the systems for sending user interface events to our code, how we draw things, fonts, colors, gestures, and so forth.

UIKit's UIApplication class is the point of contact between our code and the rest of the system. By accessing its sharedApplication() method, we can open other apps by URL, receive remote events from Apple's Push Notification service, and set a number for our app icon's badge. But a lot of apps don't do any of these things, so we don't often use UIApplication directly. Instead, the Xcode template sets up a UIApplicationDelegate class for us to customize; this class gets callbacks when common events occur, like the app being started up or opened via a URL from another app, or when it's sent to the background by the user tapping the home button.

The *delegate pattern* is frequently used in the iOS SDK, often as an alternative to subclassing. The idea is that for certain responsibilities, usually the custom behaviors specific to an app, an object can delegate its behaviors to another object. In this case, the UIApplication class handles the activities that are common to all applications, but for cases where different apps will want to do different things, it makes callbacks to our AppDelegate. Delegates don't need to be their own classes like this: they are often classes with other purposes that just implement one or two methods (usually collected as a protocol) in order to serve as a delegate.

As for the app delegate itself, we'll be revisiting it in a later chapter, when we look into what apps can do in iOS 9 even when they're not running.

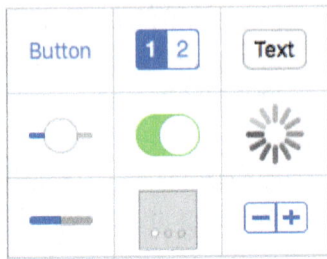

Many of the UIKit classes are views, which are the onscreen touch objects in our user interface. We've been using these in our Twitter example: our UI has a single view that fills the screen and has two subviews: the label and the button. Many other view classes are available, like switches, tables, and sliders. We saw many of these views as icons in the IB library pane (shown in the figure), and each is backed up by a subclass of UIView.

The top-level UIView defines the common functionality of all views. All views have visual properties, such as a backgroundColor, an alpha variable, and hidden and opaque flags. As we've already seen, a view can contain other views; these are accessible via a subviews property and can be added with convenience methods like insertSubview(). A child view can access whatever view it's a subview of via the superview property. Subviews are layered on top of one another by drawing them in the order of the subviews array, with the view at index 0 at the bottom, then index 1 on top of it, and so on. For visual styling needs, UIView also has a tintColor property that applies to all subviews, which makes it easier to apply custom theming to all the UI components on the screen.

Views also have frame and bounds properties that indicate their size and location. Each of these properties is a CGRect, a structure that defines an *x-y* origin (of type CGPoint, a struct inherited from the *Core Graphics* framework) and a width-by-height size (of type CGSize, another structure). The CGRect definition looks like this:

```
struct CGRect {
  var origin: CGPoint
  var size: CGSize
}
```

The difference between a view's bounds and its frame is that the bounds values are in the view's own coordinate system, while the frame is in its superview's coordinate system. So a subview's frame's origin is its top-left corner, relative to its parent's top-left corner at (0,0). Setting either property changes the other as needed, and these interact with two related visual properties, transform and center.

Along with views, UIKit provides the UIViewController class, which is meant as the place where we put the logic for our user interfaces. The view controller also has a number of life-cycle callbacks, telling it when its view is loaded from the storyboard and when the view will appear or disappear as a result of navigating to different parts of the app. We will look more at this relationship in a later chapter.

Finally, UIKit provides classes for objects that are commonly needed by user interfaces, such as UIFont and UIImage. Taken together, the UIKit classes provide an extensive and extensible user interface toolkit.

Managing an Object's Properties

Now that we've read up on the UI classes available to us, let's start putting more of them to work in our app. Our original app lets us send a tweet, but there's no way to tell if we were successful. We'll gradually improve that throughout the next few chapters. For starters, let's use iOS's built-in web browser to bring up our Twitter page inside the app.

Adding a UIWebView

Select Main.storyboard to bring up the UI in Interface Builder. We're going to add a Reload button at the top and a web view (a subview that renders web content) to fill up most of the bottom of our view. While we're at it, we can get rid of the "I finished the first project" label; having a second button named Show My Tweets, with an active verb, should provide enough context for users to know that these are both buttons.

Reworking GUIs in autolayout can be tricky, so let's go through the steps carefully. Select the label and press the Backspace key or use the Cut or Delete menu item. Before we add our new button, select the Send Tweet button and look at its constraints. The centering constraint is now orange because the surviving button's layout is now underconstrained: it depended on the distance to the label above it to know where it should go vertically. We'll have to fix that.

Using the Object library (^⌥⌘3) at the bottom right, drag a new button above the existing one, and give it the title Show My Tweets. Drag it until the center guide appears. Now drag it toward the top of the view until the top margin guide—another dashed blue line—appears. Click the autolayout Align button

Accessibility in UIKit

UIKit offers deep support for accessibility, the ability of a user interface to adapt to a user's needs, such as limitations in vision, hearing, and touch. Every UIView has accessibilityLabel and accessibilityHint attributes, along with accessibilityTraits that describe the view's behavior, that the system uses to render it to users who need help. For example, blind users can turn on the Voice Over feature to have the iOS speech synthesizer speak the names of UI elements, using the provided accessibility values if they have been set. These attributes can all be customized in the storyboard or in code.

Unfortunately, many developers don't customize their UIs for accessibility. The good news is, they often don't need to: the default behavior of iOS makes typical UIKit applications highly accessible. But it's good karma—and a legal requirement in some cases—to test the accessibility of our apps and customize these accessibility properties as necessary. And if we were to create our own views, we would have to implement these attributes on our own, so the system would know how to present our custom view to a disabled user.

at the bottom of IB and use its popover to add a Horizontal Center in Container constraint. Then click the Pin button and add a constraint pinning the distance to the Top Layout Guide as 0, which should be the value that pops up automatically because we dragged up to the top margin.

That's enough to fully specify the new button's constraints, but we still have our old Send Tweet button. Drag it up or down to position it under the other button, until a horizontal line appears between it and the Show My Tweets button. Use the autolayout Pin button's popover to pin a distance from this button to Show My Tweets, at either the current distance or Standard. This should turn the bottom button's constraints blue, indicating it is now adequately constrained.

Now we're ready for the web view that will show our tweets. Drag out a web view—as seen in the figure, its icon in the Object library resembles the Safari app icon—and put it on the bottom portion of the view. Use its handles to drag the  bottom and sides of the web view all the way to the bottom and sides of the parent view, and drag the top until a horizontal guide appears between it and the Send Tweet button. It may be easier to set the web view all the way at the bottom first, then fix the sides, and then drag up.

We want this view to always fill the entire width of the screen, always stay at the bottom, and always respect the distance to the Send Tweet button, so we will need four constraints, all from the Pin button.

- 0 distance to the left and right sides of the parent View. Be sure to *turn off* the Constrain to Margins check box to get all the way to the container's edges (the distance will initially come up as -20 points otherwise).

- 0 distance to the Bottom Layout Guide

- Standard (or the current value, 8) distance to Button - Send Tweet

Click Add 4 Constraints and the web view will be properly constrained for autolayout. It should look like the following figure.

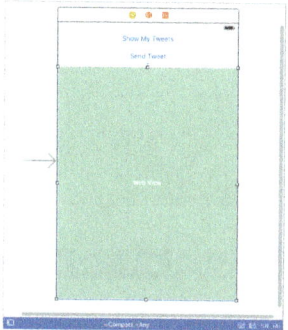

For this screenshot, we've temporarily set the width to Compact to see it as a portrait iPhone layout. It's also possible to verify that our layout will work in landscape. From the blue sizing strip, select a rectangle that is one box tall and two boxes wide. The popover window describes this as "any width | compact height," and says it is for iPhones in landscape orientation. The layout should now look like the following figure. Notice that both buttons maintain their expected spacing from the top, the web view, and each other. We don't have a lot of vertical space to work with in landscape, but for now, the design is holding up. Just make sure to go back to Any/Any mode, so we don't inadvertently create any compact-specific constraints, a problem explained back in *Autolayout*, on page 69.

Connecting the UIWebView to Code

Now let's get back to our original goal of showing tweets in the web view. For this to work, we need to write another event-handler method, one that handles a tap on Show My Tweets. That method will need to load the user's Twitter page in the web view. But wait: even if we connect the button to an action method, how is that method going to be able to call back to the web view and tell it what to display?

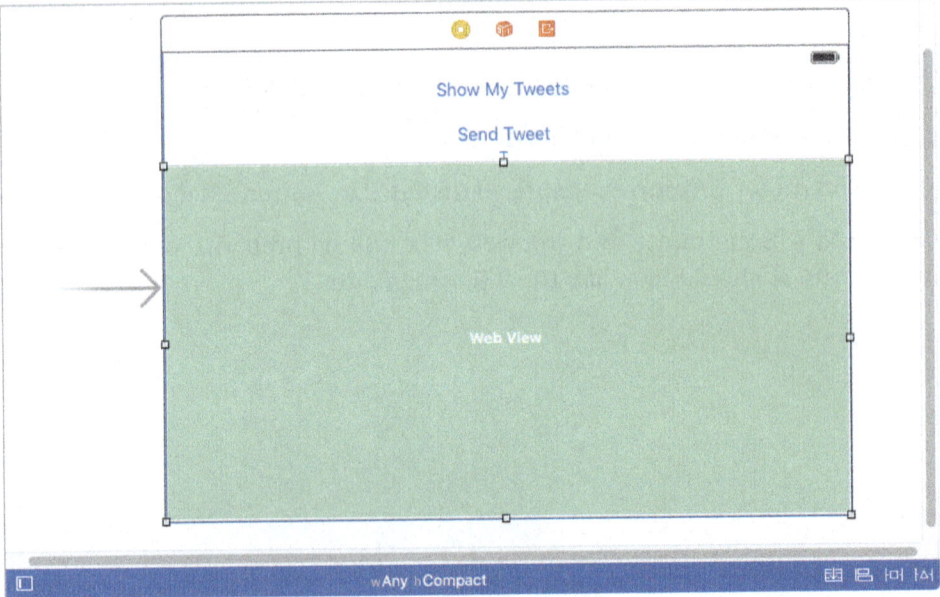

At the beginning of the chapter, we talked about outlets, which are used to connect objects in our code to objects in the storyboard. Since our view controller is a Swift class, we can use a property of the class to refer to the web view. The trick here is that preceding a property with the @IBOutlet modifier tells Interface Builder that a property can serve as an outlet, and that will let us connect the code to the UI.

Select Main.storyboard and switch back to Assistant Editor (via the "linked rings" button on the toolbar, ⌥⌘↩, or the View menu). To make room for the split view, we may want to hide the Utility area on the right. This will show the storyboard on the left and ViewController.swift on the right; if this isn't the case, check the ribbon above the right pane and make sure it's set to Automatic, which picks the most appropriate counterpart file in the right pane given the selection on the left.

To create an outlet property, we do the same thing we did to create the action method for our button: Control-drag from the storyboard into the code. Start a Control-drag from the web view in the storyboard and drag over to the source code in the right pane, as shown in the following figure.

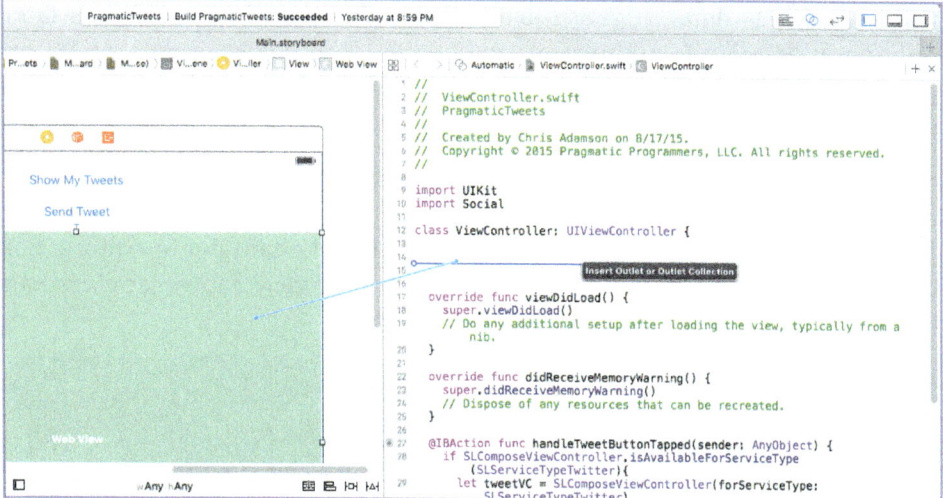

Drag over different parts of the source file without releasing the button; notice that the tip "Insert Outlet or Outlet Collection" only appears when our drop target is inside the curly brace that defines the class, and not within a method inside the class. Anywhere in here, but ideally in the whitespace just below the class declaration, release to end the drag. Xcode shows a popover to specify the outlet, much like it did when we created the action earlier. Make sure Connection says Outlet and Storage says Weak, and give it the name twitterWebView. When we click Connect, the following declaration is inserted into the source at our drop point:

connecting/PragmaticTweets-5-3/PragmaticTweets/ViewController.swift
```
@IBOutlet weak var twitterWebView: UIWebView!
```

This one line of code is doing a bunch of things: it declares the attribute IBOutlet (which lets us connect to it with Interface Builder), the weak keyword, it has a var keyword to indicate the property's value can change, and then finally declares the name twitterWebView and type UIWebView.

Notice the UIWebView type is followed by the exclamation point character (!). We saw that back in *Maybe It's There, Maybe It Isn't: Optionals*, on page 31 as an operator to force-unwrap optionals, while the optional type itself was indicated by a question mark character (?). When used on a type, the ! marks an *implicitly unwrapped optional*, an optional that does not have to be explicitly unwrapped with an if let in order to use it. That's super convenient, and there's only one catch: accessing an implicitly unwrapped optional is exactly like using the ! operator to force-unwrap it, so if it's nil, we crash instantly. But it won't be nil, so long as it's been connected in the storyboard. In fact, that's the whole point: the twitterWebView property can't be set before the initializer is done, because loading from the storyboard happens later (but prior to any of our code running). So, technically, it *has* to be an optional, but it's never really going to be nil unless we screw up something in the storyboard, so we prefer to act like it's a regular type.

So now we have a property called twitterWebView. Since twitterWebView is a property of ViewController, within the class we'll refer to it as self.twitterWebView. For properties that themselves have properties, we just chain dot operators. For example, UIWebView has a canGoBack property, so our view controller class can test this with self.twitterWebView.canGoBack.

Joe asks:
What the Heck Is the weak Keyword?

Earlier, we mentioned how Automatic Reference Counting (ARC) solves all our memory problems. Well, not *quite*. There are a few problems it can't figure out for itself. One is *retain cycles*, a problem that works like this:

- Our ViewController knows about the twitterWebView, so ARC can't free the web view from memory as long as the view controller exists. Otherwise, the view controller might go looking for the web view and it would be gone.

- But if the twitterWebView also requires the ViewController to hang around in memory, then neither can ever be freed from memory, even if we don't need them anymore.

The way to break this is to declare one side of the arrangement as weak, meaning that we don't require an object to hang around in memory if ours is the only one that knows about it.

The reason it works in this case is that the top-level view has strong references to all its children (including the web view), and the view controller has a strong reference to the view, so having an additional strong reference from the view controller to the twitterWebView would be overkill. The rule of thumb is that only "top-level" objects in a storyboard scene (like the view) need strong references, and everything else can be weak. Xcode defaulted to this behavior when we made the connection, and it solves the problem for us.

Calling into the UIWebView Property

Now that we've created the twitterWebView property, we're ready to use it in our code. We'll write an event handler for Show My Tweets that loads the user's Twitter page into the web view. How do we do that? Well, if we look up the UIWebView in the documentation viewer, the docs tells us that UIWebView has a loadRequest() method that we can use, provided we use a string to create an

NSURL (which we assume to be an object that represents a URL), and from that create an NSURLRequest.

But let's start with getting the button-tap event in the first place. Select Main.storyboard and again switch to the Assistant Editor. Make sure the right pane shows ViewController.swift. Control-drag from the Show My Tweets to anywhere inside the class's curly braces, as long as it's not within an existing method's curly braces. When the drag passes over a viable area of the source file, the drag point will show the pop-up tip "Insert Outlet or Action," which is what we want to do.

End the drag and fill in the popover, like we did earlier for Send Tweet. Change Connection to Action, enter handleShowMyTweetsTapped for the method name, and change the type from AnyObject to UIButton. Leave the defaults for event (Touch Up Inside) and Arguments (Sender). Click Connect, and Xcode will stub out a method for us:

connecting/PragmaticTweets-5-3/PragmaticTweets/ViewController.swift
```
@IBAction func handleShowMyTweetsTapped(sender: UIButton) {
}
```

Switch back to Standard Editor mode and select ViewController.swift. The method that Xcode built for us with the drag says @IBAction, which just means that Interface Builder, the storyboard editor, can work with it. It takes one parameter, sender, which is the UIButton that sent the event (that is to say, the button that was tapped). There's no return type stated, so the method doesn't return a value.

We sketched out a plan to implement this method earlier: we just have to work up a call to the UIWebView's loadRequest() method. Fill in the method like this:

connecting/PragmaticTweets-5-3/PragmaticTweets/ViewController.swift
```
Line 1  @IBAction func handleShowMyTweetsTapped(sender: UIButton) {
     2    if let url = NSURL (string: "https://twitter.com/pragsiostest") {
     3      let urlRequest = NSURLRequest(URL: url)
     4      twitterWebView.loadRequest(urlRequest)
     5    }
     6  }
```

On line 2, we create an NSURL from its initializer that takes an argument called string:. We've used http://www.twitter.com/pragsiostest here, but feel free to put in your own Twitter username. Notice this is in an if let, because the NSURL(string:) is a failable initializer: its return type is NSURL?, reserving the right to return nil if our string is garbage.

Next, line 3 takes this NSURL and makes a new NSURLRequest from it. We can then use this urlRequest on line 4 to tell the web view to load up that page, by using its loadRequest() method.

Replacing if let with guard let

One disadvantage of if let is that it forces the normal path through the code to be indented, as if it were a special case. In the earliest versions of Swift, it was almost impossible to avoid a "pyramid of doom" of nested if let indentations. And even now, it's a little weird to always have the "happy path" be indented a few spaces or tabs.

Back in *if-else Statements*, on page 29, we said that Swift now has a guard statement that inverts the usual if-else flow, but it didn't fit with how playgrounds work, because guard statements require explicit returns, and we can't return from a playground. Of course, we *can* return from a method, and doing an early return if the NSURL string is junk makes perfect sense here. So here's what handleShowMyTweetsTapped() looks like with a guard statement instead:

```
connecting/PragmaticTweets-5-3/PragmaticTweets/ViewController.swift
@IBAction func handleShowMyTweetsTapped(sender: AnyObject) {
    guard let url = NSURL (string: "https://twitter.com/pragsiostest") else {
        return
    }
    let urlRequest = NSURLRequest(URL: url)
    twitterWebView.loadRequest(urlRequest)
}
```

We test the returned NSURL? against nil with a guard let, and if it fails, we do an early return in the else block. Notice there's no curly-brace block for the success case: it's just all the code after the guard. So that spares us a bunch of junky indentation: we test everything up front, and then let the rest of the method speak for itself.

Network Security Concerns

We should be ready to go: our button tap will create an NSURLRequest and send that to twitterWebView, which will show it in the user interface. The only problem is that blindly sending requests to the Internet brings up some security concerns we must think about.

Apps built for iOS 9 or later are controlled by *App Transport Security* (ATS), a feature introduced in iOS 9 to compel developers to adhere to safe, secure, and private networking practices. If you've heard the phrase "https everywhere," you get the gist: use secure connections wherever possible. Under App Transport Security, any attempt to use a plain http-style URL fails immediately. Our app is https, but as of this writing, not all of the twitter.com SSL ciphers are up to Apple's requirements, so either our NSURLRequest will fail, or some of the images in the page won't load.

App Transport Security allows us to carve out exceptions to its policies, and since we're still early in our study, we'll use the simplest means possible. ATS has a setting that basically means "allow everything," so that's what we'll use.

ATS exceptions are implemented on an app-wide basis, so they go in our apps' settings. We can see the custom properties for our app by clicking the Pragmatic Tweets project icon at the top of the File Navigator, choosing the PragmaticTweets target, and selecting the Info tab. This view has settings for things like our app version and other metadata:

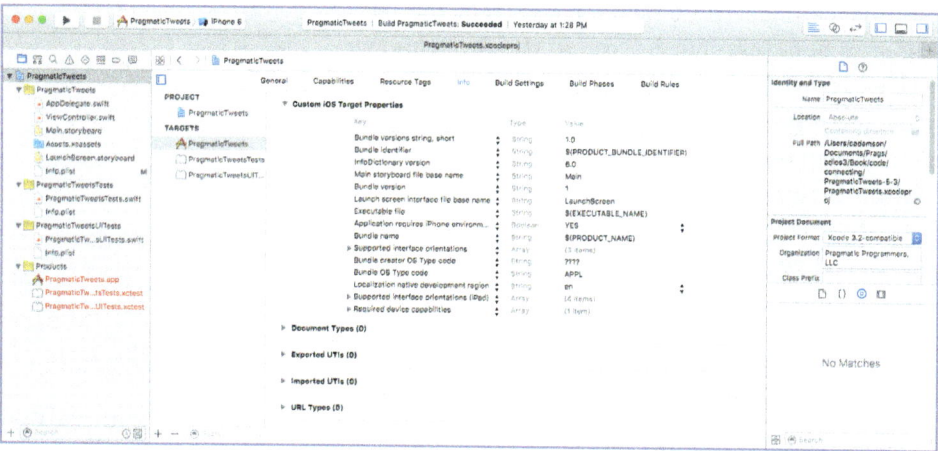

This is where the App Transport Security settings go, but this UI is hard to edit visually, and even harder to explain. (Trust us on this!) So instead, we'll go to the file where all these settings actually live. Under the Pragmatic Tweets folder icon, select the Info.plist file. That shows the same metadata in the same hard-to-use interface. Right-click or Control-click Info.plist to expose a pop-up menu, and choose Open As Source Code. This lets us edit the raw XML.

Now, we can carve out our App Transport Security exception. Right before the </dict> at the bottom of the file, add the following:

```
<key>NSAppTransportSecurity</key>
<dict>
  <key>NSAllowsArbitraryLoads</key>
  <true/>
</dict>
```

What this does is basically turn off App Transport Security for the whole app. We really shouldn't ship an app with security turned off, and we won't; we'll be able to replace this raw NSURLRequest later on. For now, this workaround gets us out of security jail.

Now that we've turned off ATS, click the Run button to launch the updated app in the Simulator, and then click the Show My Tweets button. The event sent by the new button goes to the handleShowMyTweetsTapped() method, it creates a NSURLRequest that ATS lets pass, and this request is sent to the self.twitterWebView property to load up the Twitter page in the web view:

Note that since the UIWebView is a real live web client, it acts just like Safari, so the first time we use it, we might get intercepted by an advertising page asking us to download the Twitter app for iOS, or worse yet a redirect; just look for a close button or link to dismiss it, as we would do in any other browser. At any rate, we've now got a live web view of our Twitter account, and a native control to post new tweets... not bad!

What We've Learned

We had a big job in this chapter, bringing together everything you learned about Swift programming in the first three chapters and building user interfaces in the previous chapter.

The key to doing this is creating connections in our storyboards. First, we used actions, which let us connect a UI event like a button tap to a method in our code that handles the action. Then we used outlets, which present UI elements as ordinary properties, which lets us call methods on them or change their properties.

Along the way, you also learned a little more about Swift: weak properties that make sure memory gets cleaned up when two objects reference each other, and the guard statement that's nice for early-return logic.

We've done a lot of work in this chapter, and that's something to be proud of. But what if something happens to our work? What if, while we're developing a new feature, we inadvertently break what's already working? In the next chapter, we're going to see how Xcode's testing tools will keep our app behaving as expected.

Joe asks:
Why Isn't Using https Good Enough for App Transport Security?

Apple's commitment to security and privacy is pretty serious, so just blindly using https everywhere doesn't actually cut it. In the case of Twitter, ATS flags us for not providing "forward secrecy," a more future-proof form of cryptography that can remain secure even if some of the keys it uses later become compromised. As of this writing, Twitter's SSH support isn't forward-secrecy compliant.

Turning off ATS is a blunt way around this. The nicer way to handle it is to tell ATS to carve out a specific exception, just for the twitter.com and twimg.com domains, and just for the forward-secrecy requirement. Here's how we would declare that in Info.plist:

```
<key>NSAppTransportSecurity</key>
<dict>
  <key>NSExceptionDomains</key>
  <dict>
    <key>twitter.com</key>
    <dict>
      <key>NSExceptionRequiresForwardSecrecy</key>
      <false/>
      <key>NSIncludesSubdomains</key>
      <true/>
    </dict>
    <key>twimg.com</key>
    <dict>
      <key>NSExceptionRequiresForwardSecrecy</key>
      <false/>
      <key>NSIncludesSubdomains</key>
      <true/>
    </dict>
  </dict>
</dict>
```

What this says to do is to turn off the forward-secrecy requirement for twitter.com and all its subdomains. Beyond this exception, the rest of ATS remains in effect. Clearly, if we were shipping this app, carving out a narrowly targeted exception like this would be preferable to turning off ATS altogether. To learn more, visit http://developer.apple.com and search for the "App Transport Security Technote."

CHAPTER 6

Testing the App

We have come a long way in a short time. We've got an app that can send tweets and show our Twitter web page. We now have a stable app that isn't going to crash on us, right?

Well, how do we know that? We have run the app a few times, but have we really pushed the limits of the app? Have we really tried everything that anyone could possibly do to our app? How do we prove that our app is not going to crash before we ship it off to Apple?

And as we start adding features, what proves that those changes work, or that they're not going to have weird side effects that break the stuff that had been working?

The way we deal with this is to use *unit tests*. In this chapter, we'll see how we can use our Swift programming skills to make sure that the rest of our code is doing what it is supposed to.

Unit Tests

Unit tests are exactly what they sound like. They are small, self-contained segments of code that test very small, targeted units of functionality. Rather than check to see if the whole application works, we can break the functionality into pieces to pinpoint exactly where errors and bugs are occurring.

Unit tests are designed to either pass or fail. Is this feature working the way you want it to, yes or no?

The Parable of the Dinosaur

Here is an example of unit testing gone bad.

In *Jurassic Park* (the book, not the movie), Dr. Grant asks the scientists how they can be sure that the dinosaurs are not breeding.

The scientists assure Dr. Grant that every precaution has been taken. They engineered the dinosaurs to all be female. They had the island blanketed with motion detectors to count each and every dinosaur every five minutes. They created a computer algorithm to check the number and types of dinosaurs found by the motion sensors and the number only changed when a dinosaur died. There had been no escapes. They knew everything happening on the island, and they were completely in control.

Dr. Grant asks them to change the parameters of the computer program to look for more dinosaurs than they were expecting to have. The scientists humor Dr. Grant and change the algorithm to search for more dinosaurs. Lo and behold! There are more dinosaurs. After running the program several more times with increasing numbers they eventually discover there are over 50 extra dinosaurs on the island. Oops!

The program had been set up with the expectation that the number of dinosaurs could only go down, never up. Once the program reached the number of dinosaurs it was expecting to find, it stopped counting, and the scientists never knew there was an issue. The program anticipated the outcome of dinosaurs dying or escaping the island but never the possibility that life could find a way.

Reasons We Unit Test

Bugs, like life, do find a way. The first thing to remember in computer programming is that the computer is stupid. The computer only does what you tell it to do. It can't infer what you meant. It is important to verify that you are giving the right directions to the computer and the best way to do that is to test your apps.

One major reason to unit test an application is to eliminate crashes. The single biggest reason that most app submissions are rejected by Apple is because they crash. Even if Apple doesn't catch your crash, users have a talent for finding the one combination of things that will cause your app to crash. These are the users who tend to leave one-star reviews on the store, which is something we want to avoid if at all possible.

Unit tests also expose logic errors in our code. In the Jurassic Park example, the code being run had a logic error that prevented the scientists from discovering the problem until it was too late. We don't want that to happen to you.

Writing tests also helps you write your code. Have you ever started writing a piece of code only to figure out that one feature you spent days working on wasn't really going to work out in your project? By thinking critically about what specifically you want your application to do, you can avoid writing overly complicated and unnecessary code. They can inform the design of our code: what part of the code has what responsibilities, and how we recover if something unexpected happens.

Designing Good Unit Tests

As we will soon discover, writing a unit test is not difficult. Writing a good unit test is another story altogether.

There are generally three types of unit tests:

- *Debugging:* These tests are built around bugs to ensure that when you change the code these bugs do not reappear. Sometimes when we are coding we make changes to the code that affect bugs that we have already resolved. Since we do not want to see that bug again, we need to write tests to make sure that the bug has not reappeared when we change anything.

- *Assert Success:* We are testing to make sure you are getting a result you want.

- *Assert Failed:* We are testing to make sure you are not getting a result you don't want.

We might wonder why you would need a test to assert failure. Isn't the point of testing to make sure that features we created work properly?

Think back to the Jurassic Park example. The scientists created tests to make sure they were finding all of the dinosaurs they were looking for. They asserted success once the number of dinosaurs they were looking for was reached.

Sometimes it is as important to write a test that we expect to fail to make sure that we are not getting a result we don't want. Had the scientists also included a failure assertion test, they would have discovered that they were getting results that made no sense: there are more dinosaurs in the park than there are supposed to be.

How Tests Work in Xcode

Testing functionality was introduced in Xcode 5. Apple based many of its built-in functions on accepted and open source frameworks and has been working very hard to make testing a vital and useful tool in your developer utility belt.

We are going to go over several aspects of testing in Xcode in this chapter. Since we have spent a great deal of time creating and developing the PragmaticTweets app, let's run it through some tests to see how it works.

Let's direct our attention to the File Navigator, shown in this figure. There is a group titled PragmaticTweetsTests. Xcode has conveniently created this group and sample template class, PragmaticTweetsTests.swift, for our first two tests. There is a second group, PragmaticTweetsUITests, with a file PragmaticTweetsUITests.swift; these are our user interface tests, which we'll try out later in the chapter.

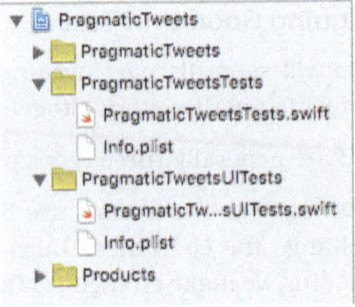

Before we move on to actually looking at the included test files, let's also look at the Test Navigator (⌘5). Rather than showing test files, this shows the tests themselves, and whether they passed or failed the last time they ran. This is another location in Xcode that makes it easy for you to get an overview of what tests you have and whether or not they are passing.

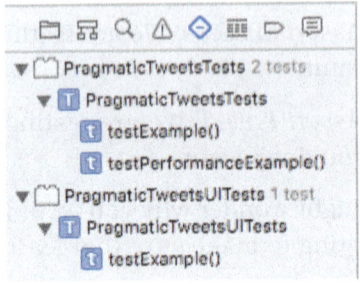

Click on the PragmaticTweetsTests.swift file in either the Project or the Test Navigator. There are four methods within this class: setUp(), tearDown(), testExample(), and testPerformanceExample(). Every test class that we create will have a setUp() and a tearDown() method. setUp() is used to instantiate any boilerplate code you need to set up your tests, and tearDown() is used to clear away any of the setup you needed to do for your tests. Whenever we find ourselves repeating code in multiple tests, it's a candidate for moving into setUp() and tearDown(). This is the principle of DRY: Don't Repeat Yourself.

Every test method we create will start with the word "test," just as the testExample() and testPerformanceExample() methods demonstrate. The first of these is an example of testing our app's logic, and the second tests its performance (that is to say, how long it takes to do something). Test classes take no arguments and return no value—this pattern is how our tests are found and executed by the test engine. A test passes if it returns normally, and fails if it fails an assertion method before it returns.

For fun, let's just run the test included in the template. There are several ways to run your unit tests:

- Keyboard command: ⌘U
- Main menu: Product > Test
- Clicking on the diamond icon next to either the test class or the specific test in Xcode

The first two ways of running tests will run all of your tests, whereas the third way will allow you to run selected tests. This is useful if you have one test that's failing and you want to focus on that one without having to run all the others.

Run the test in the manner of your choice.

Let's take a closer look at testExample().

```
testing/PragmaticTweets-6-1/PragmaticTweetsTests/PragmaticTweetsTests.swift
func testExample() {
  // This is an example of a functional test case.
  // Use XCTAssert and related functions to verify your tests produce
  // the correct results.
}
```

The XCTAssert() method mentioned by the comment is provided by the import XCTest statement at the top of the file. It exists to tell the test engine whether a test has passed or failed. Let's try it out: on a new line in testExample(), write:

```
XCTAssert(false, "Pass")
```

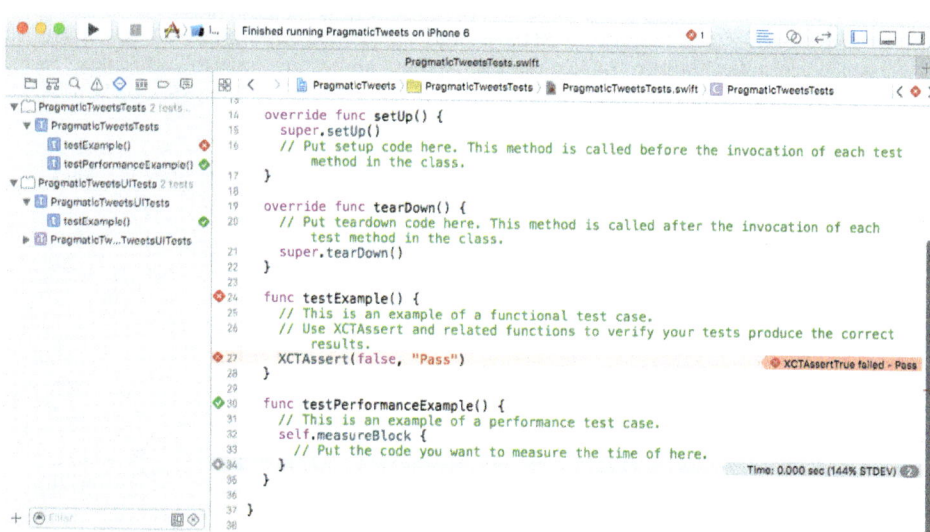

Oh no! The test stopped working! What happened?

Well, we just changed the conditions of the test. XCTAssert must pass a true condition in its first parameter for the test to pass. Since we programmed the condition to be false, the test fails, and sends the string (which indicates what was *supposed* to happen) to the test engine, which shows up as an error bar next to the test method. Option-clicking on XCTAssert doesn't give us nice documentation like most Swift methods, but we'll cover the most useful XCTest assertions later.

At first blush this might seem like a useless exercise. Why would we want to write a test that always fails when you run it?

We run a test that is designed to fail so that we verify that the testing framework itself is working properly. If we simply create nothing but tests that are supposed to pass, we can't know for certain that the tests are passing because the code is correct. There could be an error and the tests would pass regardless. By prompting a failure, we now verify that when we write a test that passes that our code is, in fact, working correctly. As one wise person put it, "How do you know your smoke detector works if it never goes off?"

Where Assertions Come From

At this point you may be wondering where we got XCTAssert() and the other testing methods from. Xcode's testing framework is called XCTest, and is built atop an older open source testing framework called OCUnit.

As we saw earlier, the method in XCTest to assert a true condition is XCTAssert(). The assertions all take the form of asserting that some condition is true, and failing the test if it is actually false. Different assertions make it easier to test numeric values, whether or not optionals are nil, and so on.

There are about twenty different assertion methods in XCTest, but the ones we will be using most often are

- XCTAssert()

- XCTAssertFalse()

- XCTAssertEqual()

- XCTAssertNotNil()

- XCTAssertThrowsSpecificNamed()

There is a complete list of every assertion in the "Testing with Xcode" programming guide in your Xcode documentation, if you want to see how deep the rabbit hole goes.

Test-Driven Development

Now that we have a good handle on how to create a unit test, we are going to delve into the realm of test-driven development (TDD). TDD, in a nutshell, is figuring out the least number of objects you need to create in order to get your application to work the way you want it to. TDD utilizes the idea that you will write your tests first rather than after you have already completed your application.

If we write tests for the app now, we'll just be checking functionality we already know works. In TDD, we write the test first, fail for lack of any working functionality, then press ahead and actually create the functionality.

Why do we want to do all this extra work before we write a line of code? Let's jump in the Way Back machine and visit your elementary school English class. Remember back when you were learning how to write stories your teacher told you to write an outline. We write outlines for our stories so that we have an idea about how our story is going to go. We want to figure out the beginning, middle, and end so that we can write a tight and cohesive story that follows a path and has an ending that makes sense. If you go into a story not sure about what is going happen, you'll wind up writing lots and lots of plot where nothing happens.

Our time is valuable. It is in our best interest to figure out exactly which features are important and which ones are not before you spend a week trying to figure out and debug a feature that we figure out later doesn't fit in with what we want our app to do.

So let's add a new feature, TDD style. Let's say we want to have the web view load itself when the app starts up, without having to tap Show My Tweets. We'll start by writing a test to make sure the web view got populated, initially failing because it's not being populated, then go back and add the feature. When the test passes, our feature is good to go.

We'll start by creating a new test class. Before you create this class, click on the PragmaticTweetsTests group. Use the menu item File > New > File to bring up a template of file types. Choose iOS Source from the left pane, and on the right, select the 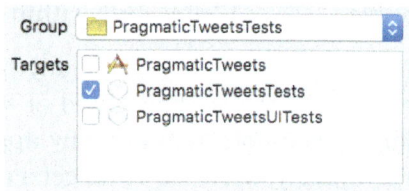 Unit Test Case Class template. Name our new class WebViewTests. Make sure this class is a subclass of XCTestCase and that it is attached to the PragmaticTweetsTests target before creating the class, as shown in the figure.

Xcode Targets

In Xcode, it is possible to create multiple applications based on the same codebase. If we wanted to make, for example, a game where we had "full" and "lite" versions where the only difference is how many levels are included, we could create two targets that mostly differed by which level files were or weren't included.

Since the primary application does not know what to do with a testing class, we don't want to include it in the codebase for that application; it would just take up space on the end user's device. Putting the test classes in their own target helps us segregate them out.

Targets can also be used for other sophisticated build tasks, like running arbitrary shell scripts prior to or after building our code. They can also be set as dependencies of one another. For example, the tests target is dependent on the main app target, so any time we run tests, any changes to the app's code will be built first.

Creating Tests

What we need to do is to write a test method that can access the twitterWebView property of the ViewController class. This actually presents a little bit of a hassle that we haven't had to consider before. Swift considers all the classes in the PragmaticTweets target to be one *module*, and classes in a module can see each other's properties and methods by default. However, PragmaticTweetsTests is a different target and thus a different module, so it cannot see the methods or properties of our app's classes. We'll have to fix that before we can test anything.

We can declare different levels of access for our classes and their members. Swift has three levels of access, set by special keywords:

Access modifier	Visibility
public	Visible everywhere
internal	Visible within the same module
private	Visible only within the class itself

In the past, we had to make anything testable a public member, and make the class itself public. That's kind of ugly, because it would expose more of our implementation than is really appropriate for good programming practices. Fortunately, in Xcode 7, we get a nice new keyword, @testable, that relaxes the access modifiers just for the purposes of unit testing, so that's what we'll use here.

Start in WebViewTests.swift by adding an import statement, just like the default one that pulls in the XCTest frameworks. In our case, we need to import the PragmaticTweets module. By annotating it with the @testable keyword, we can access the properties and method internal to the PragmaticTweets module, without having to make them public.

testing/PragmaticTweets-6-1/PragmaticTweetsTests/WebViewTests.swift
```
@testable import PragmaticTweets
```

This will let our test code access the members of the ViewController class where we wrote all our functionality in the last chapter. Now let's write a test to let us look inside that class.

Also, since we're going to be writing our own test methods in this class, we can delete the testExample() and testPerformanceExample() methods provided by the Xcode template.

Writing Unit Tests

Now we're ready to write our test. What we want to do here is to look at the contents of the twitterWebView. To keep things simple, we won't go scraping for any specific text—Twitter could always change their web page—and instead we'll just make sure the loaded page isn't blank.

The test is really an outsider, so it doesn't have direct access to the views on the screen or the logic behind them. However, we can ask the UIApplication object for the first view controller it's showing (luckily, we only have one in our app) and drill down from there. So let's write a testAutomaticWebLoad() class like this:

testing/PragmaticTweets-6-1/PragmaticTweetsTests/WebViewTests.swift
```
Line 1  func testAutomaticWebLoad() {
   -      guard let viewController =
   -        UIApplication.sharedApplication().windows[0].rootViewController
   -          as? ViewController else {
   5          XCTFail("couldn't get root view controller")
   -            return
   -      }
   -      let webViewContents =
   -      viewController.twitterWebView.stringByEvaluatingJavaScriptFromString(
  10        "document.documentElement.textContent")
   -      XCTAssertNotNil(webViewContents, "web view contents are nil")
   -      XCTAssertNotEqual(webViewContents!, "", "web view contents are empty")
   -  }
```

Lines 2–4 are how we get to the ViewController object. The shared UIApplication object has an array of UIWindows (one per screen, so usually just one unless we're doing AirPlay), and each window has a rootViewController. So we use a guard let statement to try to get that rootViewController object as our ViewController class.

Not only does this object have to be non-nil, it also has to be of type ViewController; we test for this with as?, the *type cast operator*. If we fail on either count, guard let sends us to the early return on line 5.

If that works, then we want to inspect the contents of the twitterWebView. There's no method on UIWebView to just give us its contents, but there is the method stringByEvaluatingJavaScriptFromString(), which lets us run any JavaScript string on the contents of the UIWebView (seriously!). So on lines 8–10, we evaluate the DOM property document.documentElement.textContent to get the text of the web page.

We are now ready to test whether or not this got anything. On line 11, we use XCTAssertNotNil() to make sure the webViewContents is not nil. And then on line 12, we use XCTAssertNotEqual() to make sure it's not an empty string. If we survive both of those test methods, the method executes normally and we pass the test.

We now have a test and no feature. So what do we do? This is test-driven development, so we run the test, of course! Click the diamond to the left of testAutomaticWebLoad() to run just this one test.

And we fail. We knew we'd fail, because we know the feature isn't there. The error message from the XCTAssertNotEqual() assertion appears next to that line in the source to show us where the test failed. Our pass/fail results also appear in the Test Navigator, and in the Report Navigator (⌘8), which has a nice summary of all tests run, the Simulator or device we ran them on, and which tests failed and where. See the following figure.

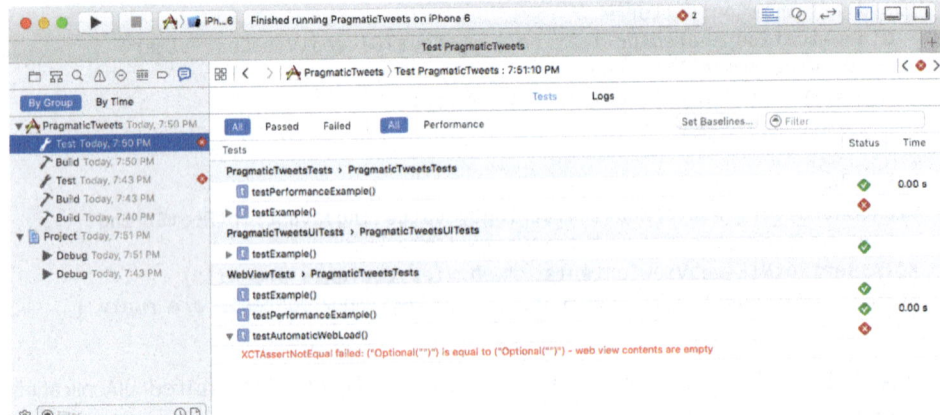

Finishing the Feature

We are following proper TDD practice: we built a test; we watched it fail. Now we can build the feature, and when the test stops failing, we know we have a working feature.

Go back to ViewController.swift. We want the web view to come up when the app does, so all the things we do in handleShowMyTweetsButtonTapped() should happen in viewDidLoad,() too. A good way to do that is to have them both call the same thing. Copy everything currently in handleShowMyTweetsButtonTapped() into a new method called reloadTweets(), and then make handleShowMyTweetsButtonTapped() just be a call to reloadTweets(), like this:

```
testing/PragmaticTweets-6-1/PragmaticTweets/ViewController.swift
@IBAction func handleShowMyTweetsTapped(sender: UIButton) {
  reloadTweets()
}

func reloadTweets() {
  guard let url = NSURL (string: "https://twitter.com/pragsiostest") else {
    return
  }
  let urlRequest = NSURLRequest(URL: url)
  twitterWebView.loadRequest(urlRequest)
}
```

Now, add the line self.reloadTweets() to the viewDidLoad() method that Xcode provided for us when it created the project. This method is called when the view loads in from the storyboard, and, therefore, is the perfect place to do our automatic web-page loading.

```
testing/PragmaticTweets-6-1/PragmaticTweets/ViewController.swift
override func viewDidLoad() {
  super.viewDidLoad()
  reloadTweets()
}
```

Run the app (not the test) with the Run button or ⌘R to make sure it works. The app comes up; the web page loads. We are good to go! Now run the test with ⌘U, and we will have finished our first TDD development.

But wait, the test is still failing! What's wrong?

Testing Asynchronously

Take another look at running the app. After the app appears, it takes a second or two for the web page to load. But from the test's point of view, as soon as the app is up and running, it is ready to be tested. What's happening is that we are testing too soon. We need a way to wait before we run our test.

What we need is *asynchronous testing*, the ability to test things that happen at unpredictable times. If we wanted to test that 2 + 2 == 4, or that a string has a certain value, we could do that right away, because the value would be there right when we asked for it. But with the web view, we don't know when (or if) its contents will be set. Asynchronous testing lets us test these kinds of unpredictable events.

Prior to iOS 8, you could not run asynchronous unit tests using XCTest, so it was impossible to do testing on the network calls, background tasks, or anything else where the value to be tested was not immediately available.

The way to deal with these situations is a testing class called XCTestExpectation. XCTestExpectation is an object that describes events that we expect to happen at some point in the near future. We tell it how long it can wait, and then perform test assertions elsewhere—in parts of the code that run asynchronously—finally notifying the expectation when we're done. And if we fail to do so in time, that's considered a failure.

> ### Joe asks:
> ## What the Heck Is an "Expectation Object"?
>
> There is a wonderful quote by the late John Pinette that goes: "Salad isn't food. Salad comes with the food. Salad is a promissory note that food will soon arrive."
>
> Expectation objects are like salad. They are not the test; they are the promise to your program that something is going to happen a little later.
>
> If you went to a restaurant and got a salad, and then waited for an hour for food that never arrives, you would realize something is terribly wrong. You were set up to expect that another part of your meal was coming, and if it never arrived, your meal would be a failure.
>
> That, in a nutshell, is how asynchronous testing with expectation objects works.

Back in the WebViewTests class, the first thing we will do is create an XCTestExpectation object:

```
testing/PragmaticTweets-6-2/PragmaticTweetsTests/WebViewTests.swift
var loadedWebViewExpectation: XCTestExpectation?
```

This expectation object will start as nil (which is why it has to be an optional), and we will populate it when we start the test. When we know the web view has loaded, we can tell it that we're done by calling its fulfill() method.

We'll also need a way to know when the web view has loaded. Some general-purpose techniques for doing asynchronous tasks are discussed later, but for now, UIWebView can help us out. It has a delegate object that gets notified when web pages load or fail to load, when the user submits a form, and when other events occur. We can use that to know that the web page has loaded, and then pass or fail the test.

To be a delegate, we have to declare that our class implements the UIWebViewDelegate protocol, which declares the methods that the web view can send to its delegate.

testing/PragmaticTweets-6-2/PragmaticTweetsTests/WebViewTests.swift
```
class WebViewTests: XCTestCase, UIWebViewDelegate {
```

We are going to rewrite the testAutomaticWebLoad() to do two things. The first is to become the web view's delegate. The second is to create our expectation object so that the tests know to wait a little while and don't just return a test fail. Here's how we do that.

testing/PragmaticTweets-6-2/PragmaticTweetsTests/WebViewTests.swift
```
Line 1  func testAutomaticWebLoad() {
   -      guard let viewController =
   -        UIApplication.sharedApplication().windows[0].rootViewController
   -          as? ViewController else {
   5            XCTFail("couldn't get root view controller")
   -            return
   -      }
   -      viewController.twitterWebView.delegate = self
   -      loadedWebViewExpectation =
  10        expectationWithDescription("web view auto-load test")
   -      waitForExpectationsWithTimeout(5.0, handler: nil)
   -    }
```

On line 8, our test class becomes the web view's delegate, so it can be notified of events from the twitterWebView.

Next, lines 9–10 create the loadedWebViewExpectation and give it the name web view auto-load test. If we have many expectations, the name helps us figure out which one failed. We create as many expectations as we need—just one for now—and kick them off with a call to waitForExpectationsWithTimeout() on line 11. If we don't call fulfill() on the expectation within 5 seconds we'll get a timeout test failure.

Now that we have created our expectation object, we need to implement the UIWebViewDelegate protocol. If you look in the documentation, you will see this protocol has four methods that it can call: one to ask if it should start loading, one to report an error, and one each when the page starts and stops loading. We will implement two of these: if the web page load fails, our test fails, and if it succeeds, we use the JavaScript call to see if the web view has any contents. Let's start with the easier failure case.

```
testing/PragmaticTweets-6-2/PragmaticTweetsTests/WebViewTests.swift
func webView(webView: UIWebView, didFailLoadWithError error: NSError?) {
  XCTFail("web view load failed")
  loadedWebViewExpectation?.fulfill()
}
```

If the web page doesn't load, we use the always-fail XCTFail() to tell the test suite we failed. Notice that we also have to fulfill() the expectation even though we've already failed; if we don't do this, we'll get a timeout that looks like a second failure.

Now we can look at the possible success case.

```
testing/PragmaticTweets-6-2/PragmaticTweetsTests/WebViewTests.swift
func webViewDidFinishLoad(webView: UIWebView) {
  if let webViewContents =
    webView.stringByEvaluatingJavaScriptFromString(
      "document.documentElement.textContent")
    where webViewContents != "" {
      loadedWebViewExpectation?.fulfill()
  }
}
```

This is like our first version in how it gets at the twitterWebView and runs the JavaScript to get the web document's contents as a string. The difference is that all we do this time is fulfill() the expectation if we ever get contents that aren't an empty string. (It turns out we don't want to fail on an empty string because this will be called with an empty string when the app starts up; by not failing at that point, we give the web view more tries to call us back with some contents.)

Whew! That was a lot of code. Congratulations, you are now capable of doing something that wasn't possible before. Now click the diamond next to testAutomaticWebLoad(). This time, we pass the test, as shown by the green icon in the Test Navigator in the figure.

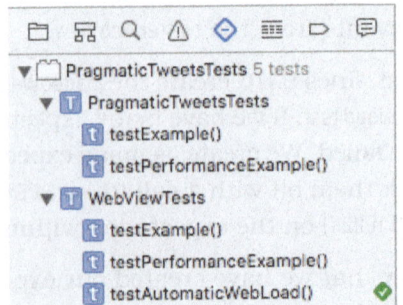

User Interface Testing

It's great that we now have the ability to automatically test our app's logic. If we inadvertently make a breaking change, or our assumptions get broken (like if Twitter goes out of business and its site disappears), then we'll discover it the next time we run our test suite.

However, one thing we haven't really exposed to testing is the user interface. If we broke the connection from a button to the method it calls, we would never know, because we test the method, not the button itself.

Testing user interfaces has always been really hard to do, which is why a lot of people don't do it! The testing culture is much stronger among web developers—where you can always post the same HTTP request and scrape the HTML you get back from a server—than among desktop and mobile developers.

Fortunately, Xcode 7 introduces a powerful new tool for testing iOS 9 user interfaces. Let's wrap up the chapter by trying it out.

Recording a UI Test

We currently test the functionality of the Show My Tweets button (if not the button tap itself), but not the Send Tweet button. Let's see how we can make sure that button still does what it's supposed to.

In the File Navigator, notice that after the PragmaticTweetsTests group we've been working with, Xcode also created a PragmaticTweetsUITests group, with a single file, PragmaticTweetsUITests.swift. Select this file and notice that it has setUp() and tearDown() methods like before, although their contents are different from what we saw in the regular unit test files. There's also an empty testExample() method, with a comment to get us started:

testing/PragmaticTweets-6-3/PragmaticTweetsUITests/PragmaticTweetsUITests.swift
```
func testExample() {
  // Use recording to get started writing UI tests.
  // Use XCTAssert and related functions to verify your tests produce
  // the correct results.
}
```

"Use recording"? How do we do that? Notice that at the bottom of the content pane (either above the Debug area or at the bottom of the window if that's now showing), we have a circular red button. That, as you might suspect, is the record button. To see how it works, put the cursor inside the testExample() method and start a blank line. Now click the record button.

This launches the app in the Simulator. After a few seconds, once the app is up and running, tap the Send Tweet button. If the Xcode window isn't covered up, you may notice that code is being written inside the testExample() for us.

Once the SLComposeViewController view comes up to let us compose a tweet, click the Cancel button. A few more lines of code get written for us. This is actually all we need to record for now, so click the record button again to stop the UI recording. Then stop the Simulator with the stop button on the top toolbar as usual.

Take a look inside testExample() to see what the recorder has written for us:

testing/PragmaticTweets-6-3/PragmaticTweetsUITests/PragmaticTweetsUITests.swift

```
Line 1  func testExample() {
     2      let app = XCUIApplication()
     3      app.buttons["Send Tweet"].tap()
     4      app.navigationBars["Twitter"].buttons["Cancel"].tap()
     5  }
```

The code here is recognizable as Swift, even if the classes are not. And that makes sense because we're not writing code to create the UI here; we're using code to discover what's on screen at a given time. The XCUIApplication object created on line 2 is a sort of proxy that lets us discover what's going on in the app. We'll use this to query for onscreen UI elements.

On line 3, our recorded code asks the XCUIApplication for an array of all buttons currently on screen, and to find the one called Send Tweet. The first part of this expression is of type XCUIElement, and it works as a sort of query. If it resolves to exactly one object, we can programmatically tap() it. If there are zero or more than one matching buttons, an error occurs and our test fails. So already, we have a test that would notice if we accidentally deleted the Send Tweet button.

Line 4 does something similar, just more complicated: it asks for any onscreen navigation bar with the title Twitter, and from that finds a button called Cancel. Again, zero or more than one of either of these would fail.

This is a nifty way to discover our UI at runtime, and with further recording we can discover how to interact with other parts of our app. We can also write this logic by hand, or clean it up after the recorder is finished: for example, we can access buttons by index rather than by name if that makes more sense to us.

Writing UI Tests

Still, this isn't much of a test: there's no condition that we're testing to be true or false. If we click the diamond next to testExample(), or run all the tests with ⌘U, this test will pass, because there's nothing to make it fail. So let's figure out what we want to test.

We know from writing the original ViewController class in the last chapter that all the handleTweetButtonTapped() method does is show the SLComposeViewController. So let's make that the thing we test: on the last line that was recorded, we don't need to tap the Cancel button—we just want to make sure it exists.

This is pretty easy: the XCUIElement expressions that the recorder creates for us have an exists property, which is true if there is one and only one matching view. And something that's true or false is something we can expose to the XCUnit methods from the last section!

Change the name of the method to testSendTweet, and rewrite the method as follows:

```
testing/PragmaticTweets-6-3/PragmaticTweetsUITests/PragmaticTweetsUITests.swift
func testSendTweet() {
  let app = XCUIApplication()
  app.buttons["Send Tweet"].tap()
  XCTAssertTrue(
    app.navigationBars["Twitter"].buttons["Cancel"].exists)
}
```

All we've changed from the recording is the last line. Now instead of tapping the Cancel button, we just check that it exists, and we wrap this in a call to XCAssertTrue(). Now we have a real test: if the button doesn't exist, the assert causes the test to fail, and then we need to look to see how this could have broken.

Click the diamond next to testSendTweet() to run the test. We see the app run in the Simulator, and, back in Xcode we fail with "XCAssertTrue failed." Yay, we finally have a failable test case! But, wait, shouldn't this work? We didn't really change that much from the recording, after all.

It turns out recording can only take us so far. Look at the code: it tap()s the Send Tweet button and then immediately looks for the Cancel button on the tweet composer. But remember that when the app is running, it takes a second or so for the tweet composer to slide in. Maybe the UI tester is trying to tap the Cancel button before it's even there, and that's why it doesn't exist yet.

This is why we sometimes need the ability to touch up our recordings as we turn them into tests. If we could just get the test runner to wait for a second or two, everything should be fine.

Luckily, we can do just that. The NSThread class has a sleepForTimeInterval() method that stalls execution for given number of seconds. That's usually a *bad* idea in an app, since we'd be stalling the app's execution. But here, the app is running in its own process, and what we're stalling is the app runner. So add a sleep statement right before testing for the Cancel button, like this:

```
testing/PragmaticTweets-6-3/PragmaticTweetsUITests/PragmaticTweetsUITests.swift
func testSendTweet() {
  let app = XCUIApplication()
  app.buttons["Send Tweet"].tap()
  NSThread.sleepForTimeInterval(2.0)
  XCTAssertTrue(
    app.navigationBars["Twitter"].buttons["Cancel"].exists)
}
```

Run the test again, and this time we pass. Huzzah! Now we can extend our XCUnit testing skills into the realm of the user interface, so if we accidentally delete something from the storyboard, break a connection, or mess up the event-handling method, tests will be able to detect it.

> ### Xcode Testing and Continuous Integration
>
> Obviously, it would be burdensome if the only way to run unit tests and UI tests was through the Xcode UI. That would be completely impractical for automated testing, in which the tests are run automatically by a server, usually after a developer has checked in his or her changes.
>
> Fortunately, our tests aren't limited by the Xcode UI. Xcode provides a command-line executable, xcodebuild, which can perform many of Xcode's functions programmatically, including building projects and running their tests. Combined with a scripting language, this gives us all we need to run our tests automatically. In fact, this is how popular continuous integration systems like Jenkins interface with Xcode.
>
> For those who prefer an all-Apple solution, OS X Server offers *Xcode bots*, which are Xcode-savvy services for building and testing Xcode projects. There's more information about bots in the "Xcode Server and Continuous Integration Guide" in the Xcode documentation.

Running and Testing on the Device

Automating our tests and testing the user interface will eliminate a lot of problems that can come up in our app. But we still have another big blind spot: what if the app behaves differently in the iOS Simulator app than it would on a real device?

This is not idle speculation. Macs are generally more powerful than iOS devices, so apps often run faster in the Simulator than on real iOS hardware. A mouse or trackpad pointer is more precise than a finger touch, so running in the Simulator might also blind us to usability problems in the app. And there is some functionality that simply doesn't exist in the Simulator: the Simulator won't pretend that the Mac's built-in webcam is either of the iPhone cameras, and we can't tilt our laptop back and forth to test motion-sensing code.

To have full confidence in our app, we need to run it on the device. Let's close out the chapter by doing that.

Preparing the Device

To start with, we need an iOS device running the current version of iOS, since this is what our app expects to run on. If your device is running something older, you can go to the app target, find the iOS Deployment Target under Build Properties, and set that to a lower version than the default.

Connect the device to the Mac with its USB cable. The first time you do this, Xcode may present a dialog asking if you want to use the device for development; be sure to approve this.

Once the device is connected, it will appear in the scheme selector above the various Simulator, but as being "unavailable." Running on the device will take a little more work than just plugging in the cable.

Preparing a Developer Account

Apple doesn't let just anyone run anything on a device. Prior to Xcode 7 and iOS 9, putting our own code on an iOS device required being a member of the developer program. That's a bridge we'll cross much later (in Chapter 17, *Publishing and Maintaining the App*, on page 289), but in the meantime, it's now possible to get our app running on our device with just a little fuss.

To put an app on a device, Apple wants to know who we are and what we're doing. That's always been the case; what's different in Xcode 7 is that they'll let pretty much anyone do it, not just paid-up members. Either way, the first step is to sign into Xcode. Open Xcode's preferences (⌘,) and select the Accounts tab. We visited this tab back in *Getting Local Documentation*, on page 12, in order to download local copies of the documentation. If you skipped that step, well, do it now: click the + to add an Apple ID, and sign in with your credentials (the same ones used for the Mac App Store to download Xcode in the first place).

Just signing in isn't enough. Go to the target's General tab, where you'll see a warning that there are "No code signing identities found." *Code signing* is the process of using cryptographic techniques to provably verify that a known developer is the one installing the app to the device, and therefore the operation can be allowed. Fortunately, we don't have to do the underlying math; there's a handy Fix Issue button. Go ahead and click it.

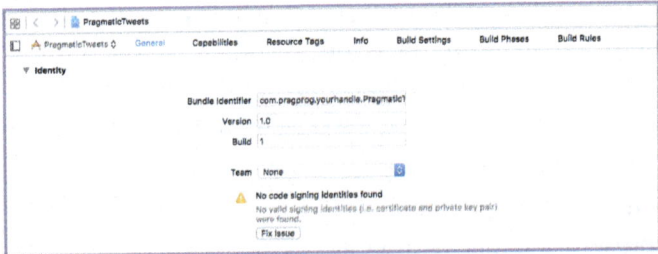

If all goes well, this will use our Apple ID from the Accounts tab to download and set up the needed credentials to allow us to put apps on the device. We'll talk more about how these actually work later, in *Member Center*, on page 290. Fixing the issue may also make you choose a Development Team; there should only be one, with your Apple ID name followed by (Personal Team), so use that.

When the issues are resolved, the warning in the target about signing identities becomes a pop-up with a choice of Team. Also, the device will be available in the scheme selector, without the (Not Available).

Select this destination and run the app as usual (be sure to unlock the screen first, since Xcode can't enter your PIN for you). After a short delay in which Xcode rebuilds the app for the device's CPU (which is different than the Simulator's, after all), it copies the app across the USB cable, onto the device.

The first time you run it, there's one more wrinkle: Xcode trusts you and the device, but the device may not trust you. This shows up as an Xcode error sheet saying "process launch failed; Security." If this happens, open the settings app on the device itself and select General. You'll see a new section called Profiles & Device Management and, within it, the section Developer App, which shows your Apple ID. Click this and, on the screen that follows, tap to trust apps from your Apple ID, as shown in the following figure.

With this last security issue resolved, running the app in Xcode will make it run on our device and behave just like before. At least we hope it does! If it doesn't, then we have a device-specific issue. And in cases where behavior differs between device and Simulator, the device always wins, since that's what our users will run the app on. In fact, it's so important to focus on the device that the testing techniques we've learned throughout the chapter all work on the device too; just choose a device in the scheme selector before running the test.

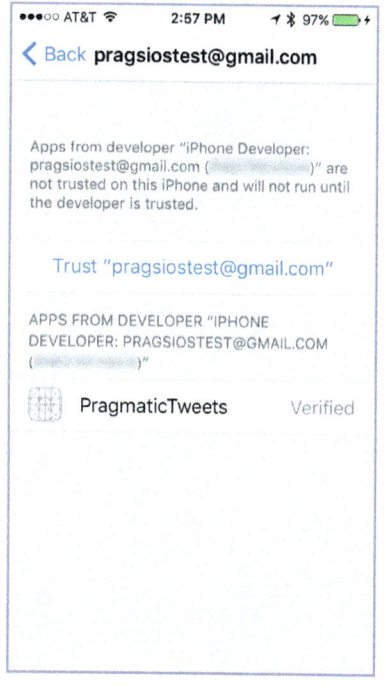

What We've Learned

In this chapter we have gone on a nice tour of unit testing and gotten a taste for the fundamentals of test-driven development. We walked through the TDD process from idea to implementation.

We have explored Apple's built-in unit testing suite XCTest, for testing both application logic and user interface. We also saw how to test the user interface and how it interacts with our code. And to top it off, we ran the app on the device, so we'll see exactly what the users will when they run it on their iPhones and iPads.

You now have the tools to go forth into the world and test your apps so that you can be sure your users will not have to deal with a crash or erroneous behavior.

Now that you know how to write tests to ensure your features work as designed, we're going to start reworking those features. In the next chapter, we'll begin moving to the table view style of presentation that's so common on iOS.

CHAPTER 7

Working with Tables

For organizing and presenting many of the kinds of data we see in iPhone and iPad apps, it's hard to beat a table view. Thanks to the intuitive flick-scrolling provided by iOS, it's comfortable and convenient to whip through lists of items to find just the thing we need, with each item visually presented in whatever way makes sense for the app. In many apps, the table view is the bedrock of the app's presentation and organization.

In this chapter, we're going start turning our Twitter application into one that's based around a table view. However, it's going to take us a few chapters to completely move away from the web view. First, we'll put some fake data into a table view, and then in the following chapters we'll get real data from the Twitter API and load it into the table view.

Tables on iOS

Coming from the desktop, one might expect a UITableView to look something like a spreadsheet, with rows and columns presented in a two-dimensional grid. Instead, the table view is a vertically scrolling list of items, optionally split into sections.

The table view is essential for many of the apps that ship with the iPhone, as well as popular third-party apps. In Mail, tables are used for the list of accounts, the mailboxes within each account, and the contents of each mailbox. The Reminders app is little more than a table view with some editing features, as are the alarms in the Clock app. The Music app shows lists of artists or albums, and within them lists of songs. Even the Settings app is built around a table, albeit one of a different style than is used in most apps (more on that later).

And while our Twitter app currently displays a web view of all the tweets we've parsed, pretty much every Twitter app out there (including the official Twitter app, as well as *Twitterrific*, *Tweetbot*, and *Echofon*) uses a table view to present tweets.

So our task now is to switch from the web view to a table view–based presentation of the tweets. We'll build this up slowly, as our understanding of tables and what they can do for us develops.

Table Classes

To add a table to an iOS app, we use an instance of UITableView. This is a UIScrollView subclass, itself a subclass of UIView, so it can either be a full-screen view unto itself or embedded as the child of another view. It cannot, however, have arbitrary subviews added to it, as it uses its subviews to present the individual cells within the table view.

The table has two properties that are crucial for it to actually do anything. The most important is the dataSource, which is an object that implements the UITableViewDataSource protocol. This protocol defines methods that tell the table how many sections it has (and optionally what their titles are) and how many rows are in a given section, and provides a cell view for a given section-row pair. The data source also has editing methods that allow for the addition, deletion, or reordering of table contents. There's also a delegate, an object implementing the UITableViewDelegate protocol, which provides method definitions for handling selection of rows and other user interface events.

These roles are performed not by the table itself—whose only responsibility is presenting the data and tracking user gestures like scrolling and selection—but by some other object, often a view controller. Typically, there are two approaches to wiring up a table to its contents:

- Have a UIViewController implement the UITableViewDataSource and UITableViewDelegate protocols.

- Use a UITableViewController, a subclass of the UIViewController that is also defined as implementing the UITableViewDataSource and UITableViewDelegate protocols

It's helpful to use the second approach when the *only* view presented by the controller is a table, as this gives us some nice additional functionality like built-in pull-to-refresh, or scrolling to the top when the status bar is tapped. But if the table is just a subview, and the main view has other subviews like buttons or a heads-up view, then we need to use the first approach instead.

Model-View-Controller

The careful apportioning of responsibilities between the view class and the controller comes from UIKit's use of the *model-view-controller* design pattern, or MVC. The idea of this design is to split out three distinct responsibilities of our UI:

- *Model*—The data to be presented, such as the array of tweets

- *View*—The user interface object, like a text view or a table

- *Controller*—The logic that connects the model and the view, such as how to fill in the rows of the table, and what to do when a row is tapped

This pattern explains why the class we've been doing most of our work in is a "view controller"; as a controller, it provides the logic that populates an onscreen view, and updates its state in reaction to user interface events. Notice that it is not necessary for each member of the design to be have its own class: the view is an object we created in the storyboard, and the model can be a simple object like an array. At this point in our app's evolution, only the controller currently requires a custom class. Still, some developers prefer the clarity of each role having its own class, so sometimes you'll see a class that exists only to implement UITableViewDataSource for a given table.

Creating and Connecting Tables

We're going to need to make some major changes to our user interface to switch to a table-driven approach. In fact, we're going to blow away our original view entirely. We'll get all our functionality back eventually, and we'll be in a better position to build out deeper and more interesting features. Eventually, we'll have an app that looks and feels like a real Twitter client.

We'll start by preparing our view controller to supply the table data. We can do this by either declaring that we implement UITableViewDataSource, or by becoming a subclass of UITableViewController. Since the table will be the only thing in this view, let's do the latter. In ViewController.swift, rewrite the declaration like this:

tables/PragmaticTweets-7-1/PragmaticTweets/ViewController.swift
```
class ViewController: UITableViewController {
```

Adding a Table View to the Storyboard

Now switch to Main.storyboard and look through the Object area at the bottom right for the Table View Controller object, shown in this figure. Drag one into the storyboard, anywhere where it won't collide with the existing view controller. This

adds a new Table View Controller Scene to the list of scenes in the storyboard.

Select the view controller from the previously existing scene and press ⌫ to delete the old scene. This leaves the storyboard with no entry point. Select the Table View Controller, bring up its Attributes Inspector (⌥⌘4), and select the Is Initial View Controller check box. The view gets an arrow on its left side, showing our app once again has a place to start. The view itself shows a status bar that says Prototype Cells above a Table View that has a single Table View Cell as a subview, as seen in the following figure.

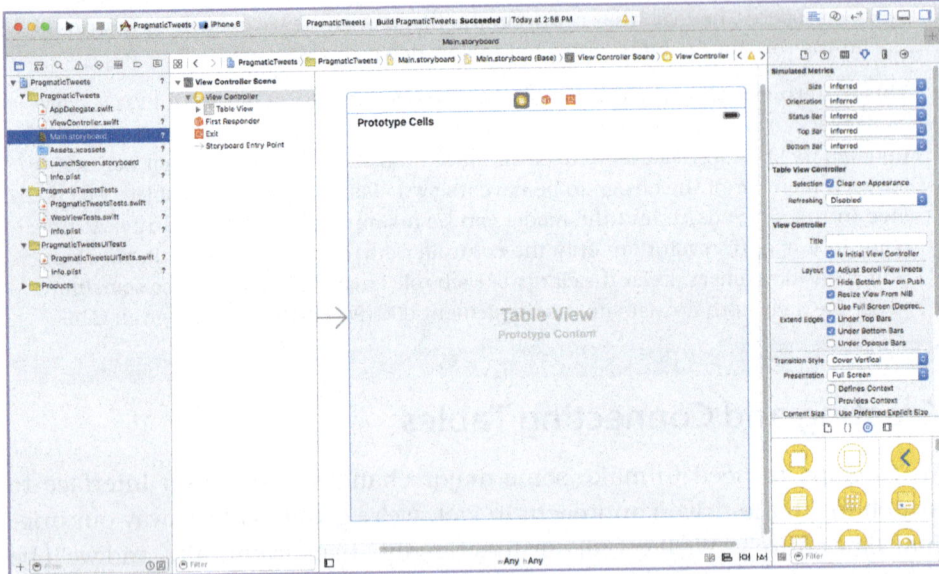

We can run this app...but it shows an empty table! That's because the table is not yet connected to a data source that can provide it with cells or even a count of how many sections and rows there are. Let's get to work on that.

Providing a Temporary Table Data Source

As it is, the table in the storyboard doesn't know to use our class; it expects to create a generic UITableViewController for the table. We want it to use our View-Controller instead. So, while still in Main.storyboard, choose the Table View Controller and visit its Identity Inspector in the right-side pane (⌥⌘3). In the Custom Class section, for the Class, enter ViewController. This should autocomplete, since we declared that our ViewController class is a valid UITableViewController, although we've done nothing to implement that behavior yet.

While here, Control-click on the table view, or visit its Connections Inspector (⌥⌘6), and notice that table view's connections to the dataSource and delegate properties are already wired up, connected to the view controller.

As a warm-up, let's provide a trivial implementation of the data source methods, just to ensure the new storyboard and its connections are good to go. To do this, our data source needs to provide a minimum of three things: the number of sections, the number of rows in a given section, and a cell for a given section and row. In ViewController.swift, provide the following trivial implementations of the UITableViewDataSource methods numberOfSectionsInTableView(), tableView(numberOfRowsInSection:), and tableView(cellForRowAtIndexPath:), as well as the optional tableView(titleForHeaderInSection:), which will let us see the section breaks.

tables/PragmaticTweets-7-1/PragmaticTweets/ViewController.swift
```
override func numberOfSectionsInTableView(tableView: UITableView)
  -> Int {
    return 5
}

override func tableView(tableView: UITableView,
  titleForHeaderInSection section: Int) -> String? {
    return "Section \(section)"
}

override func tableView(tableView: UITableView,
  numberOfRowsInSection section: Int) -> Int {
    return section + 1
}

override func tableView(tableView: UITableView,
  cellForRowAtIndexPath indexPath: NSIndexPath) -> UITableViewCell {
    let cell = UITableViewCell(style: .Default, reuseIdentifier: nil)
    cell.textLabel?.text = "Row \(indexPath.row)"
    return cell
}
```

Notice that in our quick-and-dirty table code, three of our methods are called tableView(). The reason these methods don't get confused with one another is because they're differentiated by their named parameters: one takes titleForHeaderInSection, another takes cellForRowAtIndexPath, and so on.

By convention, all these methods take the table view in question as their first argument, so if we had multiple tables, a method would be able to figure out which table it's working with.

But as for why it has to be the *first* parameter, that's more of a legacy of Objective-C, where it was somewhat more natural to incorporate the name of your first parameter into the method name, and differentiate with the rest of the parameters. Swift came later, so we're stuck with the old naming schemes, at least for now.

In this book, when we encounter cases where the method name by itself isn't unique, we'll include the parameters for clarity. That way, we'll call out the difference between tableView(numberOfRowsInSection:) and tableView(cellForRowAtIndexPath:), but we won't feel the need to write viewWillAppear(animated:) when there's only one method that starts like that, so it can be written as just viewWillAppear().

Chained Optionals

One other new thing to notice in the tableView(cellForRowAtIndexPath:) implementation is this line:

```
cell.textLabel?.text = "Row \(indexPath.row)"
```

This particular use of the ? operator is new, and quite handy. The textLabel property of UITableViewCell is an optional, so ordinarily we would want to test it with an if let or guard let. But in the middle of a chain of dot accessors, this is burdensome. And to just force-unwrap with ! would be dangerous.

One alternative is to use the ? right before a dot operator. This syntax is called the *chained optional*, and it works like this: the expression is evaluated left-to-right, and all optionals marked with ? are tested against nil. If any optional is nil, processing stops and the whole expression evaluates to nil. In an assignment like this, it's OK for the left side to be nil, because assigning a value to nil (instead of to a real variable) just quietly does nothing.

If none of the optionals are nil, then we can get the value at the end of the chain, albeit with one caveat: its type becomes optional, even if the last type in the chain wasn't optional. Again, that's fine here, because the text property of the textLabel is also an optional type: String?.

Lots of the changes since Swift 1.0 have made dealing with optionals easier. This is one we'll get a lot of mileage out of.

Anyway, while we're in the ViewController.swift file, let's delete the line that declares the twitterWebView that no longer exists, and all of the handleShowMyTweetsTapped() methods that populated it. We won't need those anymore. Also, delete the contents of reloadTweets(), but leave the method definition; we'll rebuild that one shortly. Finally, with no twitterWebView, there's no need for the WebViewTests test class, so delete that entire file.

In this implementation, we are telling the table that there are five sections, that each section has one more row than the section index (that is to say, there's one row in section 0, two rows in section 1, etc.), and that any time a new cell is needed, it should create a new UITableViewCell, get its textLabel property (a UILabel), and set the text property of the label to a string that shows the row number. When run, the table will look like the following figure.

You may be wondering why the status bar overlaps the table. This is one of the more controversial aspects of the iOS 7 visual design—view controllers default into a full-screen mode. In fact, the property wantsFullScreenLayout was deprecated in iOS 7, and since then view controllers are assumed to *always* fill the screen with their views, even the space under the status bar.

It looks horrible at first, but the idea is that once we start scrolling and see content go under the status bar, the transparency of the status bar gives us a visual cue about information that is about to come fully into view. In later chapters, we'll add a navigation bar at the top and then it'll look and feel a lot better.

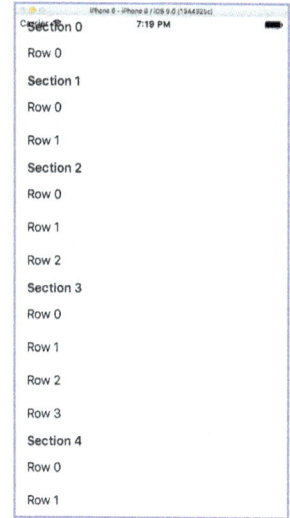

Notice that tableView(cellForRowAtIndexPath:) passes in an NSIndexPath. This is a class originally intended for representing paths in tree structures, things like "the third child of the second child of the root node." In iOS, it is pressed into service representing table entries. NSIndexPath is extended to add the properties section and row (which are implemented as just the first and second entries in the path), and this combination of section and row can uniquely identify any cell in UITableView.

Now we have a table and a way to get data into it. What we need to do next is provide a nontrivial implementation of the data source, one that actually shows some tweets.

Filling In the Table

Let's think about how we're going to go from this to a table of real tweets. Since the table can demand the contents of any row at any time, we'll want to have a data structure representing all the tweets that we want to show in the table. This doesn't have to be anything fancy; in fact, an array will do just fine.

But an array of what? Well, one approach would be to just create a data type including the parts of a tweet we care about—its text, the screen name of the person who sent it, and so forth—and then have an array of those objects.

Since starting the PragmaticTweets example, we've been dealing almost exclusively in classes, because that's what we inherit from the iOS SDK: we subclassed UIViewController to handle the UI, and subclassed XCTestCase to create unit tests. But back in Chapter 3, *Swift with Style*, on page 37, we said one of the great things about Swift was getting away from classes and pass-by-reference. Finally, we have a good opportunity to do just that: if we want a data type representing the important parts of a tweet, a struct fills the bill much better than a class. We don't need this type to maintain state or have a bunch of state-mutating functionality; we just need a container for values. That's totally perfect for a struct.

Creating a ParsedTweet Structure

To create a new struct in our project, we use File > New File (⌘N), which causes a sheet to slide out showing templates for new files, which you see in the following figure. From the iOS group on the left, choose Source, and then from the icons on the right, choose the Swift File template, and click Next.

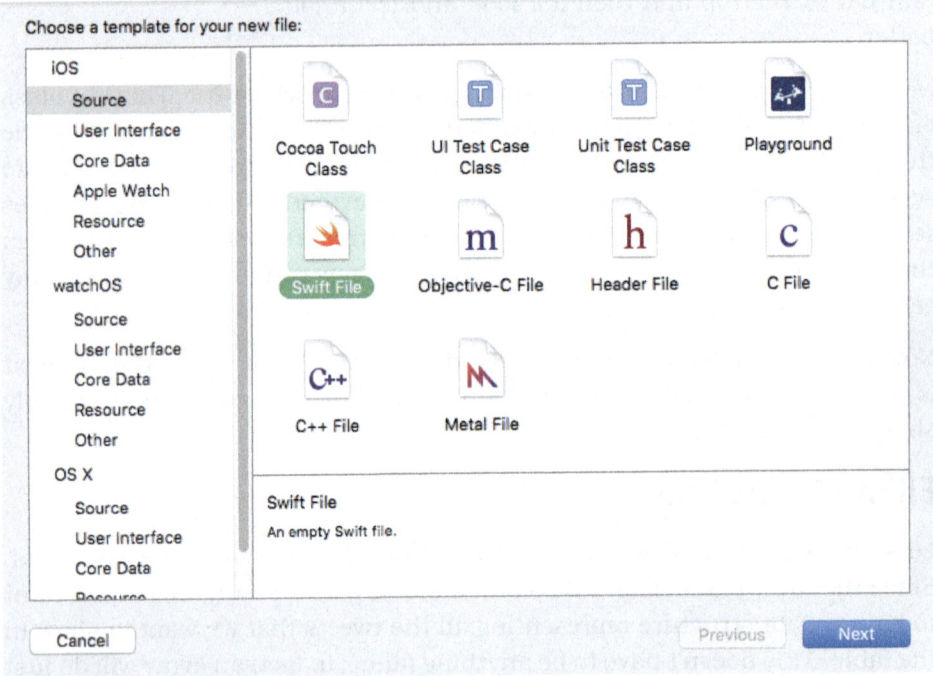

This takes us to the file dialog that indicates where to save the file and which *targets* will build the class. For the filename, use ParsedTweet. As for the targets, by default only the PragmaticTweets app will be selected, and not the PragmaticTweetsTests or PragmaticTweetsUITests testing targets. This is what we want—we only need the file built for the app itself—so click Create to create a ParsedTweet.swift file in our project.

The `ParsedTweet` structure doesn't need to hold onto every field we could get from Twitter for a given tweet—there are hundreds of them—just the ones we want to show in the UI. For now, let's figure we'll want the tweet text, the username, a created-at string, and a URL for the user's avatar. So we define public properties for those in `ParsedTweet.swift`.

tables/PragmaticTweets-7-1/PragmaticTweets/ParsedTweet.swift

```
struct ParsedTweet {
  var tweetText: String?
  var userName: String?
  var createdAt: String?
  var userAvatarURL: NSURL?
}
```

We'll make all of these optionals, since we are in no position to populate them when an instance of the `struct` is instantiated. The alternative would be to assign a value like an empty string to one of these properties, but it's more expressive to use the absence of a value to say "this hasn't been set yet," even if it might be a bit more work later to defend against the optional and make sure the property isn't `nil`.

We can now create `ParsedTweet` instances in other classes by simply writing code like this:

```
var myTweet = ParsedTweet()
myTweet.userName = "@pragprog"
myTweet.tweetText = "Check out our new iOS book!"
```

The struct also gives us a *memberwise initializer* that takes all the fields at once, so if it's convenient to do so, we could do this:

```
let myTweet = ParsedTweet(tweetText : "Check out our new iOS book!",
  userName: "@pragprog",
  createdAt: "2015-08-31 08:19:00 EDT",
  userAvatarURL: nil)
```

Keep in mind that if we use `let`, as in the second example, the `myTweet` structure, *and all its properties*, are constants and cannot be changed. It's good Swift practice to make things constant whenever they can be, but if any of the fields might need to change later, use a `var`.

Building a Table Model of ParsedTweets

Until we're ready to get real tweets from the Twitter API, we'll have to make do with some *mock data*, predictable stand-in values that will let us figure out tables and put off dealing with network stuff. We can create an array of

ParsedTweet objects, and just come up with our own values for the tweetText, userName, and createdAt strings.

Actually, let's start with the URL. Twitter's new user "egg" icon lives at a set of URLs like https://abs.twimg.com/sticky/default_profile_images/default_profile_0_200x200.png, where the 0 after profile_ can be any number between 0 and 6 inclusive, each showing a different color, and the 200x200 has several replacements for different sizes. For now, we'll just use this one image over and over. At the top of View-Controller.swift, after the imports and before the class declaration, add the following constant:

tables/PragmaticTweets-7-1/PragmaticTweets/ViewController.swift
```
let defaultAvatarURL = NSURL(string:
  "https://abs.twimg.com/sticky/default_profile_images/" +
  "default_profile_6_200x200.png")
```

We had to split the URL string into two lines for the book's formatting; feel free to write it all on one line. We would if we could.

Now, we can create an array of ParsedTweet objects to serve as our data model. After the curly brace that begins ViewController's class declaration, declare an array of ParsedTweets, and then inside square braces, use the memberwise initializer to create as many tweet objects as you like (we'll just use three to save space). The beginning of the class should look like this:

tables/PragmaticTweets-7-1/PragmaticTweets/ViewController.swift
```
var parsedTweets: [ParsedTweet] = [
  ParsedTweet(tweetText : "iOS 9 SDK Development now in print. " +
    "Swift programming FTW!",
    userName: "@pragprog",
    createdAt: "2015-09-09 15:44:30 EDT",
    userAvatarURL: defaultAvatarURL),

  ParsedTweet(tweetText : "But was that really such a good idea?",
    userName: "@redqueencoder",
    createdAt: "2014-12-04 22:15:55 CST",
    userAvatarURL: defaultAvatarURL),

  ParsedTweet(tweetText : "Struct all the things!",
    userName: "@invalidname",
    createdAt: "2015-07-31 05:39:39 EDT",
    userAvatarURL: defaultAvatarURL)
]
```

Now that we have an array that can serve as our data source, we can rewrite the UITableViewDataSource methods to use the ParsedTweets in this array to calculate the number of rows and the contents of each. Rewrite those methods as follows:

```
tables/PragmaticTweets-7-1/PragmaticTweets/ViewController.swift
override func numberOfSectionsInTableView(tableView: UITableView)
  -> Int {
  return 1
}

override func tableView(tableView: UITableView,
  numberOfRowsInSection section: Int) -> Int {
    return parsedTweets.count
}

override func tableView(tableView: UITableView,
  cellForRowAtIndexPath indexPath: NSIndexPath) -> UITableViewCell {
    let cell = UITableViewCell(style: .Default, reuseIdentifier: nil)
    let parsedTweet = parsedTweets[indexPath.row]
    cell.textLabel?.text = parsedTweet.tweetText
    return cell
}
```

Also, go ahead and delete the titleForHeaderInSection() method; we'll only have a single section from here on, so the title is superfluous.

In this new version, we have a single section, and the number of rows in this section is just the size of the parsedTweets array. Then we use the indexPath's row property to figure out which ParsedTweet to fetch from our parsedTweets array, and put its tweetText into the cell's text label.

Anyway, run the app now and behold the tweets.

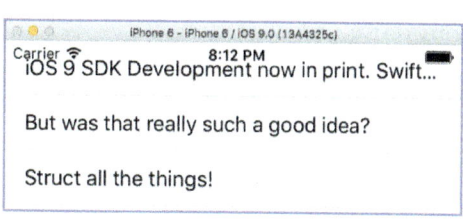

Look at that…we've got our tweets in a table view! And they scroll, so if we coded 200 in our mock data array, we could just flick through them.

Of course, the one line of text isn't big enough for most tweets. So now that we've got our data where it needs to be, let's start improving the table's appearance.

Reloading Table Contents

One thing that might not be immediately evident but that might come back to bite us later: the only reason we can see any table contents is that the app's startup will do a one-time presentation of the first view's contents. Later on, we'll be updating and changing the table's contents. So how do we refresh its contents?

We can add ParsedTweet instances to the parsedTweets array, or delete some of its contents, but the array doesn't have a way to tell the table that its contents have changed, so the table won't do anything if we just edit the array. As a controller, it's our job to keep the view and model in sync. UITableView offers methods to notify the table of distinct edits, like insertRowsAtIndexPaths() or removeRowsAtIndexPaths(). Sometimes, it's simpler to just do a full-on reload of the table, with reloadData(). So let's revise our old reloadTweets() method to do that for us:

tables/PragmaticTweets-7-1/PragmaticTweets/ViewController.swift
```
func reloadTweets() {
  tableView.reloadData()
}
```

Later on, this view won't be the first thing we see in the app, so we want to make sure to reload the table automatically any time it appears. Fortunately, we're already doing that with the call to reloadTweets() in the viewDidLoad() method.

Customizing Table Appearance

While it's great to have the Twitter data in our table cells, only having access to a single, one-line text label makes it impossible to show the various fields of the ParsedTweet; at this point, we don't even know who sent which tweet! We need to change what these table cells look like, to provide more room to show our data.

Table Cell Styles

When we create the UITableViewCell in tableView(cellForRowAtIndexPath:), our initializer takes a style argument. As it turns out, this can allay our problems somewhat.

The available styles are collected in an enumeration. Four cell styles are defined in the UITableViewCellStyle enumeration, of which we've been using UITableViewCellStyle.Default. Fortunately for our fingers, we don't have to write the whole type when we refer to an enumeration's value; we can just write the value itself, like .Default.

The UITableViewCell class itself defines certain subviews—textLabel, detailTextLabel, imageView, and accessoryView—and this style determines if and where those subviews are laid out. The figure shows a four-row table with the row number in the textLabel, and the name

of the style in the detailTextLabel. Notice that for the .Default style in row 0, the detailTextLabel is not shown at all.

This figure doesn't show the cell's other possible subviews; if an imageView is set, it appears on the left side of the cell, and an accessoryView (usually a Show Details button) appears on the right. Clearly, if all of those subviews are present, the cell is going to get pretty crowded, and that's something we'll have to deal with soon.

For now, we'll try out the two-line presentation of the UITableViewCellStyle.Subtitle, and along the way we're going to fix a problem we've created for ourselves.

Grouped Tables

Another appearance option is to use *grouped tables*, which is just an attribute we can set on the table view in the storyboard. This sets the table's style to UITableViewStyleGrouped, which in turn makes the table look like this figure.

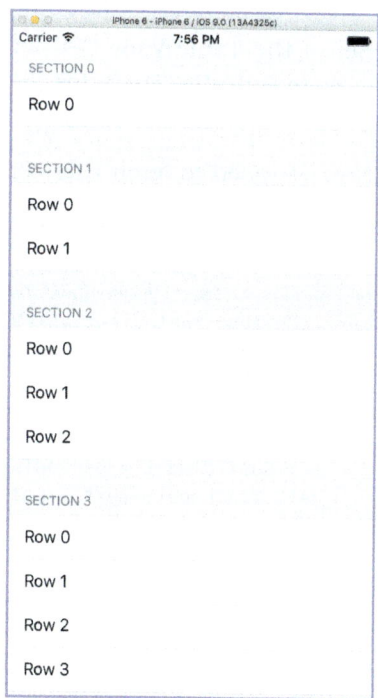

The major differences with a grouped table are that header and footer views do not "stick" to the top or bottom of the screen when scrolling, and on iOS 6 and earlier, the cells have rounded edges that make them look more like buttons. The grouped table is what the Settings app uses, and users will be familiar with its appearance from that.

Cell Reuse

Right now, we create a new UITableViewCell in every call to tableView(cellForRowAtIndexPath:). If we flick through a really long table, that might mean we create a cell that will only appear for an instant before it goes off the screen and is no longer needed. As it turns out, creating views is fairly expensive, so if we can avoid doing that frequently, it will make our app faster and more responsive.

The UITableView class is actually built to cache and reuse cells. It provides a method, dequeueReusableCellWithIdentifier(), that takes a string identifying a cell to be reused. The idea is that we can create a cell in the storyboard as a sort of template and identify it with a known string. In code, we'll ask for a cell by this name. If the table has already created a cell with this name *and* it isn't currently being shown—meaning it has scrolled off the top or bottom of the screen—the table will give us the old cell and allow us to reuse it. Otherwise, it will create a new cell from the *prototype* in the storyboard. This way, we'll create only as many cells as we need to show on the screen at one time, and our scrolling performance will be much improved.

Go to Main.storyboard and select the table view. Notice that the table header is Prototype Cells, and the table has a single Table View Cell as a child. The table's Attributes Inspector also has a field for Prototype Cells, currently set to 1. We only need the one prototype cell, because new cells will be minted from this prototype—if we had different layouts for different rows (like advertising cells that were different from tweet cells), we could add more prototypes.

Select the Table View Cell, visit its Attributes Inspector (⌥⌘4), and set its style to Subtitle. Then, for the Identifier, we need a string value that we can use to fetch this cell from our code. Let's use UserAndTweetCell.

Now we need to fetch this cell in code and customize it. We do this in table-View(cellForRowAtIndexPath:), so go back to ViewController.swift and rewrite the method as follows:

```
tables/PragmaticTweets-7-2/PragmaticTweets/ViewController.swift
Line 1  override func tableView(tableView: UITableView,
     2    cellForRowAtIndexPath indexPath: NSIndexPath) -> UITableViewCell {
     3      let cell =
     4      tableView.dequeueReusableCellWithIdentifier("UserAndTweetCell")
     5        as UITableViewCell!
     6      let parsedTweet = parsedTweets[indexPath.row]
     7      cell.textLabel?.text = parsedTweet.userName
     8      cell.detailTextLabel?.text = parsedTweet.tweetText
     9      return cell
    10  }
```

The changes we make here are to get the cell via dequeueReusableCellWithIdentifier:() (on lines 3–5), and then to use two fields from the parsedTweet: its userName can go in the textLabel, and the tweetText can go in the detailTextLabel. The result is a lot more useful.

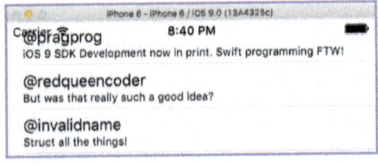

The result of dequeuing prototype cells instead of creating new cells every time doesn't have an immediate visual impact, although there is a subtle performance improvement when scrolling a few hundred cells on the Simulator, and this effect is much more pronounced when running on a genuine iOS device.

The Argument for Force-Unwrapping(!)

Admittedly, we are doing one slightly dangerous thing here. On line 5, we use as UITableViewCell! to force-unwrap the cell we get back from dequeueReusableCellWithIdentifier(). This only works if we've set up the storyboard correctly with the cell identifier. If there's no name or a misspelling, we get back nil and crash the app.

The alternative would be to do an if let or guard let, but what should we do if that fails? dequeueReusableCellWithIdentifier() *requires* us to return a UITableViewCell of some sort, so the failure case would seemingly have to just create a new, empty cell and return that. Yet that wouldn't do the user any good.

If we crash, it means we've messed up the storyboard in a way that isn't recoverable. With a programming error like this, the crash is arguably preferable: we'll see it in development and fix it, rather than ship an app with empty table cells.

This is the argument for force-unwrapping, as well as implicitly unwrapped optionals: if we know something should never be nil, and if we're honestly better off knowing sooner in the form of a crash, go ahead and use the ! operator.

While it's nice to have both the tweet and its author, longer tweets could still be truncated—we need a multiline label for those. How are we going to do that? It doesn't look like it's going to fit in the subtitle cell, and even if it does, we still would like to have a third label to show the tweet's timestamp.

Fortunately, we're not limited to the provided cell styles. We can create our own prototype cells with whatever views suit us—even tappable elements like buttons—and then use them in our table.

Custom Table Cells

To create a custom table cell, it usually makes sense to create a subclass of UITableViewCell and give it public properties for the fields that we'll need to update from tableView(cellForRowAtIndexPath:). So, in the File Navigator, select the Pragmatic Tweets group, choose File > New > File, and select the Cocoa Touch Class template. In the next pane of the assistant, name the class ParsedTweetCell, and set the Subclass of: to UITableViewCell. We don't need to do anything with the code yet, but it will help us in the storyboard to have this class already created.

Back in Main.storyboard, select the table view. We could edit the existing prototype cell, but just to prove that we can juggle multiple prototypes, let's create our custom cell as a second prototype. In the Attributes Inspector, tap the up button on the Prototype Cells field so the table has two prototypes. A second prototype is created, a copy of the first. Select the second and, in the Attributes Inspector (⌥⌘4), change its style to Custom and its identifier to CustomTweet-

Cell. Then, in the Identity Inspector (⌥⌘3), change its class to the ParsedTweetCell class that we just created; the Module should default to Current - PragmaticTweets.

Switch to the Size Inspector (⌥⌘5) and notice that the first field is Row Height, currently shown with the placeholder text Default because the Custom check box is not selected. If we want to pack a bunch of fields in here, it's pretty clear that the default row height is not going to cut it for us, so click Custom and enter a height of 125. That should give us enough room.

Now we get to lay out a UI inside the cell pretty much the same way we built the app's original view with buttons and a web view in earlier chapters. Within the cell, we can add labels, image views, whatever we like...provided that we wrangle all the autolayout constraints to put them in their place (there had to be a catch, right?). We're going to add four subviews: labels for the username, tweet text, and a created-at string, plus an image view for the user's picture. Feel free to play around; for the sample code, we've used the following views:

- An image view (use the icon with the palm tree) with height and width constraints to lock its size at 75×75 points, plus top and leading constraints of 0 points each from the margin. The image view will initially want to be much larger than this when 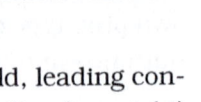 you drop it, but once you set the constraints, using Update Frames in the autolayout Resolve menu (⌥⌘=) will clean it up.

- A label for the username, with the font set to System - Bold, leading constraint of 8 points from the image view, 0 point top, and trailing (i.e., right) space constraints from the margins.

- A label for the tweet text, Lines set to 3, with the font set to System 14-point, leading and top constraints of 8 points, and trailing constraint of 0 points from the margin.

- A label for the created-at string, with the font set to Caption 1, center-aligned text, a Horizontal Center in Container constraint, and a bottom constraint of 0 points to the margin.

Once we've created the layout, we're going to connect this prototype cell to the custom class we created earlier. Since we used the Identity Inspector to assign the cell to our ParsedTweetCell, the Assistant Editor will let us connect these subviews to new IBOutlet properties in that class. With the cell selected in the storyboard, switch to Assistant Editor mode via the rings icon or ⌥⌘↵ (it may help to hide the utility pane too). Ideally, Assistant Editor should bring

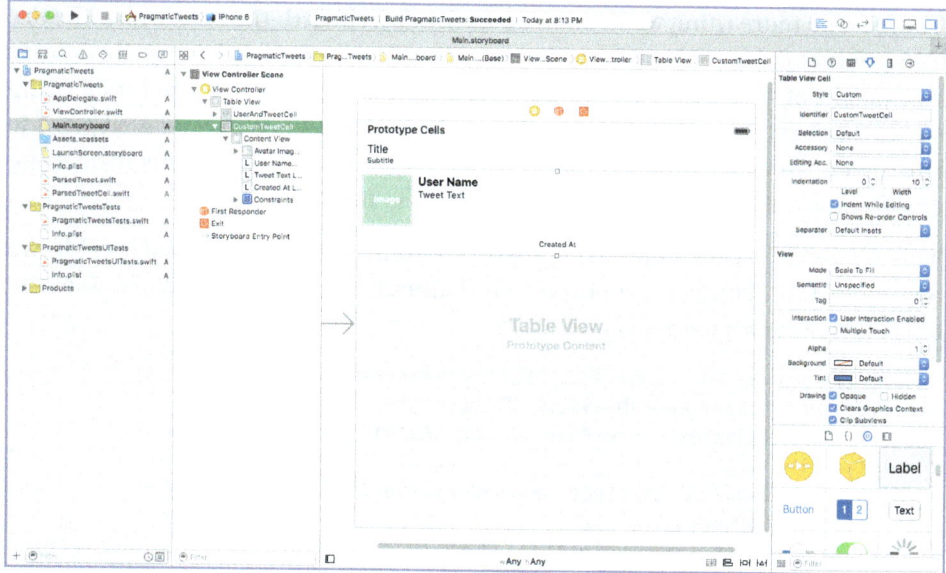

up ParsedTweetCell.swift on the right, but sometimes it chooses ViewController.swift; in that case, use the jump bar at the top of the pane to load ParsedTweetCell.swift into the right side.

Control-drag from each of the subviews over to the ParsedTweetCell.swift code, just under the class declaration and before the first method. After releasing the drag, give each property an appropriate name. With all the connections established, the properties should look like this:

tables/PragmaticTweets-7-3/PragmaticTweets/ParsedTweetCell.swift

```
@IBOutlet weak var avatarImageView: UIImageView!
@IBOutlet weak var userNameLabel: UILabel!
@IBOutlet weak var tweetTextLabel: UILabel!
@IBOutlet weak var createdAtLabel: UILabel!
```

Problems When Connecting Custom Cell Subviews

When creating connections from subviews in the custom cell, be sure that the subview (the label, image view, and so on) is selected, and not the Content View that is a superview to all of them. If the pop-up that appears at the end of the drag wants to define the class of the outlet as UIView rather than UILabel or UIImageView or what have you, chances are the connection is being made to the Content View instead of the specific subview we're trying to connect. One way to be sure is to start the drag from the subview's item in the scene's tree list, rather than from the storyboard view itself.

There's one more thing we need to do in the storyboard: the cells know they're 125 points tall, but the table doesn't, and will continue to assume the default row height of 44. Return to the Standard Editor mode, select the table, bring up its Size Inspector (⌥⌘5), and set Row Height to 125. We could also provide this height in code, which would in turn also make it possible for rows to be of different heights, but this easy approach is fine for now.

Now it's time to start populating these custom cells. Back in ViewController, we again need to update our method that dequeues and populates cells. Rewrite tableView(cellForRowAtIndexPath:) as follows:

tables/PragmaticTweets-7-3/PragmaticTweets/ViewController.swift

```
Line 1   override func tableView(tableView: UITableView,
     -      cellForRowAtIndexPath indexPath: NSIndexPath) -> UITableViewCell {
     -      let cell =
     -      tableView.dequeueReusableCellWithIdentifier("CustomTweetCell")
    5         as! ParsedTweetCell
     -      let parsedTweet = parsedTweets[indexPath.row]
     -      cell.userNameLabel.text = parsedTweet.userName
     -      cell.tweetTextLabel.text = parsedTweet.tweetText
     -      cell.createdAtLabel.text = parsedTweet.createdAt
   10       if let url = parsedTweet.userAvatarURL,
     -          imageData = NSData(contentsOfURL: url) {
     -          cell.avatarImageView.image = UIImage(data: imageData)
     -      }
     -      return cell
   15   }
```

The first big change here is on lines 3–5, where we dequeue the cell with the identifier string CustomTweetCell, and since we know it's our custom cell, we can use as! to forcibly convert it to our ParsedTweetCell class. Then, on lines 7–9, we set the values of the cell's properties that we connected.

Then we have the avatar image. The UIImageView has an image property we want to populate, of type UIImage. Unfortunately, UIImage can't be created directly from the contents of a URL. However, it will accept an NSData object containing image data, and we can initialize that with an NSURL, so we can chain those together with a chained if let on lines 10–11. If we make it into the curly braces, we have the imageData, and use it on line 12 to populate the image view.

With the image loaded into the image view, we return cell to the caller, just as before. The result looks like the figure on page 137.

This is looking a *lot* better. The avatar image is there, and the author name is nicely set off from the tweet text and created-on date. The difference in fonts lets us easily distinguish between username and their tweet, and the smaller Caption 1 font downplays the timestamp label.

There is one problem right now, though, and it's our images. If we have enough cells that we need to scroll—copy-and-paste a bunch of ParsedTweet initializers into the parsedTweets array initializer if you want to see it for yourself—the scrolling performance is pretty choppy. It's nowhere near as smooth as on a real iPhone or iPad, and this is running on the Simulator, where the power of a full-blown computer tends to run apps *faster* than they will on the device. So why is this happening?

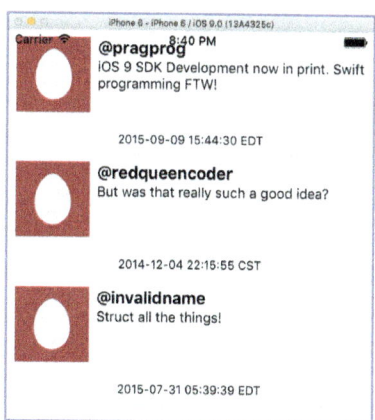

The culprit is how we're loading our images. Our approach of loading the image data from the NSURL right when the table-View(cellForRowAtIndexPath:) needs it has a big downside: it means that everything in our app just stops while we load that image from the network. We can't draw the cell, continue scrolling, or update anything else in the UI until the image data loads. Just imagine how well that's going to go over with users who are only getting one bar of cellular signal. In the next two chapters, we'll fix this problem with a more sophisticated approach.

Pull-to-Refresh

There's one other common table task we should attend to with our table: we haven't given the user a means of refreshing the tweets. We had this in the last chapter with the Show My Tweets button, but now that our whole view is a table (for now, anyway), there's no way to expose this functionality. It doesn't matter now with our mock data, but it will matter a lot if we can't get new tweets from the Internet. How are we going to fix that?

Many table-based iOS apps use a *pull-to-refresh* gesture, in which scrolling to the top of the table and then pulling down to scroll further is interpreted as a request for the app to refresh its data. There were a variety of third-party implementations of this gesture for a number of years, and in iOS 6, Apple provided a standard implementation in the form of the UIRefreshControl class.

The UITableViewController that our ViewController subclasses has a refreshControl property, meaning we inherit it, so all we need to do is to populate that with a refresh controller and default behavior will take care of the UI for us. In fact, the ease of using the refresh controller is one reason to choose to subclass UITableViewController, rather than have a plain UIViewController that also happens to implement the UITableViewDataSource protocol.

How I Gave Up Tables and Learned to Love Lists

One of the things we haven't talked about is the fact that UITableView looks a lot more like a *list* than a *table*. Isn't a table supposed to be two-dimensional? With columns and headers, like a spreadsheet? That's what a table is in most other UI toolkits.

This takes me back to a job I had back in 2002 or so, building a Java UI for a network operations center. The idea was it would feed out video clips, and the engineers there needed to see what was in the queue to go out, its priority, where it was going, and so on.

The first cut of the UI used a Java Swing JTable and, yeah, it did look like an Excel spreadsheet. I'd been playing with Mac OS X by this point—I was the only one in the office using it, and took a lot of crap for doing so—and realized that this was a lousy user interface. The wide table made it hard to trace a single item all the way across the window, and reading vertically down columns wasn't useful anyway. Also, JTable defaulted to making columns the same width, even when some of our fields were 4 characters and others were more than 40. It didn't need to be a table; it didn't work as a table.

So, I turned it into a list. I created custom cells that would group all the data together, using layout, fonts, and color to call out the stuff that mattered most, and how the items related to one another.

I liked it well enough that a decade later, with the company long gone, I still have screenshots. Here's one of the lists from the main status window:

The purple color scheme, programmer art, aliased text, and bland Windows NT fonts are hard on the eyes 10 years later, but at the time, this was a real breakthrough for us in how we thought about our in-house UI. You could easily see what was going out when, which items had priority, and why the queue was arranged the way it was. The cell layouts made the whole list more readable, and I've been a big fan of custom cells in lists and tables ever since.

Looking at the documentation, the UIRefreshControl is a subclass of UIControl and acts somewhat like a button or another generic control; when triggered, it sends an event called UIControlEventValueChanged. For us to do anything with it, we need to get a callback when that event occurs. We do that with the UIControl method addTarget(action:forControlEvents:). This method takes an object to call back to (such as our view controller), a method to call (which we'll write), and the relevant events for this callback (UIControlEventValueChanged).

So let's create and set up a suitable UIRefreshControl when our view controller first comes to life, in viewDidLoad:

```
tables/PragmaticTweets-7-4/PragmaticTweets/ViewController.swift
override func viewDidLoad() {
  super.viewDidLoad()
  reloadTweets()
  let refresher = UIRefreshControl()
  refresher.addTarget(self,
    action: "handleRefresh:",
    forControlEvents: .ValueChanged)
  refreshControl = refresher
}
```

The action, meaning the method that's invoked by the callback, is passed as a *selector*, a string that uniquely identifies a method signature. In this case, we're promising to write a method called handleRefresh() that will take one parameter, as indicated by the single colon character. By convention, these action methods take a single argument to identify the sender, and have a return type of IBAction, so they can be used for connections in the storyboard (so we could also connect it with the Interface Builder GUI rather than with code if we wanted to). So let's write this action method:

```
tables/PragmaticTweets-7-4/PragmaticTweets/ViewController.swift
Line 1  @IBAction func handleRefresh (sender : AnyObject?) {
     2    parsedTweets.append(
     3      ParsedTweet(tweetText: "New row",
     4        userName: "@refresh",
     5        createdAt: NSDate().description,
     6        userAvatarURL: defaultAvatarURL)
     7    )
     8    reloadTweets()
     9    refreshControl?.endRefreshing()
    10  }
```

This action method does three things:

- On lines 2–7, we append a new ParsedTweet to the parsedTweets array that serves as the table's data model. Notice that on line 5, we create a new NSDate object (which defaults to the current instant in time), and then use that class's description() method to turn it into a string.

- We call our existing reloadTweets() method on line 8.

- Finally, on line 9 we call endRefreshing() to tell UIRefreshControl to hide the spinning wheel. UIRefreshControl also has a beginRefreshing() method to show the spinner, but this is called for us automatically as UITableViewController processes the pull gesture.

When we run now, the spinner appears atop the table when we scroll to the top and pull again, as seen in this figure. This starts a reload of the Twitter data and dismisses the spinner, with a new row added to the table view when the reload is done. Try pulling slowly to see how the spinner only starts spinning and reloading once the drag gesture reaches a certain point. It's a handy gesture!

What We've Learned

We've put our app through a radical makeover in this chapter, and in so doing we've turned it from a toy into something that's starting to resemble real-world Twitter clients. By switching to a table view, we've adopted what's arguably the most familiar and most useful iPhone user interface. We implemented the methods provided by UITableViewDataSource (which we inherited from UITableViewController) to structure our table data as sections, rows, and cells. We tried out the basic table cell styles, and then moved on to a custom cell approach that allows us to populate, lay out, and style the cell contents in whatever way best suits the contents.

Now that our user interface is ready, we can go out to the network to get real Twitter data to populate the table. This will introduce a bunch of new challenges with how (and *when*) our code runs, but along the way we'll solve the problem with how the image loading slows down our scrolling.

CHAPTER 8

Managing Time with Closures

It's very tempting to think of our code as a series of instructions, to be executed in order. But this falls down when any of these steps takes a long time, or worse yet, an *unknown* amount of time.

Imagine that instead of programming an iPhone, we're 50 years in the future, programming a household robot to do ordinary household tasks. Let's say we want to write a program to answer the phone (OK, and imagine there are still phones 50 years from now). We might write something like this:

```
Pick up the phone.
Say "hello".
Wait for the other party to introduce themselves.
If they're a family member, let us know.
If they're a politician or an advertiser, hang up.
Otherwise, ask us what to do.
```

And so on. And this will be great, until we get a prank phone call that doesn't respond to our robot saying hello. The script will wait on step 3. If the robot is really literal-minded, it will get hung up there forever and won't attend to any of its other duties around the house.

We need the ability to express steps 4–6 as something to do once the waiting in step 3 is done. These tasks will be saved away for the future, to be performed when the other party finally responds (or maybe to be discarded when the call simply disconnects), while the robot can continue with other tasks in the meantime.

This is an example of *asynchronicity*, the occurrence of events in an unpredictable order or at unpredictable times. It's very important to us as developers, because it's a realistic model of how things happen in real life. We often don't know when things will happen or how long they will take. This is even true within the programming realm: we don't know when an event like a button tap or a rotation gesture will occur, or how long it will take to get data from the network or write a document to the filesystem.

It's very expressive to be able to say "when event *foo* occurs, do *bar*," or "do *foo*, and if and when that finishes successfully, do *bar*, but don't wait around for it."

A lot of the iOS APIs are written with an expectation of asynchronous behavior. In this chapter, we'll cover how to write "closures," blocks of code that function as completion handlers, meaning they do their thing only when some long-running or indeterminately long task completes. To use the Twitter web services, we'll have to use them in two different scenarios: asking users to let our app use their Twitter account, and making the network call to Twitter, because one makes us wait for a user response and the other makes us wait for the network.

Setting Up Twitter API Calls

When we first set up our tweet-sending button, we found the documentation for the Social framework and made use of the SLComposeViewController. To start using the rest of Twitter's features (or any other social network supported by iOS), we'll need to use another class in this framework. SLRequest lets us call the various social networks' web APIs by just providing a URL, whose contents vary by service and are documented at their various developer sites (such as http://dev.twitter.com). For Twitter, we have an additional detail to work through first: as of May 2013, all Twitter requests need to be *authenticated*, meaning they need to come from a signed-in Twitter user.

Fortunately, iOS allows a user to sign in to her Twitter account from the Settings app, and the iOS SDK will allow us to use that authentication. The key to this is that the SLRequest includes an account property that represents an authenticated user. All we need to do is to set that property before we send off our request.

To use a social-networking account, we have to ask the ACAccountStore for access to it, by means of a requestAccessToAccountsWithType() method. And that raises an interesting question: what happens if the user says no? In fact, let's consider the worst case: that the user switches out of our app, goes to the privacy settings, and changes the permission setting for our app's access to Twitter *while our app is running*. We're basically going to have to plan on asking for permission to use Twitter every time we need to make a request. And as it turns out, that has some interestingly asynchronous behavior.

The first time we call requestAccessToAc-
countsWithType(), the user will be presented with
an alert asking if she wants to grant our app
access to her Twitter accounts, as shown in
this figure. We have no idea whether the
answer will be Don't Allow or OK, and we
certainly don't want to hold up the whole app
waiting for an answer, so instead we'll make

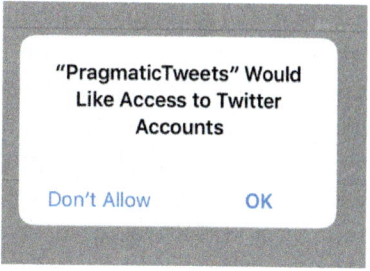

this call and move on with the rest of our app. If and when the user approves
our use of her Twitter account, then we'll go ahead and call Twitter's web
service. Actually, the user will only ever see the alert once—after that, she
can grant or deny access via the Settings app's Privacy settings—but our code
won't behave any differently; the decision about whether or not to run our
asynchronous code will just be made sooner.

Let's start by adding an import Accounts to the top of ViewController.swift, just like
we did when we added the Social framework.

asynchronicity/PragmaticTweets-8-1/PragmaticTweets/ViewController.swift
```
import Accounts
```

Then look at the requestAccessToAccountsWithType() method in the documentation
viewer. It takes an ACAccountType, which has constants for Twitter, Facebook,
and a few other services. The second argument is a dictionary of options
whose use depends on the service. The third parameter is of type ACAccountStor-
eRequestAccessCompletionHandler. That's new, so we click on its documentation
and see this:

```
typealias ACAccountStoreRequestAccessCompletionHandler =
  (Bool, NSError!) -> Void
```

What...the...heck?

Encapsulating Code in Closures

Way back in *Methods*, on page 41, we mentioned that functions use the syntax
-> to indicate the type of their return value. So, is that (Bool, NSError!) -> Void stuff
a function? Actually yes...kind of! What this syntax expresses is a *closure*, a
self-contained block of functionality. The syntax indicates what will be passed
in to this block of code (a Bool indicating if permission was granted, and an
NSError optional in case the request for access totally failed) and what will be
returned from it (Void, that is to say, there is no return value). So it's not that
this parameter is a function; it's a closure...and in Swift, all functions (and
thus all methods on objects) are just a special case of closures!

So what's so great about closures? Well, for one thing, it means we get to take some code *and treat it as if it were any other type,* meaning we can pass it to and from functions, store it as a property, and so on. In this case specifically, we get to write some code, give it to the ACAccountStore, and say "ask for permission to use the Twitter account, and run this code when done." That's precisely what we want to do here: we want to write a closure that makes a Twitter request if and when the user approves our use of her Twitter account.

Let's begin by rewriting reloadTweets to get the current Twitter account. We'll take it slowly and just concern ourselves for now with getting the Twitter account, not what to do with it yet.

```
asynchronicity/PragmaticTweets-8-1/PragmaticTweets/ViewController.swift
Line 1  func reloadTweets() {
   -      let accountStore = ACAccountStore()
   -      let twitterAccountType = accountStore.accountTypeWithAccountTypeIdentifier(
   -        ACAccountTypeIdentifierTwitter)
   5      accountStore.requestAccessToAccountsWithType(twitterAccountType,
   -        options: nil,
   -        completion: {
   -          (granted: Bool, error: NSError!) -> Void in
   -          guard granted else {
  10            NSLog ("account access not granted")
   -            return
   -          }
   -          NSLog ("account access granted")
   -      })
  15  }
```

On line 2, we create an ACAccountStore object, which we'll need for the next few steps. The requestAccessToAccountsWithType() method will require us to get the Twitter ACAccountType, which we do with a call to accountTypeWithAccountTypeIdentifier() on lines 3–4. Once we have that, we can ask for access to Twitter accounts, passing in the type (line 5), a set of options that can be nil for Twitter accounts (line 6), and a completion handler closure that will be called with the result of our request, which receives a Bool to indicate if we were granted access, and an NSError that will describe any error associated with a failed request.

Our preliminary closure ranges from the opening curly brace on line 7 down to line 14, where it ends with a telltale sequence of characters—})—which are the curly brace to end the closure, and the close parenthesis that ends the parameters to the requestAccessToAccountsWithType() call that began back on line 5. Line 8 is the signature that indicates what's being passed into the closure (the granted Boolean and an optional NSError), the return type (Void, meaning nothing), and the keyword in that begins the closure's logic. Inside this closure, our first decision to make is whether or not we can proceed; if the variable granted that's passed into the block is false, then we don't have access to Twitter accounts and should just give up. For now, on lines 9–11, we will just log a failure message and do an early return. Later on we should come back and add a proper alert so the user knows what has happened.

On the other hand, if granted is true, we will be able to start talking to the Twitter API, which means a lot more work! For now, we'll just log a success message (on line 13).

Using the Twitter Account

Now let's fill out the post-else case, replacing the simple success NSLog(). We're going to work with the accountStore that the user has graciously given us permission to use. Because it's a local variable in scope at the time of the closure's creation, we can use it within the completion handler closure.

On iOS, the user may have set up several accounts of a given type; a fancier app would show them and let the user pick one, but for now, we'll just make sure there's at least one. We can use the ACAccountStore's accountsWithAccountType() to get all configured accounts of type twitterAccountType. Code the following, directly before the }) that ends the closure.

```
asynchronicity/PragmaticTweets-8-1/PragmaticTweets/ViewController.swift
let twitterAccounts =
  accountStore.accountsWithAccountType(twitterAccountType)
guard twitterAccounts.count > 0 else {
  NSLog ("no twitter accounts configured")
  return
}
```

Once again, we're just using a guard and bailing out with an NSLog() message to the console if there are no Twitter accounts configured. We could come back later and give the user a helpful UIAlertController dialog in this case.

Continuing on the post-guard happy path, let's assume the array contains at least one Twitter account. What do we do with it? A while back—before we had to work through getting access to the account—we noted there is an SLRequest class that accesses the web service APIs of the social networks like Twitter. It doesn't have a lot of methods, and one that we should focus on is performRequestWithHandler:(), whose docs say it "performs an asynchronous request and calls the specified handler when done."

And look, it takes another closure! Well, actually it takes an SLRequestHandler, which if we click the link to its documentation, is defined as follows:

```
typealias SLRequestHandler = (NSData!, NSHTTPURLResponse!, NSError!) -> Void
```

So this is another closure, taking NSData, and NSHTTPURLResponse, and NSError as optional parameters and returning Void. We'll assume those parameters will give us everything we need to handle the response from the Twitter web service. But since we'll probably have a bunch of work to do for that, and this method is already getting pretty long, let's stub out a method to accept those parameters and deal with the response when it comes in. Somewhere outside all the existing methods' curly braces—right before the class's closing curly brace would be a great place for it—let's stub out the following method, empty but for a simple NSLog() that at least lets us know we got this far:

```
asynchronicity/PragmaticTweets-8-1/PragmaticTweets/ViewController.swift
private func handleTwitterData (data: NSData!,
  urlResponse: NSHTTPURLResponse!,
  error: NSError!) {
    guard let data = data else {
      NSLog ("handleTwitterData() received no data")
      return
    }
    NSLog ("handleTwitterData(), \(data.length) bytes")
}
```

Now we'll be able to have our performRequestWithHandler() closure just call this method, allowing us to put off for now just what's in the Twitter response and how we're going to deal with it.

Making a Twitter API Request

But what goes in our request? If we take a look at the Twitter REST API 1.1 at https://dev.twitter.com/docs/api/1.1, we'll find the call statuses/home_timeline, which is called via an HTTP GET, and which returns "a collection of the most recent Tweets and retweets posted by the authenticating user and the users they follow." Not shown on this page, but fundamental to Twitter API calls, is the fact that we can append .json to get JSON-formatted results, or .xml to get XML. Foundation's JSON parser is far easier to use than its XML parser, so our URL will be https://api.twitter.com/1.1/statuses/home_timeline.json. Since both Twitter and iOS 9 really want us to use SSL (in fact, it's a requirement for the Twitter API), our URLs will always start with https://.

So now we need to create an SLRequest. The docs show us a single convenience initializer, which takes a service type, request method, URL, and a dictionary of parameters. We already know how to fill in these four parameters:

- serviceType: The constant SLServiceTypeTwitter.

- requestMethod: The Twitter docs say we need an HTTP GET; for this, the Social framework provides the constant SLRequestMethodGET.

- url: We already figured this out as https://api.twitter.com/1.1/statuses/home_time-line.json.

- parameters: This is a dictionary of name-value pairs. The Twitter docs tell us we need to provide the screen_name or user_id parameters, so that's what will go in our dictionary.

Now we can go back into reloadTweets() and finish it up. To do so, we'll build up a call to performRequestWithHandler(), and have the handler block just call the handleTwitterData() method we stubbed out. Continuing from after we did the guard to make sure twitterAccounts has at least one member, this goes right before the }) that ends the existing closure.

asynchronicity/PragmaticTweets-8-1/PragmaticTweets/ViewController.swift
```
Line 1   let twitterParams = [
    -        "count" : "100"
    -    ]
    -    let twitterAPIURL = NSURL(string:
    5        "https://api.twitter.com/1.1/statuses/home_timeline.json")
    -    let request = SLRequest(forServiceType: SLServiceTypeTwitter,
    -        requestMethod: .GET,
    -        URL: twitterAPIURL,
    -        parameters: twitterParams)
   10   request.account = twitterAccounts.first as! ACAccount
    -    request.performRequestWithHandler( {
    -        (data: NSData!, urlResponse: NSHTTPURLResponse!,
    -        error: NSError!) -> Void in
    -        self.handleTwitterData(data, urlResponse: urlResponse, error: error)
   15   })
```

There's a lot going on here! Let's take it slowly.

- Lines 1–3 set up a dictionary of parameters to provide to the request. The available parameters depend on the web service's API. Twitter lets us send a count of how many tweets to return (the default is 20), so let's make things interesting and fetch 100.

- Lines 4–5 convert a String representation of the Twitter web service URL into an NSURL, the type needed by the SLRequest initializer.

- Lines 6–9 creates the SLRequest with the URL and parameters we've set up, along with the constant for the Twitter service type, and the SLRequestMethod enumeration value for GET requests.

- Line 10 gets the first object from the twitterAccounts array, and assigns it to the request's account property. Since the SLRequest wants an object of type ACAccount, and the array turns out to be of type AnyObject, we forcibly convert the value to the correct type with as! ACAccount.

- Lines 11–15 finally performs our request. It takes a closure as its parameter, which is executed once the request finishes. We saw before that this closure is of type SLRequestHandler, which means it receives an NSData, NSHTTPURLResponse, and NSError as parameters. Inside the closure, we just pass these parameters to the stub handleTwitterData() method we wrote earlier; we can build that out later.

  Notice that by writing a closure within the closure we were already inside of, when we're done, we will have two consecutive lines of }), the telltale end-of-closure syntax.

We've written a lot of code—and with closures two levels deep, this might be the hardest thing in the whole book so far—so let's run it to make sure it at least builds and starts up in the Simulator. Nothing interesting will happen in the Simulator, but the call from viewDidLoad() to reloadTweets() should produce a message like the following in the Debug area at the bottom of the Xcode window:

```
PragmaticTweets[6564:3175033] handleTwitterData(), 381073 bytes
```

This means the request is being sent to Twitter's web service and being responded to. Now it's up to us to act on that response.

Parsing the Twitter Response

Inside our handleTwitterData() method, we receive the raw data from the Twitter API and can use it to update our UI.

We'll start by handing the raw data over to Foundation's NSJSONSerialization, which can easily produce either an NSArray or NSDictionary of the parsed data, an object that may itself be a deep structure of nested arrays and/or dictionaries. Let's do a quick sanity check by following the NSLog() statement with this:

```
asynchronicity/PragmaticTweets-8-1/PragmaticTweets/ViewController.swift
Line 1  private func handleTwitterData (data: NSData!,
     -    urlResponse: NSHTTPURLResponse!,
     -    error: NSError!) {
     -      guard let data = data else {
     5        NSLog ("handleTwitterData() received no data")
     -        return
     -      }
     -      NSLog ("handleTwitterData(), \(data.length) bytes")
     -      do {
    10        let jsonObject = try NSJSONSerialization.JSONObjectWithData(data,
     -          options: NSJSONReadingOptions([]))
     -        NSLog ("JSON is:\n\(jsonObject)")
```

```
-      } catch let error as NSError {
-        NSLog ("JSON error: \(error)")
15      }
-    }
```

- Lines 1–3 are our method declaration. As explained a while back in *Maybe It's There, Maybe It Isn't: Optionals*, on page 31, the bang characters (!), indicate the parameters are implicitly unwrapped optionals: they're still optionals, but we can access their values directly without converting to a non-optional type if we're *sure* they can't be nil. When Apple's frameworks call back to us like this, they usually send implicitly unwrapped optionals.

- This is followed by the guard let that we wrote earlier, which bails out if data is nil. Otherwise, we have a non-optional NSData that we can parse in the lines below.

- The JSONObjectWithData()'s third parameter is listed as an NSErrorPointer. That's the old Objective-C way of handling errors, and we learned back in *Handling Errors the Swift 2.0 Way*, on page 54 that Swift 2.0 automatically converts this to a try-catch idiom. That means that we need to wrap this call (and any related statements that may throw errors) with a do (line 9). For simplicity, we'll just catch the error and log it (lines 13–15).

- We call the NSJSONSerialization method JSONObjectWithData() on line 10 to perform the JSON parsing of our data object. Since this is the method that can throw an error, we have to precede it with the try keyword.

  On line 11 we pass in our options for JSONObjectWithData(). The NSJSONReadingOptions type is a OptionSetType, which means it's a Swift wrapper around a C bit-field, a scheme where values are powers of 2, so they can be inspected with bitwise mathematical operators. That's great for C, but awkward in Swift, so in Swift 2.0, we get to treat them like Sets when we create them and inspect them, so to create an empty NSJSONReadingOptions, we pass in the empty set, [].

- For the time being, we're done: we've got an array or dictionary of parsed tweet data in parsedJSON. On line 12, we'll use NSLog() to print what we got to the Xcode console.

Run this, wait for the table view to come up, and check the console at the bottom of the Xcode window. The result will be a deeply nested structure, set off by tabs and curly-brace blocks, showing each tweet as a set of name-value pairs. The top of it will look something like this:

```
handleTwitterData(), 381073 bytes
JSON is:
(
        {
        contributors = "<null>;";
        coordinates = "<null>";
        "created_at" = "Sat Sep 05 20:06:41 +0000 2015";
        entities =            {
            hashtags =            (
            );
```

In the response, the first curly brace sets off all the data for one tweet, which has keys named contributors, "created_at", and so on. Notice that the value for entities is a curly brace, with its own child set of keys and values.

We can pick out interesting data like text, which is a string containing the tweet's text, and user, which is a dictionary of name-value pairs with items like screen_name and followers_count. Everything we could want to know about each tweet is in these entries, meaning we now have the data we need to populate the UI.

What We've Learned

Because of the complexity of closures and asynchronous code, let's take a break here and assess what we've done.

We want to get at the raw Twitter data, so we ask for access to the user's accounts and wait for that to happen (since they might be blocked on an Allow/Don't Allow alert). If we are allowed to use the Twitter account, we send off a request, wait for that to come back, and then use NSJSONSerialization to turn the received NSData into an array of dictionaries, one entry per tweet. Both of the waiting parts are done with closures, telling the iOS frameworks what work we want them to do once they're able.

We've written two closures, both using the "completion handler" pattern that is common in iOS. In the next chapter, we're going to use closures again, this time to update the user interface. But instead of waiting for things to finish, these closures will allow us to do multiple things at once, which opens the door to a lot of cool possibilities.

CHAPTER 9

Doing Two Things at Once with Closures

We started the last chapter with the example of a hypothetical household robot that would answer the phone for us. We dealt with the problem of prank callers that never respond to "Hello" by batching together all of our instructions for how to handle the greeting until after the caller responds. That leaves the robot free to do other tasks in the meantime. Now let's think about how that would work.

Some tasks will require the robot's limbs, some need its eyesight, and others its voice and hearing. If we're careful about how we divvy up tasks, the robot can do several things at once: we can prepare dinner while talking on the phone, and our robot should be able to as well.

So let's imagine we have lists of what each part of our robot's abilities can be working on: a list of manual tasks, a list of visual tasks, a list of spoken tasks. When it's time for the robot to continue dealing with the phone call, it can continue working on the manual tasks like cleaning or cooking, uninterrupted by the voice task of handling the call.

Our robot is a multitasking genius. And, if we're smart, our iPhone can be too.

In this chapter, you'll learn how Grand Central Dispatch offers the ability to break up work into distinct units—closures—and parcel that work out to whichever CPU core is most able to perform it at that point in time. You'll also see where the iOS frameworks force you to deal with concurrency, and successfully do so. With this skill in your toolbelt, you'll be able to keep your user interface fast and responsive as you get long-running tasks out of the way of the UI processing.

Grand Central Dispatch

Just like our hypothetical robot has lists of tasks to do with its hands, tasks to do with its voice, and so on, iOS has "lists" of tasks to be performed. They're called *queues*, and are part of a work-dispatching system called *Grand Central Dispatch*, or GCD. The idea of GCD is that there are multiple queues of work, each with tasks to execute. The tasks are C function calls, Objective-C blocks, or Swift closures. GCD can determine which tasks to execute based on the priority of the queue, whether the tasks are suitable for concurrent execution, how busy the CPU cores are, and other considerations.

Developers from other platforms will see an analogy to threading, and the queues are indeed performed by threads, but the difference in iOS is that the threads and their queues are managed by the system, which is in a unique position to best optimize the work. On other platforms, it's hard to reason about threads—if two threads are good, are four necessarily better? Maybe that's true on one CPU architecture, but not on another, and we can never know when we're coding. GCD takes responsibility for the problem and lets us off the hook: "Give me work to do," it says, "and I'll figure out how to best get it done."

GCD provides functions to create queues and to put work on them. The function we'll use the most is dispatch_async(), which takes a reference to a queue and a closure to execute on that queue. The async in the name means that the call doesn't wait for the closure to finish executing; the related dispatch_sync() will actually wait until the closure finishes. Mostly, we'll want to use dispatch_async() so our app doesn't wait and instead can move on to other work.

Concurrency and UIKit

In fact, GCD is already splitting our work onto multiple queues. All our user interface events run on the *main queue*, the queue that launches the app and is responsible for listening for user interface events. When we get a button tap, the call into our code is made on the main queue. When a table asks our code for the number or rows or the cell at a given index path, it's on the main queue. In fact, UIKit has a rule: calls to any method or property *must* be made on the main queue.

But when we perform certain other tasks, GCD will put that work on other queues. For example, since network calls are sometimes slow (and never predictable in how long they'll take), most of them are put onto other queues, which allows the UIKit queue to get back to work processing user events and redrawing the views.

Building a New Table Model

So let's think of where we stand right now. By the end of *Parsing the Twitter Response,* on page 148, we had used the NSJSONSerialization to convert the raw JSON (as an NSData) into a collection. If we inspect the output from the NSLog(), we see that the collection is an array, and each member of the array is a dictionary. Each dictionary contains the text of the tweet, a created_at time (as a string), and a user value that is its own dictionary to give us things like the user's name, screen_name, a profile_image_url_https for the avatar, and so on.

Back in Chapter 7, *Working with Tables,* on page 119, we built a ParsedTweet structure to hold some of these values and present them in our table view with the custom cells. So our job now is to pull values out of the array of tweets, put them into ParsedTweet objects, and use those objects to repopulate the parsedTweets array that serves as our table model.

First, since we'll finally be putting real values in the parsedTweets array, we can clear out the dummy values that we've used for the last few chapters. Replace its definition at the top of ViewController.swift with an empty array of ParsedTweets. Make sure this declaration is a var, because we *will* be modifying it.

concurrency/PragmaticTweets-9-1/PragmaticTweets/ViewController.swift
```
var parsedTweets: [ParsedTweet] = [ ]
```

Also, since we're done with fake data, we can stop appending a fake tweet in our pull-to-refresh method. So we'll cut down our handleRefresh() method (in the same source file) to just reload the tweets.

The code tag should not be here.
Let's go back to our handleTwitterData() method, specifically the if block that called NSJSONSerialization.JSONObjectWithData and then just did an NSLog() to dump the jsonObject to the debugging console. The first thing we'll do is delete that NSLog().

Next, we want to start walking the JSON array of tweets, but we can't know for sure that it's really an array, since NSJSONSerialization could have produced a dictionary, if that's what the root object in the encoding is. So we'll use an guard let to cast it to what we expect, and only enter the if block if it's safe.

```
Line 1  guard let jsonArray = jsonObject as? [[String : AnyObject]] else {
     2    NSLog ("handleTwitterData() didn't get an array")
     3    return
     4  }
```

It's not enough for something to be an array; Swift wants to know what's in the array. Put another way, it insists we say what it's an array *of.* We said earlier that the NSLog() output shows us it's an array of dictionaries...which to Swift just begs the question, "OK, buster, dictionaries of *what?*" We want to say it's a dictionary with strings for keys, but we really can't guarantee a consistent type for the values, since they can be strings, arrays, or dictionaries. So, our answer is, "The array contains dictionaries, which themselves have string keys and AnyObject values." This is what we're doing on line 1, but the syntax merits an explanation.

That's what the syntax [[String : AnyObject]] represents. The outer square braces mean array, whereas the inner square braces with a colon represent a dictionary, specifying its key and value types. We could also write this as Array<Dictionary<String, AnyObject>>, but we think the square-brace syntax is easier to write and read.

Converting JSON Values to Swift Properties

Assuming this cast works and we get past the guard block, the first thing we want to do is to remove everything currently in the parsedTweets array, by use of the removeAll() method provided for Swift arrays. Then we'll be ready to start walking the array and repopulating parsedTweets.

concurrency/PragmaticTweets-9-1/PragmaticTweets/ViewController.swift
```
parsedTweets.removeAll()
```

Now we're ready to walk the jsonArray. Our goal here is to pull out interesting values for each tweet and put them in a new ParsedTweet object, which we'll then add to parsedTweets, the model for our table.

concurrency/PragmaticTweets-9-1/PragmaticTweets/ViewController.swift
```
Line 1  for tweetDict in jsonArray {
    -       var parsedTweet = ParsedTweet()
    -       parsedTweet.tweetText = tweetDict["text"] as? String
    -       parsedTweet.createdAt = tweetDict["created_at"] as? String
    5       if let userDict = tweetDict["user"] as? [String : AnyObject] {
    -           parsedTweet.userName = userDict["name"] as? String
    -           if let avatarURLString = userDict["profile_image_url_https"] as? String {
    -               parsedTweet.userAvatarURL = NSURL(string:avatarURLString)
    -           }
   10       }
    -       parsedTweets.append(parsedTweet)
    -   }
```

Starting on line 1, we count over each tweetDict in the array, which we know is a dictionary because we only got into this if block by successfully casting as an array of dictionaries. The first thing we do in the loop, on line 2, is to create a new ParsedTweet. Instead of assigning its properties all at once with the designated initializer like we did before, we'll populate them one by one as we pull them out of the tweetDict.

Some of the values we want to put in our ParsedTweet are at the top level of the dictionary, so we assign tweetText and createdAt on lines 3 and 4, respectively. These values could be nil, but that's OK, since the ParsedTweet structure takes optionals for its various properties, so at worst we're just assigning them to nil.

There's a child dictionary with the key "user" that has user-specific details we want, like the name and avatar URL. Of course, we don't know for sure that asking the dictionary for this key will give us something other than nil, so we do an if let on line 4 to see if we can get that value as a dictionary with String keys and AnyObject values.

If we get userDict, then getting the username is as simple as the top-level properties (see line 6). For the avatar URL we want to be a little more careful: the NSURL(string:) initializer won't accept an optional, so we have to make sure there's a real string there. We can make sure with an if let on line 7, and then assign the userAvatarURL on line 8.

Finally, with all the fields of the ParsedTweet populated, we add it to the parsedTweets array on line 11. This allows our table model to pick it up when it needs a cell for that row.

Refreshing the Table Model

In fact, after the for loop, all that's left to do is to tell the table to refresh its contents. Write the following, after the curly brace that closes the for loop and before the catch line:

concurrency/PragmaticTweets-9-1/PragmaticTweets/ViewController.swift
```
tableView.reloadData()
```

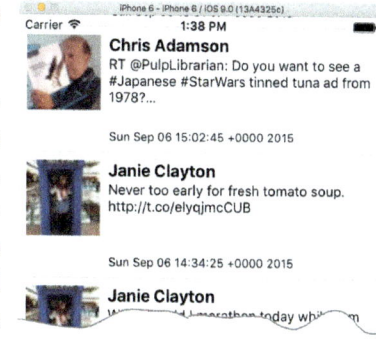

So now we should be good to go. Let's go ahead and run the app.

At first our empty table comes up in the Simulator; then we see in the Xcode window as the app reports how much data we got back. *And then it just sits there.* After about 10 seconds, the table finally updates with the tweets from our request, as seen in this figure. And there's a big problem: a bunch of errors are logged to the console that start with the following message:

PragmaticTweets[3804:330059] This application is modifying the autolayout engine from a background thread, which can lead to engine corruption and weird crashes. This will cause an exception in a future release.

Wait, what? At what point did anything we do here touch autolayout? This makes no sense. Something is up.

Putting Work on the Main Queue

Early in this chapter, we were talking about queues and how they're used to keep the multiple cores of an iOS device busy. Maybe that's part of the problem.

Unfortunately, Swift won't tell us which queue is running our code, so a definite answer will have to wait until we play with breakpoints in Chapter 16, *Fixing the App When It Breaks*, on page 275. But for now, there's an easy way to see how we've gotten ourselves in trouble. The main queue is run by the lower-level "main thread," and NSThread provides a class method isMainThread() to tell us if the current thread (and therefore queue) is main.

To try it out, plop the following line of code in any of the app's methods:

```
NSLog (NSThread.isMainThread() ? "On main thread" : "Not on main thread")
```

Inside reloadTweets(), this will print On main thread. But in handleTwitterData()—or the completion handler closure of performRequestWithHandler() that calls it—it will say Not on main thread. So, that's key to our problem. And the reason we're getting that autolayout error message is that adding new cells to the table is indeed performing layout operations, and we're not doing it on the main thread.

Actually, we're kind of lucky. The warning message says that this will become an exception in a future version of iOS, which the user will experience as a crash. But crashing or suffering 10-second delays while updating will get us angry one-star reviews either way, so we need to fix it.

Our basic problem is that any calls to UIKit classes and their method must be made on the main queue, and handleTwitterData() is being called on some other queue. We're only doing one thing that touches UIKit—reloading the table—but that's enough to get us in trouble. We need a way to move at least that one line of code back to the main thread.

A Handy Concurrency Recipe

To do this, we need two things: a way to represent a chunk of code as an object, and a method that will take that code and put it back on the main queue. We already have the first of these: closures, which we used in the previous chapter. The other piece is the Grand Central Dispatch function dispatch_async(), which allows us to put work on a queue of our choosing, such as the main queue. So we have a recipe we can always fall back on:

```
dispatch_async(dispatch_get_main_queue(),
  {() -> Void in
    // code to be performed on main thread
  })
```

dispatch_async() takes two parameters: a queue to perform the work on, and a closure with the work to be done. For the first, the point of this recipe is to use dispatch_get_main_queue(), so all we ever have to change is the contents of the closure.

In fact, our recipe gets easier. In Swift's tradition of omitting empty or unnecessary syntax, a closure that takes no arguments and returns Void (that is, nothing) doesn't even need the signature. So our recipe can be written even more simply as

```
dispatch_async(dispatch_get_main_queue(),
  {
    // code to be performed on main thread
  })
```

So let's apply our recipe. Replace tableView.reloadData() with the following:

concurrency/PragmaticTweets-9-1/PragmaticTweets/ViewController.swift
```
dispatch_async(dispatch_get_main_queue(), {
  self.tableView.reloadData()
})
```

Notice one important thing inside the closure: properties of the object, like tableView, aren't visible inside the closure, but self is, so we have to access our properties in the form self.tableView.

Run the app again, and the table should reload about a second after the app launches. This is *much* better. Our app does its network stuff on one queue so that it doesn't block the GUI; we can unpack our data on that other queue and only touch the main queue for an update when we're good and ready. It's concurrency in action, and when we're smart about it, our apps can stay nimble and responsive, which makes our users happy.

Joe asks:
Why Don't I Have to Label the Second Parameter to dispatch_async?

One of the signature traits of Swift is how the parameters of methods and functions are labeled, except for the first one. And, usually, the method or function name will indicate what the unlabeled first parameter is.

But this time, we didn't have to provide a parameter name for the second parameter either. Shouldn't it say closure: or task: or something like that?

What's going on here is that Swift parameters have "outside" names that callers see and "inside" names that are visible inside the function. Consider the definition of the JSONObjectWithData() method that parsed our JSON data:

```
class func JSONObjectWithData(data: NSData,
  options opt: NSJSONReadingOptions) throws -> AnyObject
```

The second parameter has both names: options is the outside name that we can see, and opt is what the code inside Apple's implementation would see. Notice the first parameter has only one name, data, so that is both its inside and outside name.

So what's the deal with dispatch_async()? Well, look at this definition:

```
func dispatch_async(queue: dispatch_queue_t, _ block: dispatch_block_t)
```

The outside name here is the underscore character, _, which in Swift means "ignore" or "omit." So in this case, it means "do not provide the name block."

Why does it work like this? We have a few guesses. Omitting the label makes this more like its C version that existing iOS developers already know. It would also be burdensome and messy to have to put the block: right before the curly-brace closure syntax.

There's also a related syntax that's even more concise. When the last argument to a method or function is a closure, you don't need a label, nor do you have to include it in the parentheses. Instead, just close the parens and put the curly-braced closure right after it, like this:

```
dispatch_async(dispatch_get_main_queue()) {
  self.tableView.reloadData()
}
```

We've left this syntax out of the book because we think it helps beginners to see that the closure is an argument to the method or function, but some of our colleagues really like the cleanness of this syntax.

Do-It-Yourself Concurrency

Actually, our app isn't as fast as we might like. Try scrolling the table. The scrolling is still choppy. This has been the case since way back in *Custom Table Cells*, on page 133, where we started fetching the avatar images from their URLs. So let's think about what's causing the problem and whether we can fix it.

When the table asks us for a cell—in tableView(cellForRowAtIndexPath:)—we can easily set all the labels with strings from the ParsedTweet, but what we have for the avatar image is an NSURL. So we stop and load the data for that URL, make a new UIImage from it, and assign that to our custom cell's UIImageView. This has to happen for each cell. Moreover, we can only work on one cell at a time. As a new cell comes into view, we have to wait to download the image data, and only when we have it can we continue on to the next cell. It makes swiping quickly through the table impossible.

So, we're blocking the UIKit queue on a slow network access. "Hey, wait a minute," you say, "isn't that exactly what concurrency is supposed to fix? And isn't it exactly why the Social framework does the Twitter API call on a different queue?" Exactly. And that means to fix our problem, we should do what Apple does: *get our network stuff off the main queue*.

They Don't Call It "Blocking" the Main Queue for Nothing

Lest anyone think the issue of keeping long-running tasks off the main queue is an academic problem...well, do we have a story for you.

Years ago, one of the authors of this book was working at a company with a product that worked with video. For a demo, we had to show that the application could copy this video to an analog video tape recorder (VTR). Our solution was to connect the output of the video card to the VTR, and to use an RS-232 cable to send "record" and "stop" commands to the VTR. It seemed easy: to copy the video, we start the VTR recording and play the video from the PC, and then stop the VTR when the video's done. Easy peasy.

Except that the guy who wrote this didn't know how threads work in Java, which is what the application was written in. And desktop Java works almost exactly like UIKit: there's a main thread with an endless loop that looks for events like keypresses and mouse clicks, sends them to any code that handles the event, and repaints the window.

So when the user clicked the Record button, the code to play the video and start recording on the VTR was called...on the main thread. And that code effectively said, "Wait here until the video is done," which meant that the window didn't update and no further events were processed until the video was done playing.

Some of these videos were 15 minutes long. The application couldn't do any repainting or event-handling during this time, so if you covered up the window and then foregrounded it, it wouldn't repaint. On Windows, dragging the mouse over the window would leave a trail of unerased mouse crud. Clicking a button did nothing. It was a disaster.

And this is pretty much where your author got to learn about threads, and had to completely rewrite this part of the program so that all of the video stuff happened on another thread, freeing up the main thread to immediately get back to work processing events and repainting, and then having the video thread put UI work back on the main thread only when ready.

And if you're still not convinced? Try plopping an NSThread.sleepUntilDate(NSDate(timeIntervalSinceNow:900.0)) as the first line of one of the button handlers. This will block the main queue for 900 seconds, or 15 minutes, during which time the button won't return to its untapped state, rotation events will be ignored, and the user will basically be blocked out of the app. *That's* what we're trying to avoid!

Moving Work Off the Main Queue

When tableView(cellForRowAtIndexPath:) needs an avatar, it does a slow NSURL load, makes an image from it, and sets it on the UIImageView. Only the last of these steps needs to be on the main queue, and the first shouldn't be. So we need a recipe to move work *off* the main queue.

dispatch_async() comes to our rescue again. Recall that it takes two parameters: the queue to put work on, and a closure with the tasks we want performed. What we need now is a different value for that first parameter, one that isn't the main queue, but just some other queue. For this, there's the GCD function dispatch_get_global_queue(), which takes a constant that indicates the priority of the system-provided queue we want. We're not picky, so we can use QOS_CLASS_DEFAULT to let GCD pick an ordinary background queue for us.

iOS gives us "quality of service" constants for GCD queue priorities. The priority names are meant to better express programmer intent than the low/medium/high priority system from earlier versions of iOS. Unfortunately, they're not currently searchable in the Xcode documentation viewer, and are only visible in a C header file. The following table shows the new constants, and their older equivalents, which we'd have to use for code running on iOS 7 or earlier.

iOS 8 QOS Constant	iOS 7 Equivalent
QOS_CLASS_USER_INITIATED	DISPATCH_QUEUE_PRIORITY_HIGH
QOS_CLASS_DEFAULT	DISPATCH_QUEUE_PRIORITY_DEFAULT
QOS_CLASS_UTILITY	DISPATCH_QUEUE_PRIORITY_LOW
QOS_CLASS_BACKGROUND	DISPATCH_QUEUE_PRIORITY_BACKGROUND

Anyway, now we have the pieces we need. In tableView(cellForRowAtIndexPath:), find the if let url = parsedTweet.userAvatarURL block that sets the image, and replace it with the following version:

concurrency/PragmaticTweets-9-2/PragmaticTweets/ViewController.swift

```
Line 1  dispatch_async(dispatch_get_global_queue(QOS_CLASS_DEFAULT, 0),
     2    {
     3      if let url = parsedTweet.userAvatarURL,
     4        imageData = NSData(contentsOfURL: url) {
     5          dispatch_async(dispatch_get_main_queue(), {
     6            cell.avatarImageView.image = UIImage(data: imageData)
     7          })
     8      }
     9    })
```

Lines 1–9 are one big dispatch_async() call. The difference here is that we want to get work *off* the main queue, so on line 1, we use the GCD function dispatch_get_global_queue() with the constant QOS_CLASS_DEFAULT to let GCD pick an ordinary background queue for us. That background queue gets the closure that runs from lines 2–9. This closure contains the "get a UIImage from an NSURL" logic from before, and then sets that image on the UIImageView. But since updating the image view has to happen on the main queue, we use a second dispatch_async() (lines 5–7) to wrap the UIKit work with a closure and put it back on the main queue.

And it's great! Now our table scrolls nice and fast, not blocking on the image loading at all!

There's just one more problem. Look at the figure. Every single one of the images is wrong: Chris's avatar is Janie, Janie's avatar is our publisher Andy, and then Chris appears again with the correct avatar.

Race Conditions

What's happened? A *race condition*, actually. When a cell goes offscreen and is queued for reuse, it will eventually get dequeued and filled with new data. *But the closure that fills in the image doesn't know that.* In this case, there was some cell for one of Janie's tweets that went off screen, dequeued, and repopulated with one of Chris's tweets (for the first row in the figure), but then the closure finished and filled in the image with Janie's picture. This doesn't happen often—we had to request 200 tweets, plus simulate poor network conditions to get the screenshot—but it *is* a bug, and if there's any way to make it happen in development, it's for sure going to hit someone in the real world.

The fix is to figure out when a closure has taken too long. How do we know that? Well, if the problem is that the cell has already filled in the contents from a different tweet, we can look to see if the parsedTweet that the closure started with has the same data that's displayed by the cell now. So here are the new contents for the if let url = parsedTweet.userAvatarURL block:

concurrency/PragmaticTweets-9-2/PragmaticTweets/ViewController.swift

```
Line 1  cell.avatarImageView.image = nil
   -    dispatch_async(dispatch_get_global_queue(QOS_CLASS_DEFAULT, 0),
   -      {
   -        if let url = parsedTweet.userAvatarURL,
   5          imageData = NSData(contentsOfURL: url)
   -          where cell.userNameLabel.text == parsedTweet.userName {
   -            dispatch_async(dispatch_get_main_queue(), {
   -              cell.avatarImageView.image = UIImage(data: imageData)
   -            })
  10        }
   -    })
```

We start by clearing out the possibly wrong image, on line 1. The big change is near the top of the first closure. In our if let that tries to get the imageData, a where clause (line 6) now looks to see if the text already set on the name label matches the userName of the ParsedTweet that the closure captured at the moment the closure was created. If it does, then this image belongs with this cell. If not, then the cell the closure was downloading an image for has already been reused and no longer matches, so the closure can just bail.

Now the race condition is fixed. If the image data comes in too late to use, we just don't use it. And we've once again been reminded of the promise and the hazards of working asynchronously. This figure shows our snappy and accurate app.

Janie Clayton
@invalidname Write Swift like Swift, not like Java!! ^_^

Mon Sep 07 13:18:02 +0000 2015

Chris Adamson
@RedQueenCoder Have noticed this at work. I use the completion-handler pattern a LOT.

Mon Sep 07 13:17:11 +0000 2015

Janie Clayton
@invalidname One thing that interests me about Swift is that the design patterns we used in Obj-C are not the best fit anymore.

Mon Sep 07 13:11:06 +0000 2015

Janie Clayton
@invalidname No way! @bradlarson and I have talked about how delegation doesn't necessarily make sense in Swift and can...

Mon Sep 07 13:10:21 +0000 2015

Joe asks:
Can I Slow Down the Simulator Long Enough to See the Cells Get the Wrong Image?

If your Internet connection is really good, you may load the image data too fast to see the wrong-cells bug. This shows off one disadvantage of working with the Simulator: its performance is unrealistically good, particularly for networking tasks. A Mac Pro with Gigabit Ethernet is going to get a web service response a lot more quickly than an iPhone with one bar of 3G coverage out in the woods somewhere.

Fortunately, a Mac can simulate lousy network conditions for this kind of testing. From the Xcode menu, select Open Developer Tool > More Developer Tools to be taken to Apple's Xcode downloads page. After asking for a developer ID and password, the page shows optional downloads for Xcode. Look for the latest version of the Hardware IO Tools For Xcode, download it, and double-click the Network Link Conditioner.prefPane to install it.

This adds a pane to the Mac's System Preferences called Network Link Conditioner, which adjusts the performance of the Mac's current networking device (Ethernet, AirPort, and so forth) to resemble real-world conditions an iOS device might face, from Wi-Fi with good connectivity to the outdated Edge network experiencing packet loss.

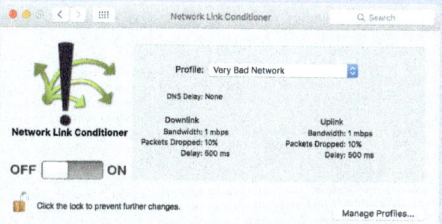

Keep in mind, however, that the Network Link Conditioner degrades *all* network traffic on the Mac, not just the iOS Simulator application. So if we forget to turn it off when we're done testing, it will make everything we do seem like we're getting one bar in the middle of nowhere.

So we have a recipe for getting work onto and off of the main thread: just call dispatch_async(), with the work to be done as a closure. For the queue, we use dispatch_get_main_queue() to put work on the main queue, or dispatch_get_global_queue() to get a system queue that can get our work off the main queue. Either way, we're exploiting concurrency, the ability of the system to do many things at once, and now we're smarter about how to let the main queue keep doing its event-dispatching and repainting thing, while we do ours.

What We've Learned

In this chapter, we furthered our command of how to determine not just "what" to run, but "when" and "how." We built on the last chapter's introduction of closures as an object wrapper for code, and used Grand Central Dispatch to put our closures onto the main thread when they need to access UIKit classes and methods, and get them off the main queue when they need to get out of its way. Between the many built-in APIs that are designed for asynchronicity and concurrency, and our own ability to make things concurrent with GCD, we've got great tools to keep our app snappy.

We've now got a pretty full screen with this table of tweets, but we still want to do a lot more with our app. The only way to do that is going to be to start having several screenfuls of information and navigate between them.

Part III

Evolving the App

CHAPTER 10

Managing the App's Growth

So far, our app interface has been restricted to a single view. We've swapped different functionality into and out of this view, but ultimately the small space of an iPhone screen limits what we can do in a single view. Most iOS apps use multiple views and switch between them with idioms like forward-backward navigation, modal alerts, iPad popovers, and so on.

Once we decide we want to start doing that, we're going to have more scenes in our storyboard, and more files in our project. Each time we want a new scene, we're generally going to have to create a new UIViewController subclass to provide its logic. And there are probably common tasks we'll want to do in many places, so we want to look for opportunities that can be spilt out into utility functions or classes.

In this chapter, we're going to reorganize the work we've done so far so it's more manageable as the app grows and so we can reuse some of the work we've done in multiple places.

Working with Multiple View Controllers

With our switch to a table view as the main interface for our Twitter app, we're starting to resemble and work like the many other Twitter apps on iOS. However, our functionality is limited: all we can do is load and display the tweets. In fact, we've actually *lost* the "Send Tweet" functionality, because the full-screen table view doesn't afford a good place for its button. So what are we going to do?

Usually, iOS tables *do something* when the user clicks on a table row. And most of the time, that something is to show the details of the thing that was clicked on, with a new interface appropriate to the detail view.

What's happening in that case is that iOS is presenting a different view controller, one that is designed specifically for the task at hand. So for our app, that means we want to go from the view controller that shows all the tweets to one that shows just the specifics of one tweet. From here, we could go to another view controller: for example, we could click on the tweeter's profile image to go to a view controller that shows details about him or her. Each view controller is built for one task—showing all the tweets, showing the details of one tweet, showing the details of the Twitter user—which allows us to divvy out functionality to different classes within our codebase.

To start adding new view controllers to our application, we'll want to make a few changes to our source code. We need the ability to arbitrarily grow our application by adding new classes and new storyboard scenes, and we need to start thinking about where we are going to put new code, and where we have opportunities for code reuse. All in all, it's a good time to tackle some much needed refactoring.

Refactoring in Xcode

Refactoring is the disciplined practice of making small changes to a codebase that alters its internal structure without changing its perceived behavior. Xcode offers a handful of refactoring tools; the rest we'll do by ourselves.

Where do we start? Well, we've sketched out our idea for using multiple view controllers, and once we've gone ahead and done that, the default name of our current ViewController is going to be a liability, since we might well ask, "*Which* view controller?" Let's rename it to clear up any future confusion.

Renaming

What should we call it? Looking at its functionality, we could call this something like TweetListViewController. However, in navigation-based apps, we typically refer to the first view controller as the *root view controller*, so let's use RootViewController as our new name.

We might be tempted to just change the name of the file in the Finder or Xcode's File Navigator, but this would cause all kinds of breakage, since other files in the project would still be looking for ViewController files. And finding all those references, particularly in the storyboard, is a tedious and error-prone process. Instead, we can ask Xcode to do the name change for us.

Switch to ViewController.swift, find the class ViewController : UITableViewController at the top of the file, and select the ViewController name. Bring up the Refactor menu, either from the Edit menu or from the pop-up menu (via a Control-click or right-click). The Refactor menu includes options to rename a selection, create a superclass, extract code into its own method, and a few others. What we want to do is to rename, so select Rename.

Oh no! An error message! Frustratingly, Xcode still isn't able to refactor Swift code, a year after Swift was released. We expect Apple to support this eventually, so keep in mind that the Refactor menu item is there, and maybe it'll actually work eventually. But for now, we'll have to do it by hand, just like we said we didn't want to. Ugh!

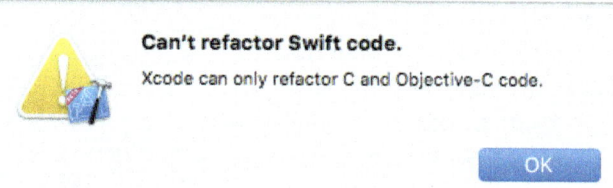

With the class name ViewController still selected, change the name in the class declaration to RootViewController. For consistency, we want the filename to match its contents, so in the File Navigator on the left (⌘1), select ViewController.swift, click again to edit the line, and change its name to RootViewController.swift

So far, that's two steps that a working Refactor menu item would have saved us, but there's one more. The storyboard still thinks that its one scene has a view controller of class ViewController. But that class no longer exists, so if we run now, our table is empty and the debug pane shows the error message Unknown class ViewController in Interface Builder file.

To fix this, go to the storyboard, select the View Controller in the scene list, and visit the Identity Inspector (⌥⌘3) in the utility pane on the right. The first section here is Custom Class, which we used before when we were telling the storyboard to use our custom table cell class. Now we want to reconnect it with our custom view controller class, so change the value of the Class field to RootViewController. Save, run, and the app works again.

The lack of a working Refactor menu item for Swift is a hassle, but at least we have a recipe: rename the class in its source file, rename the source file, and then use the Identity Inspector to rename any occurrences of it in the storyboard.

Organizing Xcode Projects with Groups

So we can rename our classes, and that's great. But if all we could do to keep our files straight was to use naming conventions, the contents of the File

Navigator would still become hard to read, once we have dozens or even hundreds of files.

One way to manage our code is to create groups. These are the folder icons in the File Navigator, several of which were created for us by the Xcode template when we started the project. We can move files into groups to organize them and strategically show and hide them, to make our project easier to manage. Note that these aren't real folders on the filesystem; they're just an organizational tool within Xcode.

A common convention in iOS development is to create a group for a view controller and any other code files used only by that view controller. For us, that would be the newly renamed RootViewController and the ParsedTweetCell. Let's do that. Click on the PragmaticTweets folder, to indicate that's the group we want as the parent of our new group, and select File > New > Group. This adds a group folder

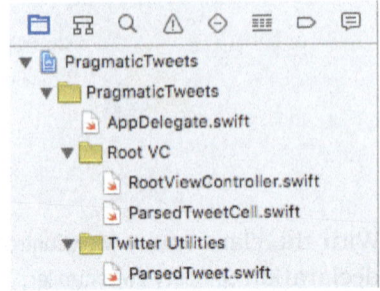

with the name New Group. Rename it to Root VC and then drag the RootView-Controller.swift and ParsedTweetCell.swift files into it. Then do the same thing to create a group called Twitter Utilities, and add ParsedTweet.swift to it. The folders in the File Navigator should now look like the figure.

There's also a quick way to create a group: select multiple files, and choose File > New > Group from Selection.

Our group's files are indented slightly and can be hidden entirely by turning the disclosure triangle on the side of the group. As we create new view controllers, we'll put them in their own groups, and we can expand just the groups we're interested in at a given time, so we don't see a bunch of files that we're not working on at the moment.

Making the Twitter Code More General Purpose

When we're ready to write these other view controllers to show tweet details and user information, we're going to need to make new calls to the Twitter API. And considering all the work we did to get our first call working—talking to the ACAccountStore and getting an account and using it to make a request and so on—we really don't want to repeat all that, right? But right now, that code is all in RootViewController. To make it more general purpose, we're going to need to *extract* it, and then generalize it.

To do this, let's think about how to make a more generic Twitter API caller. The current reloadTweets() method uses the ACAccountStore to construct an SLRequest, then calls its performRequestWithHandler(), which then calls back to our handleTwitterData() in the completion handler closure. The things that are specific to RootViewController are the URL and the parameters sent to the SLRequest (in this case, they specify the home_timeline.json call and its parameters), and the response handling, which is all in another method (handleTwitterData()). Put another way, everything in reloadTweets() other than the URL and the parameters is something we would do for *any* Twitter request, and is therefore reusable.

So what we can do to refactor is to move this code to a general-purpose version that can be called with any URL and parameters, and replace reloadTweets() with a one-line call to this new function, passing in the current URL and parameters. Everything we do in the response is already factored out into handleTwitterData(), so we don't need to change anything there.

The big difference is that the genericized Twitter request code should be in a reusable location so that classes other than RootViewController can call it. This class will go in the Twitter Utilities group, since it will work with the ParsedTweet class we've already created.

What should go here? Do we want a class? Well, no, because the Twitter request handler doesn't have to manage any mutable state; it just gets an account, makes a request, and runs arbitrary code when the data comes back. The classic iOS approach from the Objective-C days would be to create our own delegate: we could make a Twitter-calling class, and a protocol declaring a delegate method for it to call back to.

Swift lets us do things in a much more lightweight fashion. We don't need state, so we don't need a class, structure, or enumeration. Honestly, a simple function gives us everything we need: we can pass in the URL and parameters, plus a closure to execute if and when the Twitter JSON data comes back.

Creating a sendTwitterRequest() Function

With the Twitter Utilities group selected in the File Navigator, choose File > New > File to create a new file. Select the Swift File template, and name the file TwitterAPIRequestUtilities. This is where we're going to write our helper function.

We'll start at the top of TwitterAPIRequestUtilities.swift by importing the Social and Accounts frameworks, as we'll be using classes from both of them.

growing/PragmaticTweets-10-1/PragmaticTweets/TwitterAPIRequestUtilities.swift
```
import Social
import Accounts
```

Let's start declaring our generic Twitter-calling method:

growing/PragmaticTweets-10-1/PragmaticTweets/TwitterAPIRequestUtilities.swift

```
func sendTwitterRequest (requestURL: NSURL,
  params : [String : String],
  completion : SLRequestHandler) {
```

This method declaration takes three parameters: the Twitter URL and parameters for the request are what we need to create the SLRequest object that makes our Twitter call. The third parameter is the SLRequestHandler type that is sent to SLRequest's performRequestWithHandler() method. We haven't seen this type in a while, but we've been using it constantly: it's the method signature for a closure executed when the request comes back. Specifically, it's a closure that takes the argument types (NSData!, NSHTTPURLResponse!, NSError!) and returns Void. If that rings a bell, it might be because it's precisely the signature we pass through to our RootViewController's handleTwitterData() method.

Now we're ready to write the implementation. It's a lot of code, but it should look *very* familiar too:

growing/PragmaticTweets-10-1/PragmaticTweets/TwitterAPIRequestUtilities.swift

```
    let accountStore = ACAccountStore()
    let twitterAccountType =
    accountStore.accountTypeWithAccountTypeIdentifier(
      ACAccountTypeIdentifierTwitter)
    accountStore.requestAccessToAccountsWithType(twitterAccountType,
      options: nil,
      completion: {
        (granted: Bool, error: NSError!) -> Void in
        guard granted else {
          NSLog ("account access not granted")
          return
        }
        let twitterAccounts =
          accountStore.accountsWithAccountType(twitterAccountType)
        guard twitterAccounts.count > 0 else {
          NSLog ("no twitter accounts configured")
          return
        }
        let request = SLRequest(forServiceType: SLServiceTypeTwitter,
          requestMethod: .GET,
          URL: requestURL,
          parameters: params)
        request.account = twitterAccounts.first as! ACAccount
        request.performRequestWithHandler(completion)
    })
  }
```

That's a lot of code. We can write it fresh, or just copy and paste the contents from reloadTweets() in RootViewController, with the following changes:

- Remove the line that creates the twitterParams local variable.

- Remove the line that creates the twitterAPIURL local variable.

- In the SLRequest initializer, replace the twitterAPIURL and twitterParams local variables with the requestURL and params arguments.

- Simplify the call to performRequestWithHandler() by just passing through the completion closure that was passed to our function as a parameter.

Now we have a generic Twitter API request-maker that can be used by any and all view controllers that will want to make Twitter requests. To try it out, we'll finish our refactoring by having RootViewController use this class.

Back in RootViewController.swift, we can now rewrite a *much* simpler reloadTweets() to take just the arguments relevant to what this view controller needs, namely the user's home timeline:

```
growing/PragmaticTweets-10-1/PragmaticTweets/RootViewController.swift
func reloadTweets() {
  let twitterParams = ["count" : "100"]
  guard let twitterAPIURL = NSURL(string:
    "https://api.twitter.com/1.1/statuses/home_timeline.json") else {
      return
  }
  sendTwitterRequest(twitterAPIURL,
    params: twitterParams,
    completion: { (data, urlResponse, error) -> Void in
      self.handleTwitterData(data, urlResponse: urlResponse, error: error)
  })
}
```

We still set up our NSURL with a guard let, but after that, all the Twitter stuff has moved to our utility function. Plus, our splitting off the response-handling still pays off, as the completion closure is just a trivial call to handleTwitterData().

Run it and...nothing's changed! And that's exactly what we want! The point of refactoring is to change the code while maintaining the same behavior, and that's just what we've done—only now, it will be easier to grow the project, since much of the Twitter-specific code (and everything relating to the Accounts framework) is no longer in this view controller class, and what's left is directly related to the specifics of this view controller's Twitter request, and the specifics of the handling the response. The latter is still in handleTwitterData(), unchanged from where we started the chapter.

Now that we've completed this refactoring, any other view controllers we write that need to call the Twitter API can use code much like what's now in reload-Tweets() in that they'll just need to provide a URL and a parameters dictionary, and parse the response in the completion handler closure. The details will be specific to the Twitter API they're calling (tweet details, user info), but that's exactly what we'd want anyway: genericize the common Twitter behavior, and let callers specify their unique details.

Trying Out Our Function

To prove all this refactoring has been worth it, let's see how much easier it'll be to add Twitter calls to our existing classes or those we may yet create.

Just for kicks—and with the understanding we'll undo this silly code in a few minutes when we're done with it—take a look at AppDelegate.swift. This class has to do with how our app interacts with the rest of the system, something we'll talk about more later. For now, notice there is a method called application-WillEnterForeground(). This is called when the app is brought back to life from the background. Let's do a Twitter call every time this happens.

Let's use a simple Twitter API: users/suggestions. This sends us some suggested topics, based on who we follow. Thanks to our TwitterAPIRequest class, asking for this is really simple; just rewrite applicationWillEnterForeground() as follows:

```
growing/PragmaticTweets-10-1/PragmaticTweets/AppDelegate.swift
func applicationWillEnterForeground(application: UIApplication) {
  guard let url = NSURL (string:
    "https://api.twitter.com/1.1/users/suggestions.json") else {
      return
  }
  sendTwitterRequest(url,
    params: [ : ],
    completion: { (data, urlResponse, error) -> Void in
      do {
        let jsonObject = try NSJSONSerialization.JSONObjectWithData(data,
          options: NSJSONReadingOptions([]))
        NSLog ("suggestions JSON: \(jsonObject)")
      } catch let error as NSError {
        NSLog ("JSON error: \(error)")
      }
  })
}
```

Our call is pretty simple. If the URL is legit, then we make a call to our genericized sendTwitterRequest() that passes in the URL and an empty parameters dictionary. Our completion handler tries to parse the JSON and, if that doesn't throw an error, dumps it to the console.

Now, run the app. Our table appears as usual. Our new code only runs when the app returns to active duty from the background, so use the Simulator's Hardware > Home (⇧⌘H) to background the app, then bring it to the foreground by tapping its icon, or select it from the running apps list by double-tapping home (that is, ⇧⌘H twice, quickly). The request will go out and populate our debug pane:

```
PragmaticTweets[7147:692392] suggestions JSON: (
        { name = Sports;
          size = 15;
          slug = sports; },
        { name = Television;
          size = 11;
          slug = television; },  …
```

With about 10 lines of new code we fired off and handled a new Twitter API request. That's how we're going to build out the functionality of our application, creating new view controllers and letting them reuse this general-purpose Twitter function we've created for ourselves. Of course, this was a somewhat silly exercise—feel free to delete the changes in AppDelegate.swift—but it does prove out our general-purpose sendTwitterRequest() function pretty nicely.

What We've Learned

In this chapter, you learned techniques that are helpful as projects get bigger. We started by organizing our files into groups, which we can expand, put away, and nest within one another, so we can look at just the files we need at any one time.

Then we looked at Xcode's support for refactoring…which unfortunately still doesn't exist. Instead, we did our own refactoring to change class names. Then we took on a bigger project: taking the Twitter code in RootViewController and making it a general-purpose function that can be reused by other classes we'll be creating later. Since it didn't need to maintain state, we didn't have to create a helper class, and instead could split it into a function callable from anywhere in our app. Thanks to the completion handler pattern, callers can send this function an arbitrary closure to perform when the request comes back, which we exercised by having the AppDelegate call Twitter's suggested topics API.

Now that we've genericized our Twitter code, we're ready to move beyond the single view and give the user the ability to navigate between scenes, each able to take advantage of the work we've done so far.

CHAPTER 11

Moving Between View Controllers

Thanks to our refactoring work in the previous chapter, we're now ready to add lots of new view controllers and their corresponding views, each with its own ability to make, receive, and parse Twitter API requests. Thing is, where do they go? We can't just plop another view controller scene onto the storyboard, because the storyboard would have no way to get to it. What we need is a way to navigate between view controllers.

In this chapter, we're going to add view controllers that can show things like tweet and user details, and use three different ways of navigating between multiple view controllers. These are the common idioms we use for moving around in an app on the iPhone and iPad, and they let us choose whether to use the entire screen, split things on different parts of the screen, or even have it both ways, depending on how much screen space we have.

Navigation Controllers

The most common way to work with multiple view controllers is to use a *navigation controller*—a view controller that manages a stack of child view controllers. This UINavigationController will become the new point of entry to the storyboard. Our current RootViewController is the the first thing it shows. Then we'll add more view controllers, and the navigation controller will keep track of which one we're looking at and how to go back to earlier ones in the stack.

We won't have to write a new class for this, as the UINavigationController is meant to be used as is and is seldom subclassed.

Actually, we don't need to write code at all to use a navigation controller; we can do everything in the storyboard. In fact, the best thing about the storyboard is how it visualizes complex navigation schemes. Ours will be pretty simple, but it's nice to know we can grow.

Switch to the storyboard and then locate the Navigation Controller
icon in the Object library; it looks like a yellow circle with a blue
back arrow in it.

Drag this into the storyboard. During the drag, it will appear as two views
connected by an arrow. Drop it close to the existing view controller, but above
it. Once you've dropped the icon, the storyboard will have three scenes and
three view controllers with their attached views: our original root view controller, a navigation controller, and a table view controller, as shown in the
following figure. Note that we've zoomed out to get all three scenes on screen
at once, although all we can do at this zoom level is move scenes around, not
edit their views.

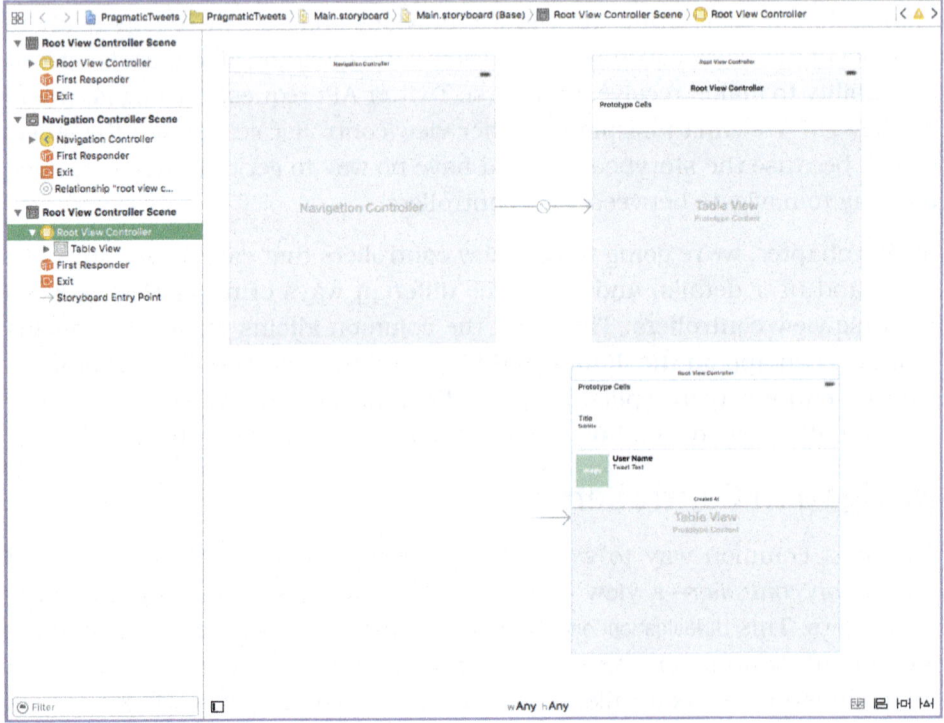

Run the app now and…nothing's different! That's because there's no way in
the storyboard to reach the navigation controller or its child view controller.
We can change that by selecting the navigation controller—either in the scene
list or from the yellow ball in the bar under its view—and bringing up its
Attributes Inspector (⌥⌘4). Find the Is Initial View Controller check box and
select it. In the storyboard graph, the arrow that went into our root view
controller now goes into the navigation controller.

Run again and...now our tweets are gone, replaced by a table with the title Root View Controller. What we're seeing is that the app now enters via the navigation controller, which in turn shows its first (root) child controller, which is the empty table view controller that Xcode gave us when we dragged in the navigation controller. But we don't want this controller: all our custom table cell work is back in our old view controller.

What we need to do is to tell the navigation controller to use our old view controller as its root view controller. Notice that in the scene list, the last entry in the Navigation Controller scene is Relationship "Root View Controller." That needs to change. Control-click on the navigation controller, or bring up its Connections Inspector (⌥⌘6). Under Triggered Segues, there's a connection called Root View Controller. Starting from the connection's circle, begin a drag (which will stretch out a blue line) and drop the connection on our old view controller, as shown in the following figure.

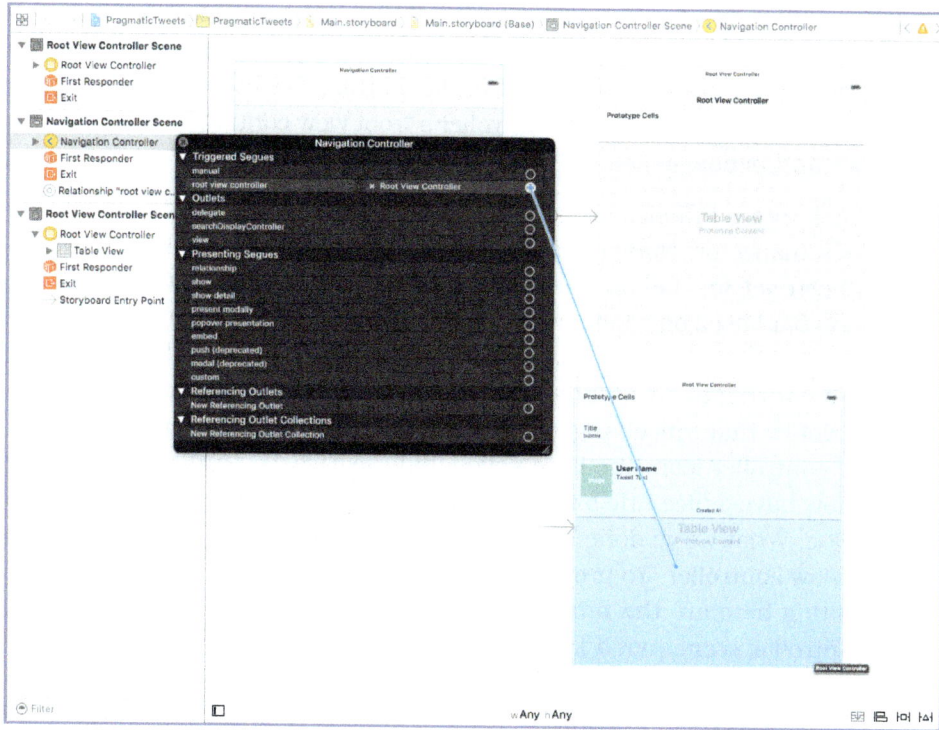

Run again and our app is pretty much back to normal, showing all our tweets as before. The only change is that there's now a big blank space at the top of the screen. Still, progress!

The Navigation Bar

The space at the top of the screen is the *navigation bar*, which appears atop any view controller managed by a UINavigationController. The navigation bar has room for three UI elements, from left to right:

1. A left-side *bar button item*. For anything but the root view controller, this is typically a Back button, and a default back button will be provided if we don't set a different bar button item of our own.

2. A title, either as a string or as a custom view.

3. A right-side bar button item.

We can easily customize all these things in the storyboard. First, as a bit of cleanup, we can get rid of that empty table controller that Xcode gave us, the one that was attached to the navigation controller. Select its view controller and press ⌫; the entire scene disappears. We can also grab the title bar atop our root view controller and move it around the storyboard to get it closer to the navigation controller; notice that as we do this, the arrow connecting the two (representing the navigation controller's "root view controller" relationship) stretches and bends as needed to keep the two connected.

Zoom back into a full-size view of the Root View Controller and bring up its Attributes Inspector. Notice that the top bar says Inferred. This is what it's always been set to; the storyboard figures out whether or not to show the navigation bar based on whether the view controller has a navigation controller as a parent, which it now does. Double-click in the center of the navigation bar and it'll turn into an editable text field. Type Tweets and press ↵ to finish editing. Notice that this changes the name of the scene to Tweets Scene, and the view controller icon (the little yellow ball) to Tweets. Run again and our tweets now have a nice title bar. Keep in mind that we haven't added a UILabel or UITextField. What we've done here is tell the navigation bar what title to use for this view controller. To prove this point, notice in the scene list that what we're editing here are the properties of a "navigation item" within the Root View Controller scene, not a label or any other sort of view.

The two bar button items in the navigation bar also give us an opportunity to add functionality to our app. In fact, they give us a very nice way to bring back our New Tweet feature! In the Object library, scroll down to the smaller Item icon; this is the bar button item, shown in the figure. The UIBarButton is very different from the UIButton we've used before; in fact, it's not even a subclass of UIView! It's an object that contains just enough state to be drawn in a bar and to be able to call a method when tapped.

Drag the bar button item to the right side of the top bar in the Root View Controller scene. A highlight to accept the drop will appear, and after the drop, the bar button item will appear as Item in the bar. We can edit its text in place, but there's a better option. Select the bar button item and bring up the Attributes Inspector. The second attribute listed is System Item, with a default value of Custom. Custom bar button items are those that have custom labels. However, there are about 20 other choices, representing common actions like Search, Refresh, and Trash. From this list, choose Add. This turns the bar button item into a plus (+) symbol, which is a reasonably intuitive way to tell users that this is how they'll compose a tweet, and more practical in limited space than text like Compose Tweet would be. The next figure shows our finished navigation bar.

Now that we've customized the button's appearance, we need to give it some functionality. Fortunately, our functionality already exists: it's the handleTweet-ButtonTapped() method we wrote way back in *Making Connections*, on page 75. So we just need to wire up a connection. Control-click the add button to bring up the heads-up display (HUD) showing its connections, and notice that instead of the UIButton's various events (Touch Up Inside, for example), there's just a Triggered Segues action and a Sent Actions selector. What we want now is to just call a selector, so drag from the "selector" line over to the Root View Controller icon (the yellow ball that now says Tweets). When we complete the drop, a pop-up will show us the selectors we can connect to.

Unfortunately, the one we want, handleTweetButtonTapped(), isn't in the list. The reason for this is in the code. handleTweetButtonTapped() currently takes a UIButton as an argument, and a bar button item isn't actually a button. So, in RootViewController.swift, edit that method definition to take AnyObject instead.

navigation/PragmaticTweets-11-1/PragmaticTweets/RootViewController.swift
```
@IBAction func handleTweetButtonTapped(sender: AnyObject) {
```

Now, back in the storyboard, select the "+" bar button item, Control-drag from the selector to the view controller icon, and after completing the drop, choose handleTweetButtonTapped(). Note that there's a faster way to do this: rather than bring up the pop-up, just Control-drag from the bar button item to the view controller, which figures out that you want to connect the selector, since the other kinds of connections don't make sense here.

At any rate, run the project again and tap the add button. The tweet compose view controller returns, although at this point the default "I just finished the first project" text seems totally out of date. We've gotten a *lot* further since then! With the addition of the navigation bar, our app much more closely resembles the other major Twitter apps on iOS.

Navigating Between View Controllers

Now that we have our root view controller managed by a navigation controller, we're ready to start navigating. Where shall we go? Since our root view shows a table of tweets, let's allow the user to select one of those tweets to inspect in detail. To do this, we'll add a new view controller scene to the storyboard, indicate how we navigate to it, and write a custom UIViewController subclass to provide the behavior for the new scene.

 We can begin in the storyboard. From the Object library, choose the generic View Controller icon, which looks like the rectangular UIView icon inside a yellow circle, as seen in the figure.

Drag the icon (which turns into a view with the usual title bar underneath) into the storyboard, dropping it to the right of the existing root view controller. Once dropped, it appears as a completely empty view, and when not selected, the title bar above the view simply says View Controller. This view controller has no visible contents and cannot be reached from any other view controller, but we can change that easily enough.

From the Root View Controller scene on the left, select CustomTweetCell, which is the one we customized with the styled labels and the icon. Control-drag from there to the new view controller (either its entry in the scene list or its icon, or its view out on the storyboard; any of these will work). This gesture indicates that you want to create a *segue* from the cell to the new view controller when the cell is tapped. Optionally, instead of Control-dragging, we can bring up the connections pop-up with a Control-click and drag the Triggered Segues: Selection connection over to the new view controller.

Whichever gesture we use, upon ending the drag, a pop-up menu asks us to clarify what we want the connection to do, as seen in the figure. For a selection segue, we have five main choices: Show, Show Detail, Present Modally, Popover Presentation, or Custom. Choose Show.

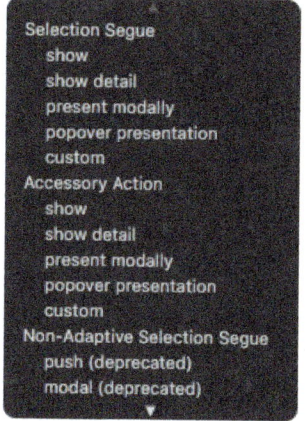

Once we do this, two interesting things happen to our new view controller. First, it gets a simulated navigation bar, just like when we connected the root view controller to the navigation controller. That's because Interface Builder knows this view controller is now managed by a navigation controller, so a navigation bar will be provided at runtime. However, we can't double-click in this one to set its title. The reason is that to customize the appearance of a non-root view controller, the scene needs to have a navigation item, which tells the navigation controller what's different about this scene, usually meaning a title and a right bar button item.

Drag a Navigation Item icon from the Object library to the new scene. You should now be able to double-click in the navigation bar and change its name to Tweet.

The other thing that changed when we dragged the segue between the two scenes is that there's now an arrow connecting the root view controller to our new view controller. In the middle of the arrow is a circular icon that represents the segue, which is the object managing the transition between the two view controllers. We'll have more to say about using segues a little later.

For now, let's run the app and see what we have. Once the tweets table gets populated, tap one of them. The tweets view will slide out to the left while the new view slides in from the right. Although it's empty, we can easily get our bearings thanks to the navigation bar, which shows our Tweet title. The navigation controller also provides a back button on the left, which by default uses the title of the previous view controller: Tweets. Not bad, getting navigation for free without having written any code for it!

Using the Storyboard Segue

When we tap a cell in the list of tweets, we navigate to the new view controller, which we'll customize to show the details for the selected tweet. But hold on —how do we know which tweet was selected? And how will we communicate that to the other view controller?

This is where the segue can help us. Prior to performing a transition between view controllers, the current view controller gets a callback on the method prepareForSegue(), passing in details of the transition in a UIStoryboardSegue object. As inherited from UIViewController, this method does nothing, but we can override it to take some interesting action, based both on our current state and details of the segue.

The UIStoryboardSegue object provides properties for the sourceViewController, destinationViewController, and an identifier, which is a string that we can use to distinguish between different segues in the storyboard. It's a good habit to name any segue we intend to use in code, so click on the segue's circle icon between the two view controllers and display the Attributes Inspector. The main attributes we can edit are the Identifier string and the segue kind (which is whatever we set in the HUD when we created the segue: Show, Show Detail, Present Modally, and so on). There is also a Segue Class and Segue Module, which would be used for running custom code to perform the segue. All we need at this point is to name the segue, so for the identifier, enter showTweet-DetailsSegue.

Now visit RootViewController.swift. Write a new method to override prepareForSegue():

```
navigation/PragmaticTweets-11-2/PragmaticTweets/RootViewController.swift
override func prepareForSegue(segue: UIStoryboardSegue,
  sender: AnyObject?) {
    if segue.identifier == "showTweetDetailsSegue" {
      if let row = tableView?.indexPathForSelectedRow?.row {
        let parsedTweet = parsedTweets[row]
        NSLog ("tapped on \(parsedTweet.tweetText)")
      }
    }
}
```

When called, this looks at the segue argument to see if it matches the identifier we put in the storyboard: showTweetDetailsSegue. If it does, it gets the selected row from the table, looks up the corresponding tweet, and logs its text to the console. Run the app and tap a row to verify this is working; if not, check the spelling of the segue identifier in the storyboard and the code to make sure they match *exactly*.

Sharing Data Between View Controllers

Now that we can get the selected tweet, we need a way to communicate between the view controllers. Actually, our tweet detail view controller may want more information than we have in the ParsedTweet, or things that the home_timeline API doesn't even provide, so we'll need a way to pass the tweet's unique identifier to the second view controller, and then let that view controller get whatever details it needs via a new Twitter API call.

So, add a tweetIdString to ParsedTweet.swift:

navigation/PragmaticTweets-11-2/PragmaticTweets/ParsedTweet.swift
```
var tweetIdString: String?
```

In the Twitter API response, the tweet's unique ID string is identified with the key id_str, so that's what we need to get from the response dictionary and set on the ParsedTweet. Put this assignment in RootViewController's handleTwitterData(), where we do the rest of our JSON unpacking. A good place for it is right before the line with the if let that creates the userDict.

navigation/PragmaticTweets-11-2/PragmaticTweets/RootViewController.swift
```
parsedTweet.tweetIdString = tweetDict["id_str"] as? String
```

Now we're ready to send the tweet ID to the second view controller, and let it get more detailed tweet information.

Sending Data to the Second View Controller

Next we need to put some code behind that second view controller, which we can do with a custom class. It's good practice to put each view controller class and any helper classes in their own group. So, in the File Navigator, create a new group called Tweet Detail VC. Then select this group and choose File > New > File to create a new Cocoa Touch Class file. Call it TweetDetailViewController, and make sure it's a subclass of UIViewController and the language is Swift.

This class will have one public property, a tweetIDString. When we set this property, we want the view controller to immediately take that ID and fetch the details of the tweet from Twitter. We can do that with the didSet keyword introduced way back in *Computed Properties*, on page 40. Let's stub it out like this:

navigation/PragmaticTweets-11-2/PragmaticTweets/TweetDetailViewController.swift
```
var tweetIdString: String? {
  didSet {
    reloadTweetDetails()
  }
}
```

This will cause the reloadTweetDetails() method to run anytime the tweetIdString is set. Of course, that method doesn't exist yet, so quickly stub out an empty implementation so we don't get build errors.

navigation/PragmaticTweets-11-2/PragmaticTweets/TweetDetailViewController.swift
```
func reloadTweetDetails() {
}
```

Sending Data via a Segue

The storyboard doesn't know that the second view controller is supposed to use this class. Fix that by selecting the second view controller, the tweet detail scene, in the storyboard and bringing up the Identity Inspector (⌥⌘3). Under Custom Class, change the class from UIViewController to TweetDetailViewController (it should autocomplete as you type).

Now the pieces are all in place to deliver the tweetIdString from the first view controller to the second when the transition happens. Go back to RootViewController.swift, and rewrite the prepareForSegue:sender:() method as follows:

navigation/PragmaticTweets-11-2/PragmaticTweets/RootViewController.swift
```
Line 1  override func prepareForSegue(segue: UIStoryboardSegue,
     -    sender: AnyObject?) {
     -      if segue.identifier == "showTweetDetailsSegue" {
     -        if let row = tableView?.indexPathForSelectedRow?.row,
     5          tweetDetailsVC = segue.destinationViewController
     -          as? TweetDetailViewController {
     -          let parsedTweet = parsedTweets[row]
     -          tweetDetailsVC.tweetIdString = parsedTweet.tweetIdString
     -        }
    10      }
     -  }
```

The big change here is lines 4–6. First, we check to see that there is a non-nil row selection (line 4), and then ask the segue for its destinationViewController (line 5), and attempt to cast it to a TweetDetailViewController (line 6). If this works, then we can assign the tweetDetailVC's tweetIdString on line 8, which will kick off the setter method we wrote before.

Designing the Second View Controller

Now let's give the second view controller some UI elements to fill in. Add the following UI elements and their constraints:

- A button at the upper left, with fixed width and height of 60 by 60, the top edge pinned 8 points from the top layout guide, and the leading edge pinned 0 points from the margin. Use the Attributes Inspector to change its type to Custom, which will allow us to change its image. Unfortunately, this will make it effectively invisible in the layout view, but it can still be selected, and it's still present in the scene list. Our reasons for making this a button will be revealed later in the chapter.

- A label called Real Name top-aligned to the button. We do this by selecting both the button and the label, bringing up the alignment constraints from the Align popover, and in the Add New Alignment Constraints section, choose Top Edges. Then use the pin constraints to pin the leading space 8 points from the button, and stretched all the way across so its trailing edge is 0 points from the margin. Change the font to "Title 1" rather than a specific font name and size combination; this kind of *dynamic type* text style allows the user to make onscreen text more readable by adjusting font sizes in the Settings app.

- A label called Screen Name just below the Real Name label, leading space 8 points from the button, with a top edge 8 points down from the label above it (a fixed distance to the superview will also work), and trailing space of 0 to the right margin. Use Title 3 for the font style.

- A label called Tweet Text, leading edge and trailing edges 0 points in from the side margins, 8 points down from the button, and set to 0 lines so it can grow as needed to accommodate the tweet text. Use text style Body.

- An image view, top edge 8 points down from the Tweet Text label, leading and trailing edges 0 points from the margins, bottom edge 20 points in. Use the Attributes Inspector to set its mode to Aspect Fit, which will scale the image to fill one or both dimensions, without cropping or stretching (but without necessarily filling the entire space).

When finished, the layout should look something like the screenshot on page 188 (we've selected the button for this figure so you can see it's there).

Switch to the Assistant Editor, and make sure that TweetDetailViewController.swift is visible in the right pane (use the jump bar to bring up the right file if necessary). Control-drag from each of these UI components in the view to create outlets in the class file, using the names userImageButton, userRealNameLabel, userScreenNameLabel, tweetTextLabel, and tweetImageView. The resulting outlets should look like this:

navigation/PragmaticTweets-11-2/PragmaticTweets/TweetDetailViewController.swift
```
@IBOutlet weak var userImageButton: UIButton!
@IBOutlet weak var userRealNameLabel: UILabel!
@IBOutlet weak var userScreenNameLabel: UILabel!
@IBOutlet weak var tweetTextLabel: UILabel!
@IBOutlet weak var tweetImageView: UIImageView!
```

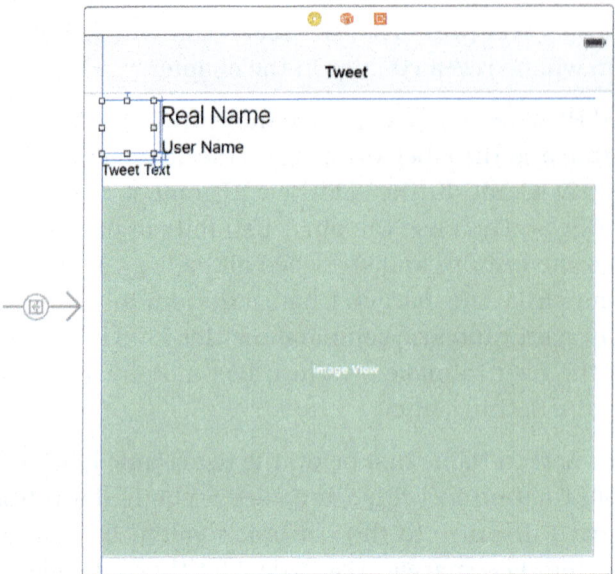

Coding the Second View Controller

Now we need to add the code to make our second view controller get to work. We can wait until our view controller's viewWillAppear() method is called so that if the tweetIdString has been set, it can immediately update the UI.

navigation/PragmaticTweets-11-2/PragmaticTweets/TweetDetailViewController.swift
```
override func viewWillAppear(animated: Bool) {
  super.viewWillAppear(animated)
  reloadTweetDetails()
}
```

Notice that since we're overriding the viewWillAppear() method inherited from UIViewController, we have to put an explicit override in the method declaration, and call the superclass's implementation as part of our own.

Now we're ready to use the Twitter code we refactored in the previous chapter. We're going to call sendTwitterRequest() to ask for the details, and then parse the response.

The Twitter API provides the statuses/show.json call to get details about a single tweet, and takes a single parameter, id, with the unique ID of the tweet, so that's what we'll call in our reloadTweetDetails().

navigation/PragmaticTweets-11-2/PragmaticTweets/TweetDetailViewController.swift
```
func reloadTweetDetails() {
  guard let tweetIdString = tweetIdString else {
```

```
      return
  }
  if let twitterAPIURL = NSURL (string:
    "https://api.twitter.com/1.1/statuses/show.json") {
  let twitterParams = ["id" : tweetIdString]
      sendTwitterRequest(twitterAPIURL,
        params: twitterParams,
        completion: { (data, urlResponse, error) -> Void in
          dispatch_async(dispatch_get_main_queue(), {
            self.handleTwitterData(data, urlResponse: urlResponse,
              error: error)
          })
        })
    })
  }
}
```

This is similar to the code we refactored in RootViewController's reloadTweets() in the last chapter: we create a TwitterAPIRequest, set its URL and parameters, and fire off the request. We also have to provide a closure telling our reloadTweetDetails() what to do with the response. As before, we'll call a yet-to-be-written handleTwitterData() method, and wrap it in a dispatch_async() to do its work on the main queue.

A trivial implementation of handleTwitterData() could just convert the data parameter into an NSJSONSerialization object, and log it out to see what Twitter sends back to us. To save you that step, the response provides the tweet text, along with a user dictionary that contains a name, screen_name, and much, *much* more. Let's pull out the easy stuff first.

navigation/PragmaticTweets-11-2/PragmaticTweets/TweetDetailViewController.swift
```
func handleTwitterData (data: NSData!,
  urlResponse: NSHTTPURLResponse!,
  error: NSError!) {
    guard let data = data else {
      NSLog ("handleTwitterData() received no data")
      return
    }
    NSLog ("handleTwitterData(), \(data.length) bytes")
    do {
      let jsonObject = try NSJSONSerialization.JSONObjectWithData(data,
        options: NSJSONReadingOptions([]))
      guard let tweetDict = jsonObject as? [String : AnyObject] else {
        NSLog ("handleTwitterData() didn't get a dictionary")
        return
      }
      NSLog ("tweetDict: \(tweetDict)")
        self.tweetTextLabel.text = tweetDict["text"] as? String
        if let userDict = tweetDict ["user"] as? [String : AnyObject] {
          self.userRealNameLabel.text = (userDict["name"] as! String)
```

```
            self.userScreenNameLabel.text =
              (userDict["screen_name"] as! String)
            self.userImageButton.setTitle(nil, forState: .Normal)
            if let userImageURL =
              NSURL (string: userDict["profile_image_url_https"] as! String),
              userImageData = NSData (contentsOfURL: userImageURL) {
                self.userImageButton.setImage(UIImage(data:userImageData),
                  forState: .Normal)
            }
          }
      } catch let error as NSError {
        NSLog ("JSON error: \(error)")
      }
  }
```

The handling of the jsonResponse is identical to what we did in the RootViewController; the only difference is which values we pull out of the tweetDict and then use to update our user interface. It's also different in that we are using a button for the user's icon, something we'll take advantage of in a bit.

Once the response is received, the various labels and the image button are all updated, including the tweet text, which, thanks to autolayout, can grow or shrink to as many lines are needed to contain all the text. Try it now and verify that everything's OK. We can also see the effect of using the dynamic type font styles by opening the Settings app, choosing General > Accessibility > Larger Text, and adjusting the text size slider.

Adding an Image to the Detail View

So far, we aren't making much use of the extra space in our second view controller, and not showing much more information than could fit in a carefully designed table cell. Let's fill in the image view that we added in the storyboard.

If the selected tweet has an image that was uploaded with Twitter's own image-hosting service (not a third-party service like TwitPic or img.ly), the tweetDict will contain an entities dictionary with extra attachments. Within this, there may be a media array, each describing one attachment as a dictionary. Assuming this is the case, we can take the first element of this array, which will be a dictionary, and look for a media_url_https (there's also a media_url, but for best practices, we should use the more secure URL).

We can dig into the tweetDict for any image attachments as part of the closure we just wrote. Just after the part that set the button image, and still inside the closing curly brace of the if let userDict block, add the following logic:

```
navigation/PragmaticTweets-11-2/PragmaticTweets/TweetDetailViewController.swift
if let entities = tweetDict["entities"] as? [String : AnyObject],
  media = entities["media"] as? [[String : AnyObject]],
  mediaString = media[0]["media_url_https"] as? String,
  mediaURL = NSURL (string: mediaString),
  mediaData = NSData (contentsOfURL: mediaURL) {
    tweetImageView.image = UIImage(data: mediaData)
}
```

Wow! That's a busy if let. It's doing *five* things in a row, drilling down the tree structure for keys entities, media, and media_url_https; trying to create an NSURL from that; and then trying to create an NSData from the contents of that URL. If all the keys are found and the URL and data objects are non-nil, we get to the inside of the curly braces, where we create a new UIImage from the data and assign it to the UIImageView. In Swift 1.0, these were five separate if lets, and a textbook example of the "pyramid of doom" that Swift's language changes have cleaned up.

But now that we can dig for a media_url_https if there is one, try selecting a tweet that you know has an image attached to it, and you should see it in the detail view, as shwon in the screenshot.

So, now we have a more interesting Twitter app, one that lets us pick a tweet and show it in detail, including whatever information we'd care to pull out of the response, such as presenting location information on a map. More importantly, we have a way forward for expanding the capabilities of the app: as we need new features or new ways to enter or present data, we can navigate to new view controllers, building them out in our storyboard and custom classes.

Modal Navigation

We'll close out the chapter with a different approach for presenting view controllers, and how it ties into one of the neatest things about navigating through storyboards.

In the tweet detail controller, we used a button rather than an image view to present the user's icon, and this is where we're going to use that: we'll allow the user to tap the icon to go to a third view controller, one that presents details about the user.

Modal Segues

Add another view controller to the storyboard, to the right of the tweet detail view controller (again, it may be necessary to zoom out to organize the views nicely). Scroll so that both the tweet detail view controller and the new view controller are visible at the same time, and Control-drag from the user image button to the new view controller; this can also be done by Control-dragging through these entries in the scene tree on the left. When we end the drag and release, Interface Builder infers that we want to make a segue to the new view controller, triggered by a tap on the button, and shows a pop-up asking what kind of segue to create. This time, choose Present Modally.

The storyboard will add an arrow connecting the second and third view controllers, with a circle-shaped segue icon in the middle.

Notice that this icon is different from the icon for the push segue we used earlier. And there's another thing to notice: *the new view controller doesn't show a navigation bar*. That's because modal navigation is different. Showing another view controller modally doesn't require a navigation controller like a "show" presentation does, so we're always free to create this kind of transition in a storyboard. This is handy because we often need to do something modally, meaning we need to stop users to either show them something or get some input from them before we continue.

On the other hand, no navigation bar means no back button, and we'll have to deal with that eventually.

While we're thinking about the segue, click its icon and bring up the Attributes Inspector, so we can give it an identifier string: showUserDetailSegue.

Stack Views and the User Detail View Controller

For now, let's build some utility into this third view controller. Since we've had a lot to do in this chapter, let's try out a new tool that will make our layout easier.

For this view, we'll just have an image of the user, and then several labels on successive lines: their real name, screen name, location, and so on. We could lay these out with autolayout, carefully setting their spacing relative to each other and to the side margins. But for such simple layouts, iOS 9 provides a simple option: the *stack view*. The stack view is a container view that holds other views. It lays out its subviews either vertically or horizontally, and manages the spacing between them. Basically, all we need to do is decide whether the subviews should be left-, center-, or right-aligned, and then just add them to the stack view, one by one.

Start by finding the vertical stack view icon (shown in the figure) and adding it to the new scene. This will be the only direct child of the view, and thus it needs some layout constraints. Use the pin popover to give it a top constraint of 0 to the superview, and leading and trailing constraints of 0 to the margins. Don't choose Update Frames to force a layout just yet, because with no contents the stack view will assume it has a height of zero. Even if you do, it's not that bad, since we can still add children by dragging them to the scene list.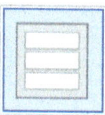

Select the stack view and bring up the Attributes Inspector (⌥⌘4). Set the alignment to Center so that any subviews we drop into the stack view are centered within it.

Now drag and drop the following subviews into the stack view, customizing as you go:

- An image view with width and height pinned to 100
- A label called User Name, with text style Title 1
- A label called Screen Name, with text style Title 2
- A label called Location, with text style Title 2
- A label called Description, set to 0 lines so it can wrap as needed, with text style Title 3
- A button titled Done

It's nice not having to fiddle with lots of constraints for every view, right? When finished, the layout should look like the following figure.

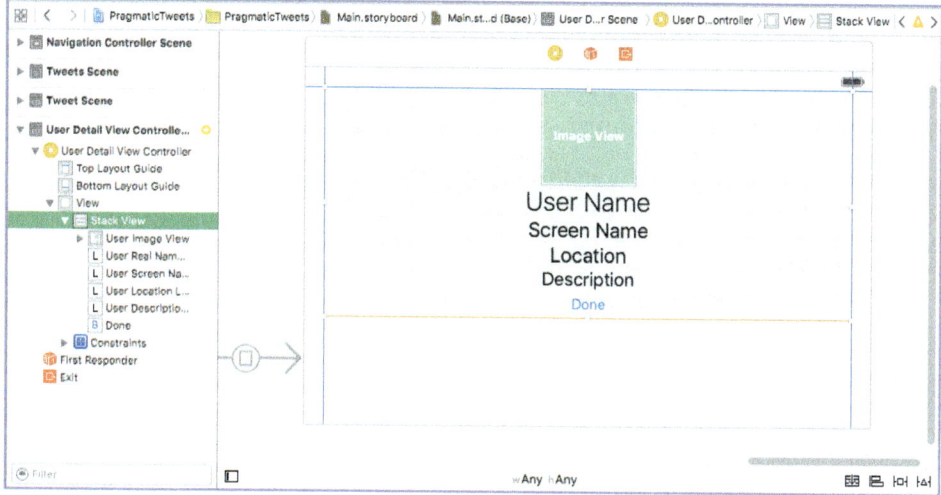

Now we want to tie this into code, so we'll need a custom view controller, like we did before with the tweet details scene. In the File Navigator, create a group called User Detail VC. Within that group, create a new file, using the iOS Cocoa Touch Class template, calling it UserDetailViewController and making it a subclass of UIViewController, written in Swift.

Back in the storyboard, select the view controller icon for this scene (from the scene list on the left or the scene's top title bar), and use the Identity Inspector (⌥⌘3) to set the class to UserDetailViewController. That will allow us to bring up the Assistant Editor (making sure that UserDetailViewController.swift is in the right pane) to Control-drag outlets for the image view and all the labels. When done, the properties should look like this:

navigation/PragmaticTweets-11-3/PragmaticTweets/UserDetailViewController.swift
```
@IBOutlet weak var userImageView: UIImageView!
@IBOutlet weak var userRealNameLabel: UILabel!
@IBOutlet weak var userScreenNameLabel: UILabel!
@IBOutlet weak var userLocationLabel: UILabel!
@IBOutlet weak var userDescriptionLabel: UILabel!
```

Coding the User Detail View Controller

Our code for this third view controller is going to be a lot like the second: we'll expose a public property, and let it use that to refresh itself from the Twitter API every time it needs data. Twitter lets us get the user details from just a screen name, so let's make that a public property in our new UserDetailViewController.swift file:

navigation/PragmaticTweets-11-3/PragmaticTweets/UserDetailViewController.swift
```
var screenName: String?
```

Since we want to update the view whenever it appears, we'll make our Twitter call in viewWillAppear(). To get the user details, we'll use Twitter's users/show.json request, which takes just a screen_name parameter. As before, we'll fire off a sendTwitterRequest() to make our request:

navigation/PragmaticTweets-11-3/PragmaticTweets/UserDetailViewController.swift
```
override func viewWillAppear(animated: Bool) {
  super.viewWillAppear(animated)
  guard let screenName = screenName else {
    return
  }
  let twitterParams = ["screen_name" : screenName]
  if let twitterAPIURL = NSURL (string:
    "https://api.twitter.com/1.1/users/show.json") {
      sendTwitterRequest(twitterAPIURL,
        params: twitterParams,
        completion: { (data, urlResponse, error) -> Void in
```

```
            dispatch_async(dispatch_get_main_queue(), {
              self.handleTwitterData(data, urlResponse: urlResponse,
                error: error)
            })
          })
  }
}
```

This is just like the other calls we've made to sendTwitterRequest(), except for having a different URL and parameters. As before, we'll parse the result in a new handleTwitterData() method.

navigation/PragmaticTweets-11-3/PragmaticTweets/UserDetailViewController.swift
```
func handleTwitterData (data: NSData!,
  urlResponse: NSHTTPURLResponse!,
  error: NSError!) {
    guard let data = data else {
      NSLog ("handleTwitterData() received no data")
      return
    }
    NSLog ("handleTwitterData(), \(data.length) bytes")
    do {
      let jsonObject = try NSJSONSerialization.JSONObjectWithData(data,
        options: NSJSONReadingOptions([]))
      guard let tweetDict = jsonObject as? [String : AnyObject] else {
        NSLog ("handleTwitterData() didn't get a dictionary")
        return
      }
      userRealNameLabel.text = (tweetDict["name"] as! String)
      userScreenNameLabel.text = (tweetDict["screen_name"] as! String)
      userLocationLabel.text = (tweetDict["location"] as! String)
      userDescriptionLabel.text = (tweetDict["description"] as! String)
      if let userImageURL = NSURL (string:
        (tweetDict["profile_image_url_https"] as! String)),
        userImageData = NSData(contentsOfURL: userImageURL) {
          self.userImageView.image = UIImage(data: userImageData)
      }
    } catch let error as NSError {
      NSLog ("JSON error: \(error)")
    }
}
```

This is our third time unpacking a Twitter response, so it should be looking pretty familiar: use NSJSONSerialization to convert the data to a [String : AnyObject] dictionary, and then use known keys in the response to pull out interesting values and set them in the UI.

The last thing we need to do is to set the screenName property. That's something the second view controller (tweet detail) will do as it begins the segue to the third (user detail). Switch to TweetDetailViewController.swift and add an implementation of prepareForSegue().

navigation/PragmaticTweets-11-3/PragmaticTweets/TweetDetailViewController.swift

```
override func prepareForSegue(segue: UIStoryboardSegue, sender: AnyObject?) {
  if let userDetailVC = segue.destinationViewController
    as? UserDetailViewController
    where segue.identifier == "showUserDetailSegue" {
      userDetailVC.screenName = userScreenNameLabel.text
  }
}
```

Run this version of the app, choose a tweet to view in detail, and then click the user icon. This will perform a modal transition to the user detail view controller, showing the user in all his or her glory.

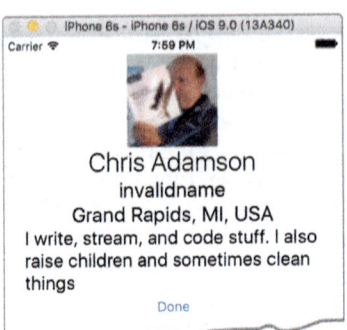

This looks great, but there's just one little problem: *we're trapped*. There's no back button, and the Done button does nothing. Now what do we do?

Exit Segues

There are a few ways we could implement the back button, but the most generally useful is the *exit segue*. With an exit segue, we can go backward in a navigation, regardless of whether we came by way of push or modal segues.

What's tricky about exit segues is that they don't appear on the storyboard the same way push or modal segues do. Instead, their existence is implicit. We can only perform an exit segue if a previous view controller has exposed a method for us to come back to. These methods, commonly called *unwind methods*, have to follow a certain signature—they take a UIStoryboardSegue parameter and have return type IBAction—but they don't have to have any code—they just have to exist.

We want our user detail view controller to unwind to the tweet detail view controller, so write the following method in TweetDetailViewController.swift:

navigation/PragmaticTweets-11-4/PragmaticTweets/TweetDetailViewController.swift

```
@IBAction func unwindToTweetDetailVC (segue: UIStoryboardSegue) {
}
```

An unwind method needs to have the @IBAction annotation (so we can make connections to it in the storyboard), needs to take a UIStoryboardSegue as a parameter, and should return nothing. This particular unwindToTweetDetailVC()

implementation does nothing, but if we did need to collect data from the other view controller, this would be a great place to do so. In a sense, the unwind method is a counterpart to the prepareForSegue() method, in that the prepare method can send data to a view controller that we're transitioning to, and the unwind method can get data from it when it's done.

In the storyboard, click on the user detail view controller's Done button and Control-drag up to the orange box on the right of the title bar above the view, which shows the tooltip Exit as we hover over it, as shown in the figure. When we complete the drop, a popover appears showing all the unwind methods we can connect to.

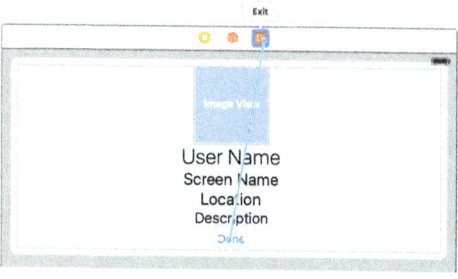

Now run the app, drill down to the user details, and tap Done. The modal transition unwinds and we're back at the tweet details view controller. All this with no code...well, no code that does anything, anyway. We could put an NSLog() in the unwindToTweetDetailViewController() method to see that it's being called.

Perhaps more interestingly, we can unwind to *any* earlier view controller. For example, if we go to RootViewController, write an unwindToRootViewController() there, and connect to an exit segue that uses that method instead, our Done button would take us all the way back to the root view controller, skipping over the tweet detail view controller entirely. This can be immensely helpful in complex storyboards where our navigation controllers get four or five view controllers deep, and we find the user may want a nice "start over" or "go home" button; exit segues make this really easy.

Programmatic Segues

It's possible to perform segues programmatically, which can be useful if we have a long-running action that should perform a segue when it's completed, like a login screen dismissing itself when a remote server sends us a response that the password has been accepted.

To programmatically go forward, a view controller can call the performSegueWith-Identifier() method. The identifier parameter it takes is the same string we've been using in prepareForSegue(), reminding us why we always want to put identifier strings on segues in the storyboard.

Programmatically performing exit segues is a little trickier, since they don't initially appear in the storyboard in a way that we can give them identifiers. But we can force the issue by Control-dragging from the view controller icon to the exit segue icon, as shown here. This adds an Unwind Segue From entry to the view controller's children scene list, which we can then select and edit its attributes to give it an identifier. And then we can call performSegueWithIdentifier() to perform the unwind programmatically.

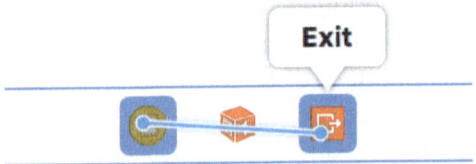

What We've Learned

This has been a very long chapter, in which we've radically reworked our app into one that is far more capable and extensible than when we started. We've gone from being tied to one screen to having as many as we care to create.

To do this, we reworked the storyboard from a single-view design to a navigation metaphor, putting a navigation controller at the beginning of the storyboard and letting it manage the user's progress through our root view controller and a new tweet detail view controller, giving us forward/back navigation pretty much for free. We saw how to use storyboard segues to deliver information between view controllers, which allowed our root view controller to tell the tweet detail view controller just which tweet the user tapped on. Then we tried out a modal transition to show the user detail view controller, and we saw how exit segues let us return to any previous view controller and deliver data back to them in the unwind method.

This is how many popular apps work: navigating forward and backward through view controllers, each specific to some part of the app's overall functionality. From here, we can add any new features we might think of.

In the next chapter, we're going to look at another way of managing multiple view controllers, one that's particularly well suited to the iPad.

CHAPTER 12

Making the Most of Big Screens

We've got a pretty nifty Twitter app at this point, one that lets us scroll through tweets, navigate into a detailed view of a tweet, and then drill down to details about the account that sent it. It's pretty nice on an iPhone.

But, come to think of it, we haven't tried running it on an iPad. And we did make it a universal app in the beginning. So let's see what that looks like. Use the scheme selector in Xcode's toolbar to change to a model of iPad—we often use iPad 2, because as a non-Retina device it fits on the Mac screen—and run the app. In landscape, it looks like this:

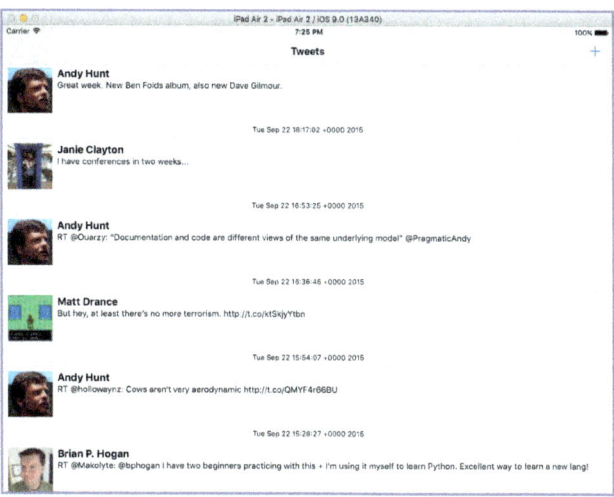

It's…*OK*. Kind of. It's not like any of the views are in the wrong place or anything. And it works fine. It just doesn't take any advantage of all the extra room on the screen. In fact, it looks a lot like the Android screenshots that speakers at Apple events used to use to demonstrate how stretching a phone UI to a tablet screen doesn't work.

So, let's not do that. In this chapter, we're going to take advantage of some unique options that let us use the iPad screen to a better effect, while still working the way we want on iPhone. We'll adapt to larger screens—starting with the iPad and then the iPhone 6s Plus—so that our app can have the best of both worlds.

Autolayout and the Many-Screen-Sizes Problem

Actually, this chapter isn't really where we start dealing with bigger screens. By using autolayout, we've been dealing with differing screen sizes all along. Instead of nailing our UI components to specific coordinates and sizes, we've used constraints like "center this button horizontally," "put this text view 8 points below this other one, wherever it is," and "let this label use whatever space is available inside the superview's margins." Thinking that way, and using these kinds of relative layout instructions, works on screens of different sizes and shapes.

Apple calls this an *adaptive* user interface, one that adapts not only to the physical factor of the device, but also to user preferences, like larger fonts for vision-impaired users.

Split Views on iPad

When the iPad was first introduced, Apple changed the name of the operating system from iPhone OS to iOS, and added some iPad-specific features to the SDK. The most distinctive is probably the *split view*. This is a UI metaphor that combines a narrow view on the left side of the screen with a wide view on the right. In portrait orientation, the left view usually can be shown or hidden, whereas in landscape view the left view is always present.

Several built-in apps on iOS use the split view. Mail shows message senders and subjects in the left view and the message content on the right. Settings has the master list of settings categories on the left and the UI for the selected topic on the right. The split view lends itself well to this sort of a "master-detail" metaphor: the main list of items is in a table on the left, and selections in this table populate the contents of a detail view on the right.

Conveniently, this is also how our Twitter app works. We have a list of tweets, and when we tap one of them, we bring up details on it in a new view. For starters, let's adapt our app to use the split view like this.

Adding a Split View to the Storyboard

To adopt the split view, we need to go to the storyboard and zoom out for a view of our current view controllers. Right now, they're in a left-to-right flow, starting with the navigation controller, and proceeding through the root view controller, the tweet detail view  controller, and the user detail view controller. Go to the Object library, find the Split View Controller icon (shown in the figure), and drag it to the storyboard. The drag will put four scenes on the storyboard, so do the drop someplace where there's lots of room to work with.

Post-drop, the default split view goes off in a couple of different directions, as seen in the following figure. On the left, the split view controller scene has one connection that goes up and right to a navigation controller, and from there to a table view controller. The split view controller also has another connection that goes down and right, to a plain and empty view controller.

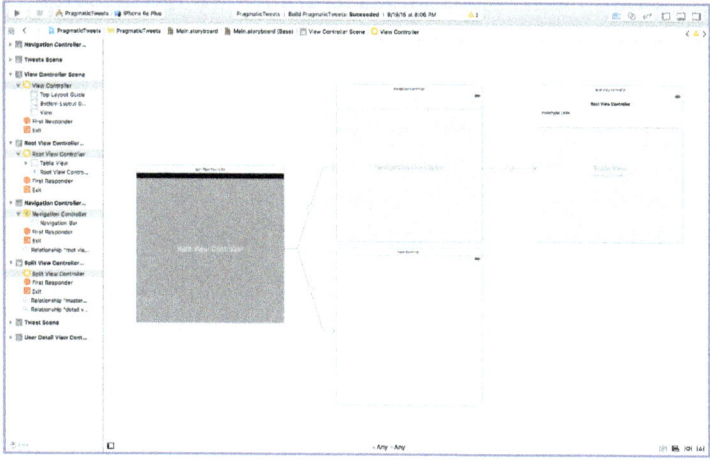

With the default arrangement of scenes, the navigation controller exists largely to provide a navigation bar for the master table view, since the table will often need to have add and edit buttons. Meanwhile, the default detail view is empty, since its contents will totally depend on the content presented by the table and which row is selected.

We already have suitable view controllers to play both of these roles, so rather than customizing the default scenes, we will delete them and replace them with our own. Our RootViewController, the scene currently labeled Tweets, will replace the default one, and our TweetDetailViewController will become the detail scene. Here's how we're going to do that:

- Start by deleting the split view's default table view controller, the one at the upper right that says Root View Controller. We do this by selecting the scene, or its view controller icon in the scene list, and pressing the Delete key (⌫).

- The split view is going to control the relationship between the Tweets view controller and the various detail view controllers, so we need to let it move around the storyboard by breaking its existing connections. First, Control-click our old initial navigation controller to bring up its connections HUD, and click the X to break the connection to the root view controller. Next, select the segue—the circle in the arrow between the Tweets scene and the Tweet Details scene—and delete it as well.

- Now that it's free, we can connect our Tweets table to the master portion of the split view. Drag the Tweets scene up to the right of the split view's navigation controller. Control-click on the navigation controller and find the connection called Root View Controller. Drag from this connection over to the Tweets scene to make the connection.

- Now for the detail part of the split view controller. Delete the empty default detail scene that came with the split view controller. Drag our original navigation controller into the space that was just vacated. Control-click the split view controller to see its connections. The Detail View Controller connection is now empty; drag this to the Navigation Controller scene.

- But where does this navigation controller go? After all, we broke its connection to the Tweets scene that it was originally connected to. Instead, Control-click the navigation controller to bring up its connections HUD, and connect the root view controller to the Tweet Detail View Controller scene. Now the bottom half—the "detail" flow—of our split view controller goes from Navigation Controller to Tweet Detail to User Detail.

- Finally, select the split view controller, bring up its Attributes Inspector (⌥⌘4), and select the Is Initial View Controller check box so that the split view will get to do its thing when the app comes up.

Wow! That's a lot of clicky-draggy! Well, if nothing else, this should allay any fears about deleting and reconnecting storyboard scenes. And if things ever go truly bad, there's always the Undo command. At any rate, the storyboard should now look like the following figure, with the upper branch of the split view going to a navigation controller and our Tweets table, and the lower branch going to the Tweet Detail scene, and then on to User Detail.

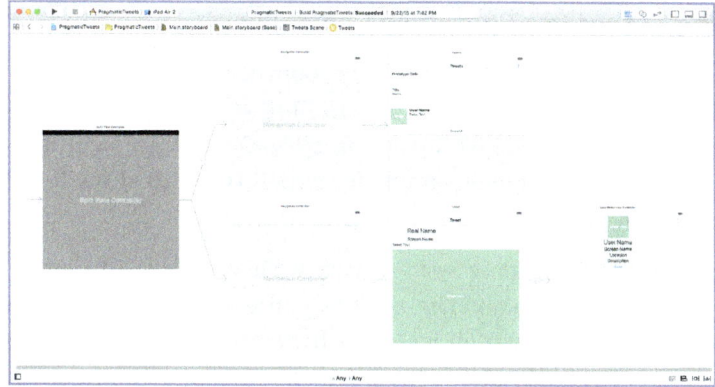

Go ahead and run the app like this, with the scheme selector still set to some flavor of iPad. In portrait, all we'll see is the unpopulated detail view with its empty labels for the username and tweet text. However, a left-to-right drag gesture will reveal the master view, the list of tweets, on the left. Rotating the Simulator to landscape (⌘← or ⌘→) will cause the master list to always be visible, as seen in the following figure.

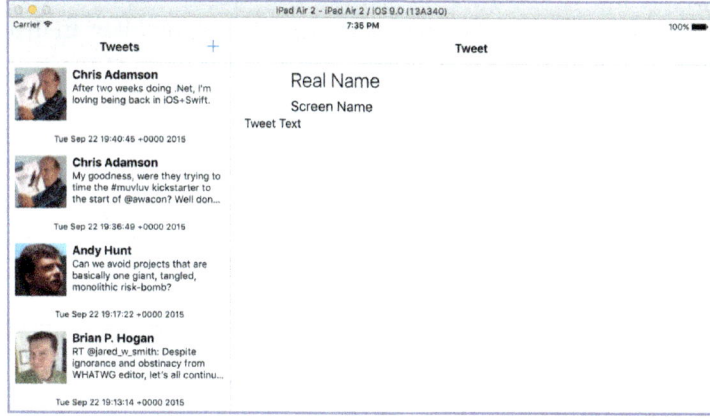

So far, so good! The master view appears when it needs to in landscape and can be brought up in portrait, and everything we did to populate the list of tweets is still working as before.

There's just one thing: *tapping on the rows no longer does anything.* Previously, we had created a segue to connect the table to the Tweet Detail scene, which gave us the navigation between scenes. But we deleted that segue, and now there's no way to send data between the scenes. So what do we do now?

Connecting Scenes in a Split View Controller

When we built our navigation in the storyboard, creating the segue from the table to the detail scene took care of handling taps on the table for us, and telling us (in prepareForSegue()) which destinationViewController was coming in, which is how we told the second view controller which tweet to show in detail. With that gone, we will have to handle things on our own.

First we go to RootViewController.swift, where we'll write an implementation of tableView(didSelectRowAtIndexPath:). The trick is going to be getting information to the TweetDetailViewController, which we don't have a reference to: it's not a property, and we don't get told about it via a prepareForSegue() method anymore.

The only thing these two view controllers have in common anymore is that they're both connected to the same UISplitViewController. As it turns out, that's exactly the key we need. The UIViewController class has an optional property, splitViewController, defined as "the nearest ancestor in the view controller hierarchy that is a split view controller."

Now let's think about what we can do with that. The UISplitViewController has an array property, viewControllers, that represents the child view controllers it manages. So there should be two: a navigation controller in front of our RootViewController, and another navigation controller in front of the TweetDetailViewController.

```
bigscreens/PragmaticTweets-12-1/PragmaticTweets/RootViewController.swift
Line 1  override func tableView(tableView: UITableView,
   -       didSelectRowAtIndexPath indexPath: NSIndexPath) {
   -       let parsedTweet = parsedTweets[indexPath.row]
   -       if let splitViewController = splitViewController
   5         where splitViewController.viewControllers.count > 1 {
   -           if let tweetDetailNav = splitViewController.viewControllers[1]
   -               as? UINavigationController,
   -               tweetDetailVC = tweetDetailNav.viewControllers[0]
   -                 as? TweetDetailViewController {
   10                 tweetDetailVC.tweetIdString = parsedTweet.tweetIdString
   -           }
   -       }
   -       tableView.deselectRowAtIndexPath(indexPath, animated: false)
   -  }
```

This short method starts on line 3 by getting the ParsedTweet from our model that corresponds to the clicked row, just like in the navigation segue case.

Next, we make sure the structure of the scenes is what we expect. Lines 4–5 test to see if the splitViewController property is non-nil (since we don't need to do any of this if we're in a split-view scenario) and if the splitViewController has at least two child view controllers, since we will need to work with the second one. Lines 6–7 check that the first VC in the detail flow—the bottom half of the split in the storyboard—is a navigation controller, and that its root VC is a TweetDetailViewController (lines 8–9).

If all of this works out, then line 10 assigns the tweetIdString property. As a handy side effect, this kicks off the reloadTweetDetails() method called by the didSet() property setter that we wrote back in *Sending Data to the Second View Controller*, on page 185. In fact, this is the reason we needed to write that setter: in the navigation case, we could always count on viewWillAppear() to call reload-TweetData(), but in the split view scenario, the detail view will appear at launch and just stay there, so we need to make sure that setting tweetIdString will update the display.

Finally, outside all our storyboard-hierarchy logic, line 13 always runs at the end of the method and deselects the tapped row so it doesn't stay highlighted.

Run again and our selecting a tweet populates the detail view as expected. With all the space afforded by the iPad, tweets that have images make particularly good use of the screen, as seen in the following figure.

Actually, though, the images introduce a small bug. Now that the detail view is always visible, once we set an image in the image view, nothing ever unsets it. That wasn't a problem in our navigation flow, which was creating and populating a new detail view every time, but now if we click a tweet without an image, the old one hangs around. We need to fix this in TweetDetailViewController, in the part of handleTwitterData(urlResponse: error:) that sets the image:

bigscreens/PragmaticTweets-12-1/PragmaticTweets/TweetDetailViewController.swift

```
Line 1  if let entities = tweetDict["entities"] as? [String : AnyObject],
     2    media = entities["media"] as? [[String : AnyObject]],
     3    mediaString = media[0]["media_url_https"] as? String,
     4    mediaURL = NSURL (string: mediaString),
     5    mediaData = NSData (contentsOfURL: mediaURL) {
     6      tweetImageView.image = UIImage(data: mediaData)
     7  } else {
     8    tweetImageView.image = nil
     9  }
```

The only thing that's new here is the trivial else block from lines 7–9. It says, "if the tweet doesn't have an image URL, nil out the image in the UIImageView."

Split Views on the iPhone

So it's great that we have our app making better use of the space on the iPad, but that begs the question of what's happening on the iPhone. Does it have a side-by-side split view too? How will that fit on a dinky iPhone 4s? We'd better check what's going on, so use the scheme selector to switch to one of the smaller iPhone models (the 4s, 5, or 5s) and run the app again.

What happens is pretty unexpected:

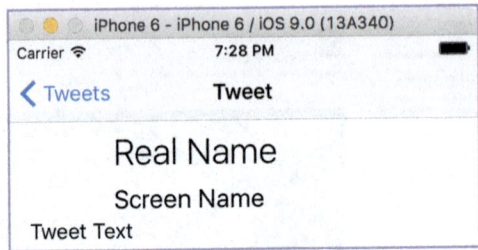

Somehow, our changes have caused us to start on a full-screen detail view instead of the master view with the list of tweets. Also, there's a navigation bar over the detail view, even though there wasn't one on top of the right pane of the split view on the iPad.

Why? The split view controller realizes there's not enough space on the screen for both view controllers, so it has switched into a navigation-like metaphor for showing the two parts of the split on separate pages. This is actually a handy feature, since it lets us use a split view controller for both iPad and iPhone. Prior to iOS 8, we had to have completely separate storyboards for iPhone and iPad. So this is a big win for building Universal apps—those that run on iPhone and iPad—if only it did the right thing out of the box.

Notice that the back button at the top left says Tweets (the title of the master view, which it gets from a navigation item), and we can tap it to go back to the list of tweets. However, if we tap one of the tweets, it doesn't populate the detail view and take us to it. So we have two things to fix: we want to start on the master view controller (the list of tweets) instead of the detail, and we want tapping a table row to fill in the detail like it did in the old navigation app, and in the iPad version of the split view.

Handling Collapsing Split Views

The first step to dealing with the user starting on the wrong scene is knowing that our code is even in this scenario and that we need to do something different. Actually, we can gain the ability to address the problem by becoming the split view controller's delegate. The delegate gets told about changes like rotation, which cause it to rework how it presents its contents. It gets these callbacks at startup too, including one that says it's running in the compact space of an iPhone.

Start in RootViewController.swift by appending UISplitViewControllerDelegate to the comma-separated list of protocols in the class declaration. This will allow our RootViewController to become the split view controller's delegate.

We want to become the delegate as soon as possible, so viewDidLoad() is a good place to do so. At the bottom of that method, add the following code:

bigscreens/PragmaticTweets-12-2/PragmaticTweets/RootViewController.swift

```
if let splitViewController = splitViewController {
  splitViewController.delegate = self
}
```

All this does is check if there's a splitViewController parent, just like we checked when we handled the table row tap. If there is, we become its delegate.

Actually, removing the second view controller, the detail scene, is exactly what we want. If we just return true, the split view controller will give up on the detail view controller, leaving us with just the master view controller, which is the list of tweets. So implement the method like this:

bigscreens/PragmaticTweets-12-2/PragmaticTweets/RootViewController.swift

```
func splitViewController(splitViewController: UISplitViewController,
  collapseSecondaryViewController secondaryViewController: UIViewController,
  ontoPrimaryViewController primaryViewController: UIViewController)
  -> Bool {
  return true
}
```

Run the app on one of the iPhone models now, and we come up on the list of tweets.

Restoring Discarded View Controllers

Well, that's great, except that tapping on a row still doesn't do anything. And the reason for that is in our tap-handling logic in tableView(didSelectRowAtIndexPath:). When we implemented that before, we made sure the split view controller had two child view controllers, so we could take the second one (the TweetDetailView-Controller) and populate it.

But we can't do that now, because *there is no second view controller*. We just told the split view controller that it was OK to discard the second view controller. So that's just great.

Maybe we'll just have to remake that view controller ourselves! Fortunately, it's pretty easy to do so with storyboards. There's a UIStoryboard class that offers just three methods, two of which are for creating scenes from within the storyboard. The one we need is instantiateViewControllerWithIdentifier(), which takes a string and gives us back a UIViewController, with its view and all its subviews laid out exactly like we created them in the storyboard.

For this to work, we need to give the Tweet Detail scene a unique ID string. In the storyboard, select the Tweet Detail View Controller, and bring up its Identity Inspector (⌥⌘3). In the Storyboard ID field, enter TweetDetailVC, as shown in the following figure.

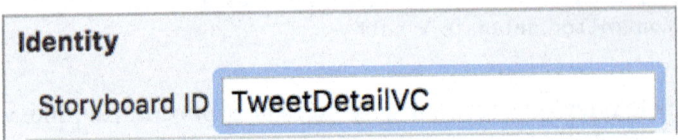

Perform a clean build (Product > Clean, or ⇧⌘K), since changes to storyboards aren't always picked up by Xcode's build process, and we want to make sure this scene is findable by that string.

Now we can re-create this view controller when we need it. The place we're going to do so is in RootViewController's tableView(didSelectRowAtIndexPath:). We want to handle the case where the split view controller has only one child view controller, so find the closing brace that matches if let splitViewController = splitViewController where splitViewController.viewControllers.count > 1 {, and replace its closing brace with the following else block.

bigscreens/PragmaticTweets-12-2/PragmaticTweets/RootViewController.swift

```
Line 1  } else {
2    if let storyboard = storyboard,
3      detailVC =
4      storyboard.instantiateViewControllerWithIdentifier("TweetDetailVC")
5        as? TweetDetailViewController {
6          detailVC.tweetIdString = parsedTweet.tweetIdString
7          splitViewController?.showDetailViewController(detailVC,
8            sender: self)
9    }
10  }
```

On lines 2–5, we check to see that we're in a storyboard, that it has a scene called TweetDetailVC, and that we can cast it to a TweetDetailViewController. If all that works, then we've got our detail view controller, and its whole view hierarchy, just as laid out in the storyboard. In turn, that means we can get it to load its contents like we always have, by setting its tweetIdString (on line 6). Then we just have to navigate to it. UISplitViewController gives us that ability with the showDetailViewController() method, on lines 7–8.

And that's it! Run the app on a simulated iPhone, and it works just like the navigation version did from the previous chapter, perfectly well suited to the small space of the iPhone. Back on the iPad, we get a side-by-side split that makes better use of all the screen real estate. Best of both worlds, and with the split view controller we get it all with one storyboard and this little bit of tricky code.

Split Views and iPad Portrait Orientation

Actually, we're not quite done. Run the app on an iPad and rotate to portrait orientation. Adding the UISplitViewDelegate has killed the gesture that showed the master view controller (that is, the list of tweets). Maybe it's just as well, since the gesture wasn't very discoverable, but we need a way to hide and show the list.

Two things will help us here: the UISplitViewController has a UIBarButton that shows its master view controller. We could add this on the fly, if we knew when to do so. Fortunately, the UISplitViewControllerDelegate gives us that, too.

We'll need to add the bar button in two places: when the UI first comes up, and when the split view controller changes its display mode. So let's stub out an empty method in RootViewController for performing the fix:

```
func addShowSplitPrimaryButton(splitViewController: UISplitViewController) {
}
```

The first place we'll call our helper method is in viewDidLoad(), right after we set ourselves as the UISplitViewController's delegate:

bigscreens/PragmaticTweets-12-2/PragmaticTweets/RootViewController.swift
```
if let splitViewController = splitViewController {
  splitViewController.delegate = self
  addShowSplitPrimaryButton(splitViewController)
}
```

The second time we need to call our helper is when we get rotated: we need to show it in portrait orientation, which shows only the detail view controller, but not in landscape, which shows both master and detail. A delegate method called splitViewController(willChangeToDisplayMode:) helps us here. It passes in a UISplitViewControllerDisplayMode, which is an enum whose values are .Automatic, .PrimaryHidden, .AllVisible, and .PrimaryOverlay. When we rotate to portrait, this will get called with the .PrimaryHidden value, and in landscape, it will be called again with .AllVisible. So we need to call our helper when the primary view controller, our list of tweets, becomes hidden:

bigscreens/PragmaticTweets-12-2/PragmaticTweets/RootViewController.swift
```
func splitViewController(svc: UISplitViewController,
  willChangeToDisplayMode displayMode: UISplitViewControllerDisplayMode) {
    if displayMode == .PrimaryHidden {
      addShowSplitPrimaryButton(svc)
    }
}
```

Now, for the main attraction: how do we actually get this button to show the primary view controller? It's available from UISplitViewController, via the method displayModeButtonItem(), so getting it is easy. What to actually do with it is a little trickier. Here's the recipe:

bigscreens/PragmaticTweets-12-2/PragmaticTweets/RootViewController.swift
```
func addShowSplitPrimaryButton(splitViewController: UISplitViewController) {
  let barButtonItem = splitViewController.displayModeButtonItem()
  if let detailNav = splitViewController.viewControllers.last
    as? UINavigationController {
      detailNav.topViewController?.navigationItem.leftBarButtonItem =
      barButtonItem
  }
}
```

After we get the barButtonItem, the trick is what to do with it. Our detail view controller has a navigation controller in front of it, which gives it a navigation bar (and also the "Tweet" title in that bar). So what we're doing here is asking if the split view controller's last view controller (the last member of its viewControllers array) is a UINavigationController. If it is, then we can ask for that navigation controller's first view controller, get its UINavigationItem, and set its leftBarButtonItem.

Run the app on an iPad simulator and rotate a few times. Whenever the screen is in portrait orientation, there will now be a blue "back" chevron, as seen in the following figure. Tap it to slide the list of tweets over the detail view. Now it works just like the side-by-side presentation in landscape: select a tweet from the list, and its contents pop up in the detail view. Also, tapping outside the list of tweets (that is to say, in the detail view) dismisses the list of tweets, but we can always get back to it with our handy left bar button.

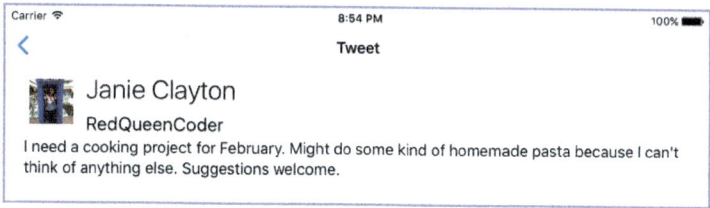

Size Classes and the iPhone 6

So it's great that the split view gives us one behavior for the iPad and another for the iPhone.

Except, well, that the iPhone 6-series devices are *really* big. Maybe not iPad big, but it at least makes you wonder whether it's really appropriate to lump all iPhones together. After all, iOS 9 runs on everything from the 4s (with its 320×480, 3.5-inch screen) to the iPhone 6s Plus (414×736, 5.5-inch screen). Even within the iPhone range, there may be times we want to go to a side-by-side mode with our split view.

To do so, we need to understand how iOS represents screen sizes and their contents.

Size Classes

In iOS, screens, view controllers, and views all have a collection of sizing information called a *trait collection*. These traits are collected by the UITraitCollection class, and include things like the points-to-pixels scaling factor (2.0 for Retina devices, 3.0 for the iPhone 6s Plus, 1.0 for the old iPad 2), the device idiom (phone or pad), whether it supports 3D touch, and a very general way to represent the available space in each dimension.

The available space is represented as a *size class*, and has two values: compact and regular. Those should sound familiar, because they're the values of the sizing bar at the bottom of the storyboard pane, which we saw way back in *Managing an Object's Properties*, on page 85. Let's think back to the grid that appeared in the pop-up, and the descriptions it provided: regular width and height were described as an iPad, whereas compact width and regular height represented an iPhone in portrait orientation.

Traits are inherited from the screen, to the one window that's always on the screen, through view controllers, and views, down to each individual view, like a button or table. Along the way, they can be changed. So an iPad screen will have regular width size class in either orientation, but the left side of a split view will have compact width, since the layout of the split view constrains how much space it can use.

The split view's decision about whether to use a side-by-side or a two-screen layout is based on the width size class it inherits. If it thinks it's in a compact space, it will use the navigation-style two-screen approach; if it inherits regular width, it will use a side-by-side presentation.

The size classes are also used to support the new multitasking features in iOS 9. To try it out, run the app in the Simulator for an iPad Air, Air 2, or Pro, the devices that support iOS multitasking. Use the home button (⇧⌘H) to go back to the home screen. Launch another app in the Simulator, like Safari, and rotate to landscape. Drag a little bit from the right side of the screen to enter multitasking mode. From here, you'll see a list of apps and their icons. Choose PragmaticTweets to open it in the right side of the multi-tasking interface, running side-by-side with Safari, as seen in the figure.

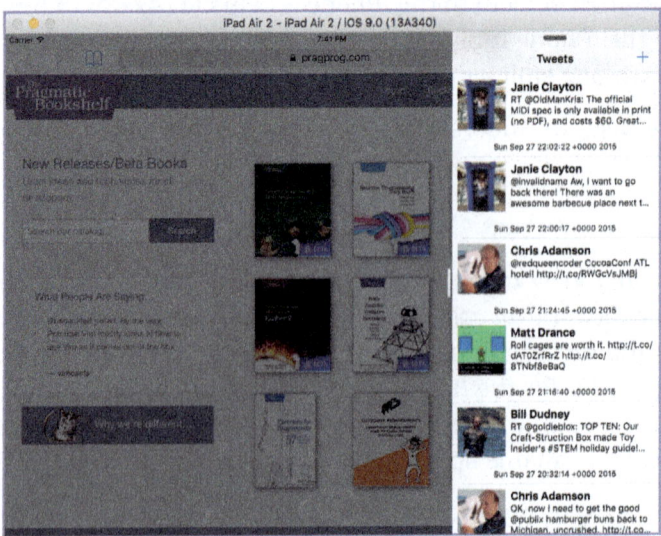

Notice that as long as our side of the split uses only part of the screen, it is considered to be in a horizontally compact size class, and so we get the iPhone-style behavior of navigating from the list of tweets to their details. Only by dragging out to consume the rest of the screen (and thus becoming the sole foreground app) can we achieve our regular-width, two-pane split view.

Now let's use size classes for our own purposes. When an iPhone 6-series device is in landscape, there's surely enough room to do the two-pane split view, rather than just have table rows stretch across the screen. So let's do that. The trick to do this is simple: we have to convince the split view that it has regular width to work with, not compact. Let's do that.

Container Controllers

We can't just tell the split view controller that it has regular width: it has to inherit this from a parent view or view controller. We can do that by creating a *container controller*, a view controller that contains other view controllers. This parent will own the split view controller and will be in a position to give it a trait collection that says it has regular width, if we decide we want to go side by side.

To get started, go to the storyboard, look through the Object library (^⌥⌘3), and find the plain View Controller icon, a yellow ball with a dashed box inside it. Drag this icon to the left of the split view controller.

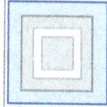

The way we get this view controller to "own" the split view controller is pretty weird. We need to use a *container view*, instead of the usual UIView that comes with a view controller. So, in the scene list, find the view that's a child of this new view controller and delete it. This will also delete the top and bottom layout guide objects from the scene. Now, in the Object library, find the Container View icon, shown in the figure as a gray box inside a white box inside a gray box. Drag it onto the new view controller icon or its box in the storyboard; it will become the sole child of the view controller.

This also adds a new view controller scene to the storyboard, connected by a segue. What's interesting is that this isn't a segue that transitions between scenes; it's an embed segue that tells the container scene which view controller to show first. So it's great that Xcode gave us a default view controller to embed, except we don't want that one; we want to embed the split view controller.

So, Control-click on the container view to show its connections HUD. The first one will show that viewDidLoad() has an embed segue connected to that blank view controller. Drag from the circle in this connection to the split view controller. This will allow us to make a segue connection. At the end of the drag, choose Embed as the segue type. We should always name our segues, so click the segue icon between the two scenes, bring up its Attributes Inspector (⌥⌘4), and give it the storyboard identifier embedSplitViewSegue.

Now the empty view controller that the container view supplied for us has no connections at all, so we can delete it.

Control-click on the container view to show its updated connections. For Triggered Segues, it will show viewDidLoad() via an embed segue to the Split View Controller. This is the weird part: this segue isn't performed as part of a navigation like in the last chapter; it happens when the view loads, at which point the container view controller will get its one and only look at the child view controller that it's going to contain.

This scene is going to be the beginning of our app, so choose the view controller, go to the Attributes Inspector (⌥⌘4), and select the Is Initial View Controller box. This won't visually change anything, since control will flow immediately to the split view controller child. But it will ensure that this view controller loads first, which we need. The beginning of the storyboard should now look like the figure on page 215.

Now we're at the point where we need to write some code, to grab the reference to the split view controller and be able to change its trait collection. In the File Navigator, select the Pragmatic Tweets group and use New Group to create the group Size Class Override. Within this group, choose New File to create a new Cocoa Touch Class, with the name SizeClassOverrideViewController, a subclass of UIViewController written in Swift. Finally, in the storyboard, select the view controller with the container view, bring up its Identity Inspector (⌥⌘3), and change the class to SizeClassOverrideViewController. Now the container view controller will be our custom class.

What we need to do with this code is grab a reference to the split view controller, and send it our preferred size class traits. In SizeClassOverrideViewController.swift, start by creating a property to refer to the UISplitViewController.

bigscreens/PragmaticTweets-12-3/PragmaticTweets/SizeClassOverrideViewController.swift
```
var embeddedSplitVC: UISplitViewController!
```

As implied by the name of the embed segue, our one look at the split view controller happens when the view loads. This will make a call to prepare-ForSegue()—just like when we're navigating between scenes—so we override that method to grab the reference to the destinationViewController.

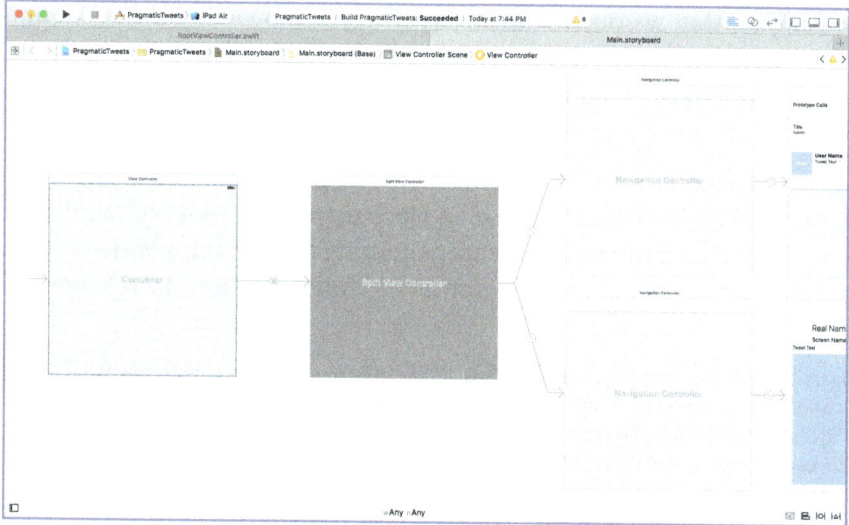

bigscreens/PragmaticTweets-12-3/PragmaticTweets/SizeClassOverrideViewController.swift

```swift
override func prepareForSegue(segue: UIStoryboardSegue, sender: AnyObject?) {
  if segue.identifier == "embedSplitViewSegue" {
    embeddedSplitVC = segue.destinationViewController
      as! UISplitViewController
  }
}
```

Now we're in a position to start changing the split view's sense of how much room it has to work with!

Overriding Trait Collections

Now let's think about what we want to tell the split view controller, and when. It will use a side-by-side view when it thinks its width size class is regular and not compact. We could probably swing the side-by-side view on an iPhone 6s, but not a 4s. Let's look at our sizes.

Model	Dimensions (points)	Scale factor
iPhone 4s	320×480	2.0
iPhone 5/5s	320×568	2.0
iPhone 6/6s	375×667	2.0
iPhone 6 Plus/6s Plus	414×736	3.0
iPad 2	768×1024	1.0
iPad Retina/iPad Air	768×1024	2.0
iPad Pro	1024×1366	2.0

So, assuming that we don't want to try to go side by side on the 4s, and we definitely want to do so on the big iPhone 6 models, let's pick a value in the middle. We'll just say that any width bigger than 480 is enough for us to try side by side.

When the device is rotated, view controllers get a callback to the method viewWillTransitionToSize(). That's the perfect place to pull our trickery. We'll override that method, check the size we're transitioning to, and if it's wide enough for us, we'll override the split view controller's trait collection. Here's how we do that.

```
bigscreens/PragmaticTweets-12-3/PragmaticTweets/SizeClassOverrideViewController.swift
override func viewWillTransitionToSize(size: CGSize,
  withTransitionCoordinator coordinator:
  UIViewControllerTransitionCoordinator) {
    if size.width > 480.0 {
      let overrideTraits = UITraitCollection (
      horizontalSizeClass: .Regular)
      setOverrideTraitCollection(overrideTraits,
        forChildViewController: embeddedSplitVC!)
    } else {
      setOverrideTraitCollection(nil,
        forChildViewController: embeddedSplitVC!)
    }
}
```

We look at the incoming width on line 4. If it's greater than 480.0, lines 5–6 create a new UITraitCollection. The initializers for this class take either one of the four traits—horizontalSizeClass, verticalSizeClass, userInterfaceIdiom, or scaleFactor—or an array of already initialized trait collections to merge together. All we care about is setting the horizontalSizeClass to the enum value UIUserInterfaceSizeClass.Regular.

Then all we have to do is pass this to our embeddedSplitVC. A parent view controller can override a child's trait collection with setOverrideTraitCollection(), which is what we do on lines 7–8. This is only possible from a parent view controller—other VCs can't go changing each other's trait collections willy-nilly—which is why we had to go through the whole rigmarole of setting up our custom container controller.

Finally, if our width isn't big enough for the split view controller to go into side-by-side mode, we use setOverrideTraitCollection() with nil, on lines 10–11, which lets it inherit its traits as before.

With our sneaky override of the size class now complete, run the app again on different models in the Simulator (keeping in mind you'll have to sign into Twitter on each one if you haven't already, as they store their system settings separately from each other). On a sufficiently large device, the split view controller will now go into side-by-side mode when rotated to landscape, as seen in the following figure.

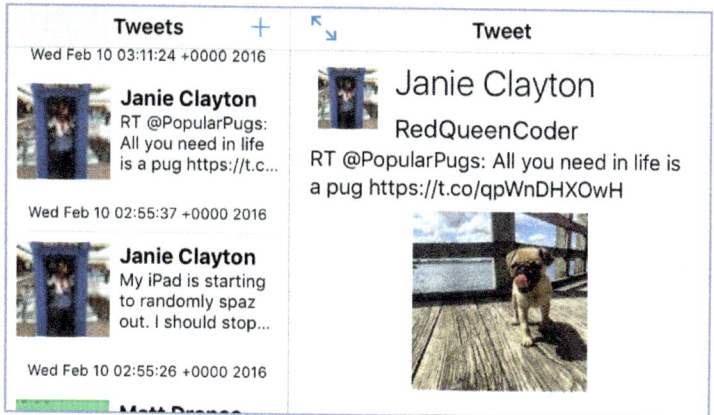

What We've Learned

In this chapter, we stopped looking at our app through iPhone goggles. We thought about how it used the space available on an iPad, and switched to a split view to make better use of all the screen real estate. We discovered that this gives us a navigation-like experience for iPhone sizes when the side-by-side view doesn't really make sense, although we did have to put in some effort to make it work like we wanted it to. And in between the extremes of the little iPhone 4s and the iPad, there are now several iPhone models at intermediate sizes, so we saw how to inspect our size classes and even change them.

So, we've done some work on how users see our app. Now it's time to enhance how they interact with it. In the next chapter, we'll look at how to create and handle touch gestures on our own, so our app won't just look great, it will literally feel great, too.

CHAPTER 13

Handling Touch Gestures

Touch is the defining trait of user interfaces on the iPhone and iPad. It's what makes working with the data seem so direct: flicking a table to scroll it, pinching a photo to resize it, or drawing freehand with our fingers. iOS builds in sensible touch controls for all of its provided views, and we can build upon those further by creating our own.

Gesture Recognizers

The first versions of the iPhone SDK gave us only low-level raw touch data via the UIView methods touchesBegan(), touchesMoved(), touchesEnded(), and touchesCancelled(). These delivered sets of UITouch events, and from the raw geometry and timing of these events, we could track events like swipes, using logic like "if the touch moved at least 50 points up, and not more than 20 points to either side, in less than 0.5 seconds, then treat it as an upward swipe."

As one might expect, this was a huge pain in the butt to implement and led to variations in user experience as different developers interpreted the touch data differently, based on what "felt right" to them.

Fortunately, the situation was cleaned up in later versions of iOS thanks to *gesture recognizers*. With these classes, iOS determines for us what counts as a swipe or a double-tap, and calls into our code only when it detects that a matching gesture has occurred.

The top-level UIGestureRecognizer class represents things like a gesture's location in a view, its current state (began, changed, ended, and so on), and a list of target objects to be notified as the recognizer's state changes. Subclasses provide the tracking of distinct gestures like taps, pinches, rotations, and swipes, and these subclasses also contain properties representing traits specific to the gesture: how many taps, how much pinching, and so on.

Segue Gestures

One handy trick for our Twitter app would be to give the user a better view of a given tweeter's avatar. From the user detail screen we built in the last chapter, we could go to a new screen that shows the image in a larger view, and allow our user to pinch-zoom and move around the avatar in detail.

To do this, we'll need a new "user image detail" scene in the storyboard. Find the View Controller icon in the Object library, and drag it into the storyboard, to the right of the User Detail View Controller scene that is currently the end of our storyboard. To this new scene, add the following:

- An image view, with width and height pinned to 280 points, vertically and horizontally aligned in its container

- A button, with the title Done, pinned 20 points up from the bottom of the container, horizontally aligned in the container

We'll put some logic into that scene later, but for now, we just need to create a way to get to it from the user detail scene. We could do that by replacing the detail scene's image view with a button and then adding a segue on the button tap. But to show how flexible gesture recognizers are, we'll do functionally the same thing by giving the existing image view the ability to handle taps, thereby turning it into a de facto image button.

Scroll through the Object library and find the gesture recognizer icons. They're displayed as blue circles against dark gray backgrounds, some with swooshes that represent movement. Find the tap gesture recognizer, which is represented as a single static circle, shown in the figure.

Drag this icon onto the UIImageView that's above the User Name label in the User Detail View Controller scene. This won't cause an immediate change to the image view, but the gesture recognizer will become a top-level member of the scene, a sibling to the view controller and the various segues, in the list on the left. Select it from this list and view it with the Attributes Inspector (⌥⌘4). As shown in the

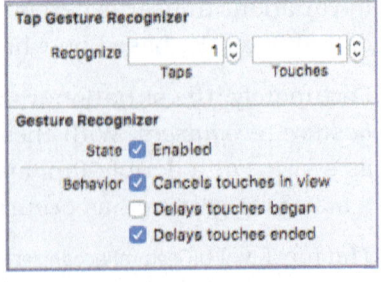

figure, the gesture recognizer allows you to configure the number of sequential taps (single-, double-, triple-, and so on) and the number of touches (how many fingers touching the screen) required to trigger the recognizer.

Connecting Gesture Recognizers

One thing we don't see here is how the gesture recognizer is related to the image view. For that, go to the Connections Inspector (⌥⌘6). There we see that the Referencing Outlet Collections have a property called gestureRecognizers that is connected to the Image View (if it just says View, you probably dropped it on the full view and not the image view; delete the recognizer from the scene and try again).

So it's not that the recognizer refers to the view; instead, the view knows that the recognizer is one of its potentially many gestureRecognizers. Now let's address the question of the what the recognizer does when it's tapped. In the Connections Inspector, we see a few interesting properties: a triggered segue action, a delegate outlet, and a sent action selector. The delegate doesn't help us here: the UIGestureRecognizerDelegate is meant to let our code adjudicate when two gesture recognizers want to handle the same gesture. What's useful for us are the selector, which calls a method when the gesture begins, ends, or updates, and the segue action, which takes us to a new scene.

What we want is the segue, so draw a connection line by dragging from the circle next to action in the Connections Inspector to anywhere in the new image detail scene. It would also work to do a Control-drag from the gesture recognizer in the user detail scene over to the image detail scene; Xcode will figure out that a connection between scenes can only be a segue (and not some other kind of connection). At the end of the drag, a pop-up asks what kind of segue

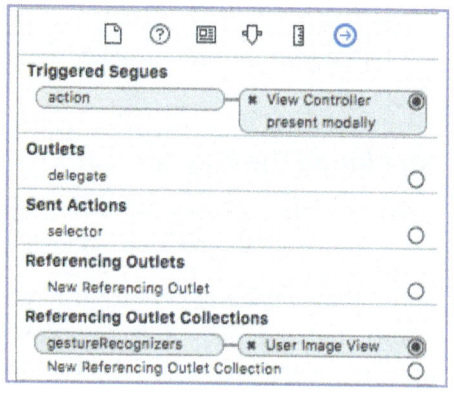

we want; coming from a modal scene, the only choice that will work is another Present Modally segue. Our gesture recognizer's connections should now look like the figure.

We can try running now, choosing a tweet, and drilling down to user details, but clicking the image won't perform this segue yet. To see why, select the image in the user detail scene, and bring up the Attributes Inspector (⌥⌘4). Notice that User Interaction Enabled is unchecked, since image views by default don't handle user input. But this means that it won't process touch events, which in turn means our gesture recognizer will never fire. Simple fix here: just check the User Interaction Enabled box.

Run the app now and we can drill all the way to our new scene, which at this point only shows a Done button, since we haven't populated the image view yet. Moreover, the Done button doesn't work, and we're trapped on this scene. Let's fix that before we move on. The fix is to use an unwind segue. Back in UserDetailViewController.swift, add an empty implementation for unwindToUserDetailVC():

gestures/PragmaticTweets-13-1/PragmaticTweets/UserDetailViewController.swift
```
@IBAction func unwindToUserDetailVC (segue : UIStoryboardSegue) {
}
```

Now, we can go to the image detail scene in the storyboard, and Control-drag from the Done button to the orange Exit Segue button. At the end of the drag, we have two methods we can unwind to: choose the unwindToUserDetailVC() method we just created. Run again, and we can go back from the image detail scene.

So what we've accomplished at this point is to bring tap handling to a UIImageView, a class that ordinarily supports no user interaction whatsoever. And we did it without really writing any code—we just created the gesture recognizer in the storyboard, connected it to a new segue, and gave ourselves a no-op method to unwind to.

But we're just getting started. There's a lot more we can do to the default image view.

Populating the Image

Before we start gesturing around with the image view, it'll help to actually have an image we can see. So let's deal with that now.

In the File Navigator, create a new group called User Image Detail VC, and within that, use New File to create a new class UserImageDetailViewController, a subclass of UIViewController. At the top of this new UserImageDetailViewController.swift file, declare a property for the user image URL:

gestures/PragmaticTweets-13-2/PragmaticTweets/UserImageDetailViewController.swift
```
var userImageURL: NSURL?
```

We'll set that property every time we follow the segue to the new scene, so we have some work to do in the storyboard. First, select the image detail scene's view controller icon (either from the frame below the scene or in the scene's object list), go to the Identity Inspector (⌥⌘3), and change the class to UserImageDetailViewController. Since we will need to know when we're taking the segue to this scene, select the segue, bring up the Attributes Inspector (⌘⌥4), and set the identifier to showUserImageDetailSegue.

Now we're going to be able to set the image URL when we segue to the new scene. We do this back in UserDetailViewController.swift, where we will need to save the URL of the image. Right now, the user detail scene just creates a UIImage to populate this class's image view, but there's a good reason it should save off the URL: it will let us get a higher-quality image. Currently, it uses the key profile_image_url_https to get an image URL from the Twitter response. The value is a URL string like https://pbs.twimg.com/profile_images/290486223/pp_for_twitter_normal.png. As it turns out, that _normal is used by Twitter to indicate an icon at a standardized 48×48 size. That's OK for the user detail view controller, but it will be very blocky in the 280×280 image view in the next scene. Fortunately, if we just strip the _normal, we can get the image in the original size uploaded by the Twitter user, and that will look nicer in the next scene. So start by giving the UserDetailViewController this new property:

gestures/PragmaticTweets-13-2/PragmaticTweets/UserDetailViewController.swift

```
var userImageURL: NSURL?
```

You're not seeing double; that's the same property we previously added to UserImageDetailViewController. We want to save the URL in this view controller, and pass it to the next one. To save it here, down in handleTwitterData(), inside the closure, change the last few lines (after the userDescriptionLabel.text = (tweetDict["description"] as! String) line) so they save this property and use it to create the userImageView.image, rather than use a local userImageURL variable.

gestures/PragmaticTweets-13-2/PragmaticTweets/UserDetailViewController.swift

```
if let userImageURL = NSURL (string:
    (tweetDict["profile_image_url_https"] as! String)),
  userImageData = NSData(contentsOfURL: userImageURL) {
    self.userImageURL = userImageURL
    userImageView.image = UIImage(data: userImageData)
}
```

Now we're ready to send the good version of the user image URL to the UserImageDetailViewController by writing a prepareForSegue:() method:

gestures/PragmaticTweets-13-2/PragmaticTweets/UserDetailViewController.swift

```
Line 1  override func prepareForSegue(segue: UIStoryboardSegue, sender: AnyObject?) {
     -    if let imageDetailVC = segue.destinationViewController
     -      as? UserImageDetailViewController,
     -      userImageURL = userImageURL
     5    where segue.identifier == "showUserImageDetailSegue" {
     -        var urlString = userImageURL.absoluteString
     -        urlString = urlString.stringByReplacingOccurrencesOfString("_normal",
     -          withString: "")
     -        imageDetailVC.userImageURL = NSURL(string: urlString)
    10    }
     -  }
```

We begin with a big if let where that verifies that the destination view controller is of the correct class (lines 2–3), that the userImageURL property is non-nil (line 4), and that the segue has the correct identifier (line 5). If *all* that is true, we can then get a String version of the URL (line 6), and strip out the _normal substring (lines 7–8). Finally, we make a new NSURL for the full-size image and send it to the user image detail view controller on line 9.

Once the segue is performed, the UserImageDetailViewController will have the URL for the full-size image. Now all we need to do is to populate the image view in that scene. Start by going to the storyboard, going to the last scene (the User-ImageDetailViewController), and selecting the 280×280 image view. Bring up the Assistant Editor (the "linked rings" toolbar button, or ⌥⌘↩), with UserImageDe-tailViewController.swift in the right pane, and Control-drag from the image view in the storyboard to somewhere inside the class (perhaps right after the userImageURL we created), to create an outlet that we'll name userImageView.

gestures/PragmaticTweets-13-2/PragmaticTweets/UserImageDetailViewController.swift

```
@IBOutlet weak var userImageView: UIImageView!
```

Now that we can see the image view in code, go back to the standard editor, visit UserImageDetailViewController.swift, and add a viewWillAppear() method:

gestures/PragmaticTweets-13-2/PragmaticTweets/UserImageDetailViewController.swift

```
override func viewWillAppear(animated: Bool) {
  super.viewWillAppear(animated)
  if let userImageURL = userImageURL,
    imageData = NSData (contentsOfURL: userImageURL) {
      userImageView.image = UIImage(data: imageData)
  }
}
```

Run the app now, and we can navigate all the way to the image detail scene, which will show the higher-quality user image and not the 48×48 icon. As seen in the figure on page 225, we've drilled down for a look at Janie's Twitter avatar.

That's a nice, normal-looking image for now. But we're about to start letting our fingers have some fun with it.

Pinching and Panning

How can we play with images on iOS? The whole point of a touch interface is to provide the feeling of interacting directly with our data, so we should be thinking of moving the image around with a drag, zooming in and out of it with pinch gestures, and so forth.

Let's take a look at what gesture recognizers give us. Here's a table summarizing the concrete subclasses of UIGestureRecognizer and the important properties and/or methods exposed by each:

Class	Important Properties and Methods
UILongPressGestureRecognizer	minimumPressDuration, allowableMovement
UIPanGestureRecognizer	translationInView:, velocityInView:
UIPinchGestureRecognizer	scale, velocity
UIRotationGestureRecognizer	rotation, velocity
UIScreenEdgePanGestureRecognizer	edges
UISwipeGestureRecognizer	direction
UITapGestureRecognizer	numberOfTapsRequired, numberOfTouchesRequired

As we look at the names of the gesture recognizers, we can start to get some ideas: UIPanGestureRecognizer handles dragging a finger around, so we can use that to move the image around. The UIPinchGestureRecognizer seems like it would be a natural for pinch-to-zoom functionality. So it looks easy enough to recognize the gestures we want. Question now is: what do we do with it? How is a scale or translationInView() going to help us change the appearance of the image view?

Affine Transformations

The properties and methods provided by the gesture recognizers work well with a trait common to all graphic objects in iOS: *affine transformations*. A transformation, speaking generally, changes how we draw something. More technically, transformations indicate how points in one coordinate system map to another. Affine transforms are special, because they maintain parallel lines between the two coordinate systems.

A specific example of how we already use affine transforms may be helpful here. Think of how when you print out a document, you can save paper by using the printer dialog to print two pages of the document on one sheet of physical paper, putting two portrait-oriented pages side by side on one land-scape page. To do that, each page of your document goes through three transformations:

- The page is rotated 90°, so that it prints "sideways."

- The page is shrunk down (*scaled*) by about 50% (well, for a US letter page anyway...legal or A4 would have slightly different math).

- The page is moved (*translated*) so that odd pages are left-aligned against the edge of the portrait page, and even pages are left-aligned approximately along the center fold of the page.

Each of these can be represented as an affine transform. Moreover, all of them can go in a single transform by simply applying each transform to the one that came before it.

For our purposes, every UIView has a transform of type CGAffineTransform. This is a struct, not a class, and consists of just six CGFloats: a, b, c, and d, tx, and ty. These six values represent any combination of rotation, scaling, skewing, and translation (movement) operations. Technically, they represent six members of the matrix in the following equation.

$$[x'\ y'\ 1] = [x\ y\ 1] \times \begin{bmatrix} a & b & 0 \\ c & d & 0 \\ t_x & t_y & 1 \end{bmatrix}$$

What this equation provides is the transformed values for any point, x' and y', given their original values (x and y) and the contents of the affine transform matrix. This works out to a pair of simple equations:

x' = ax * cy + t_x
y' = bx * dy + t_y

Notice that the t_x and t_y values stand alone as terms in the equations. These are the "transform" values. If a, b, c, and d are all 1.0, then t_x and t_y can be used directly along the x- and y-axes.

On the other hand, if we only work with a, b, c, and d, we can easily scale an object while maintaining its aspect ratio: if we set a and d to 2.0, then every coordinate value will double, and this transform will represent doubling the size of an object. Or we can use sines and cosines to represent rotation. Or we can use all the terms to combine scaling, rotation, and translation.

Transforms and Layers

The CALayer objects that provide the actual drawing of our views have a different way of representing transforms, the CATransform3D. As its name implies, this transform works in three dimensions, with a z-axis that comes out of the screen toward the viewer. Any time we want to do transforms that work with a sense of depth, like views that flip over or are viewable from the side, we need to work at the CALayer level.

Fortunately, we don't have to use the members of CGAffineTransform directly here. In fact, we almost never do. Core Graphics provides a set of convenience functions to create affine transforms for rotation, scaling, and translation operations, either as absolute values or as modifications of existing affine transforms. So if we ever found ourselves writing the printer driver that had to do side-by-side printing as described earlier, we could create one affine transform to the rotation, use that to create a transform to do the scaling (of the rotated page), and then use that to make the translation (of the rotated and scaled page).

Transforming the Image View

Now that we see what affine transforms offer us, the properties and methods exposed by the gesture recognizers start to make more sense. The pinch gesture recognizer provides a scale that we could use to make a scale transform, and the pan recognizer offers translationInView() that will be perfect for making a translation.

To make use of these transforms, we have a few options. UIView has a transform property, so we can set that directly. The underlying CALayer that provides the view's appearance also has a transform property, although that one is of type CATransform3D and works in three dimensions. A more advanced option would be to write our own subclass of UIView or CALayer that draws its own contents; the Core Graphics library used for drawing allows us to set an affine transform on our drawing operations, and is the only way to use multiple transforms. To keep it simple for now, we'll just reset the UIImageView's transform property, which it inherits from UIView.

The Pan Transform

 Let's start with a pan transform to move the image around. In the storyboard, go to the user image view detail scene, the one with the 280×280 image and the Done button. In the Object library, find the Pan Gesture Recognizer icon, which looks like a blue circle leaving a streak below it. Drag and drop the pan recognizer on to the image view.

Now we need to give the recognizer a method it can call. Select the pan gesture recognizer in the scene's object list, and switch to Assistant Editor (⌥⌘↩), making sure UserImageDetailViewController.swift is in the right pane. Control-drag from the gesture recognizer (either in the scene's object list or from the bar atop the scene), to any free space inside the class, perhaps down by the closing curly brace. At the end of the drop, a pop-up asks for what kind of connection to make—be sure to change from Outlet to Action—and for a name for the action method. Let's call it handlePanGesture(). Also, before clicking Connect, change Type from the default AnyObject to UIPanGestureRecognizer.

This connection will call handlePanGesture() when a pan gesture starts, updates, or ends on the image view. At least it *would*, if image views processed touch events by default. Just as with the image in the previous view controller, we have to explicitly enable user interaction with this image view to make it respond to touch events. Switch back to the storyboard's standard editor, select the image view, bring up its Attributes Inspector, and select the User Interaction Enabled check box.

Switch back to the standard editor and bring up UserImageDetailViewController.swift so we can write this method that we just connected. This is where we're going to ask the gesture recognizer how far it's moved, and use that to update the image view's affine transform.

For this to work, we need to understand what the gesture recognizer tells us. If we look up translationInView() in the documentation for UIPanGestureRecognizer, we find it returns "a point identifying the new location of a view in the coordinate system of its designated superview." There's also an important note in the discussion of the method:

> The x and y values report the total translation over time. They are not delta values from the last time that the translation was reported. Apply the translation value to the state of the view when the gesture is first recognized—do not concatenate the value each time the handler is called.

What this is telling us is that as we get new callbacks as handlePanGesture() is repeatedly called during the drag, the value reported back to us is relative to the image view's initial transform, not the last value we set it to. That means we should plan on saving the image view's transform the first time we get called. Define that as a property up in the top of the class:

gestures/PragmaticTweets-13-2/PragmaticTweets/UserImageDetailViewController.swift
```
var preGestureTransform: CGAffineTransform?
```

Now we can assign that property the first time we're called back by the gesture recognizer. When we're called back, we can ask the gesture recognizer for its state, which can be started, changed, ended, canceled, or a few other administrative and error states. When the value is UIGestureRecognizerState.Began, we'll save off the initial transform of the image view. Begin the handlePanGesture:() like this:

gestures/PragmaticTweets-13-2/PragmaticTweets/UserImageDetailViewController.swift
```
@IBAction func handlePanGesture(sender: UIPanGestureRecognizer) {
  if sender.state == .Began {
    preGestureTransform = userImageView.transform
  }
```

When a pan gesture begins, this if block saves the image view's transform to our preGestureTransform property, since all subsequent event coordinates will be relative to this initial transform. Now we're ready to handle moving the view around. So, finish up handlePanGesture() with a second if, as follows:

gestures/PragmaticTweets-13-2/PragmaticTweets/UserImageDetailViewController.swift
```
Line 1    if sender.state == .Began ||
  2         sender.state == .Changed {
  3           let translation = sender.translationInView(userImageView)
  4           let translatedTransform = CGAffineTransformTranslate(
  5             preGestureTransform!, translation.x, translation.y)
  6           userImageView.transform = translatedTransform
  7       }
  8   }
```

We get the translationInView() on line 3. This is a CGPoint whose x and y members represent how far we have moved along each axis from where the pan began. With that information, we can use the CGAffineTransformTranslate() function to create a new transform that represents that distance from the original preGestureTransform (lines 4–5). Then, on line 6, we just set that as the new transform property of the image view.

Does this work? Try it. Drill down to an user image detail and try dragging the picture around. You should have total freedom to put it wherever you like, even under the Done button or partially offscreen, as seen in the following figure. Pretty cool, but we should clean up after ourselves before we go further.

The Identity Transform

So it's great that we can drag the image wherever we like...but that does mean we can drag it completely off the screen. Problem!

Let's give ourselves a "panic button": if the user double-taps the image, it'll go back to its default position.

In the storyboard, add a new tap gesture recognizer to the image view. Select the tap gesture recognizer icon from the scene's object list or the title bar atop the scene, bring up the Attributes Inspector, and set the number of taps to 2. This means it will take a double-tap for the recognizer to fire.

Next, switch to Assistant Editor, and Control-drag from the tap gesture recognizer into UserImageDetailViewController.swift to create a new action method. When the pop-up appears at the end of the drag, call the method handleDoubleTapGesture(), and switch the type from AnyObject to UITapGestureRecognizer.

So how do we write this method? We want to go back to the image view's original transform, before any of our changes. By default, UIViews have an *identity transform*, which means no scaling, rotation, or translation. This is a CGAffineTransform where a and d are 1.0, and b, c, t_x and t_y are all 0.0. Run that through the earlier formulas and we find that makes x' equal x and y' equal y. This "do nothing" is provided to us as the constant CGAffineTransformIdentity.

```
gestures/PragmaticTweets-13-2/PragmaticTweets/UserImageDetailViewController.swift
@IBAction func handleDoubleTapGesture(sender: UITapGestureRecognizer) {
  userImageView.transform = CGAffineTransformIdentity
}
```

Restoring the identity transform on a UIView is a one-line call. Run the app, drag the image around, and double-tap to send it back to where it started. Easy peasy!

The Scale Transform

The other common gesture we should add to our image viewer is a pinch-to-zoom feature. Again, this naturally links the scale property of the gesture recognizer—in this case a UIPinchGestureRecognizer—to the ability of affine transforms to perform scaling operations.

Back in the storyboard, go to the Object library and locate the pinch gesture recognizer icon. As before, drag it on to the image view to add it to the scene. Switch to the Assistant Editor with UserImageDe-tailViewController.swift in the right pane, select the icon in the scene or the title bar, and Control-drag to create a new action method. Name the action han-dlePinchGesture() and change the parameter type to UIPinchGestureRecognizer.

What does the pinch gesture's scale give us? According to the docs, it's "the scale factor relative to the points of the two touches in screen coordinates." And, as was the case with the pan recognizer, this value is relative to the beginning of the gesture, not to the last time we were called. So, once again, we need to make use of the preGestureTransform to hold on to our initial value.

```
gestures/PragmaticTweets-13-2/PragmaticTweets/UserImageDetailViewController.swift
Line 1 @IBAction func handlePinchGesture(sender: UIPinchGestureRecognizer) {
  -     if sender.state == .Began {
  -       preGestureTransform = userImageView.transform
  -     }
  5     if sender.state == .Began ||
  -       sender.state == .Changed {
  -         let scaledTransform = CGAffineTransformScale(
  -           preGestureTransform!, sender.scale, sender.scale)
  -         userImageView.transform = scaledTransform
 10     }
  - }
```

As with the pan recognizer, we use the start state to save off the image view's initial transform, on lines 2–4. Then on lines 5–6, we deal with the scale value of a started or changed event. On lines 7–8, we use CGAffineTransformScale() to create a new CGAffineTransform by taking the original preGestureTransform and applying the scale value to both the x and y factors of the scaling transform. And then on line 9, we set this as the new value of the image view's transform.

Run the app and give it a whirl. To simulate a pinch gesture in the Simulator, hold down the Option key on the keyboard, which will show the pinch points as two circles that move with the mouse or trackpad. By adding the Shift key, we can move the pinch points without registering as a pinch. In the following figure, we've panned to the right and pinch-zoomed in to pick out two *Neon Genesis Evangelion* cosplayers coming off the escalator behind Janie (yes, her Twitter avatar is from an anime convention, how did you guess?).

To better understand the math behind the transform, try changing the x- and y-scaling values sent to CGAffineTransform-Scale(). For example, if we set the last argument, sy, to the constant value 1.0, then the pinch will become a horizontal stretching operation, because the y value will always be the same after the transform (since it's being multiplied by 1). Another fun trick is to multiply the scaling value by -1.0, which causes the image to flip around the axis, making it an upside-down mirror image.

Subview Clipping

Thanks to the natural pairing of the gesture recognizers and the affine transforms, we've added the dragging and pinch-zooming functionality that will be familiar to our users from many other apps they use. However, views that are allowed to just sprawl all over the screen aren't something we usually see on iOS. It may be fun, but it feels wrong, and we hardly want to let the user make a mess of our user interface.

Let's rein in the madness a little bit. We'll put the image view into another view, and have it clipped off at that view's edges. That will put an end to sliding the image offscreen or under the Done button.

In the storyboard, select the image view and delete it (with the Backspace key or the Edit > Cut menu item). Notice that the three gesture recognizers survive this, because they are top-level objects in the scene, and not children of any view or view controller.

From the Object library, find the plain view (the popover will show its class as UIView), and drag it to the middle of the scene's main view. Use the autolay-out popovers to pin its width and height to 280 and to horizontally and verti-cally align it in the container. Then go to its Attributes Inspector and check the Clip Subviews box. What this does is to constrain ("clip") drawing to the bounds of the view, so if the contained image view goes beyond those boundaries, it will just get cut off.

Next, drop an image view into this subview. It should allow itself to fill the parent subview; one way to make this work for sure is to drag the image view onto the subview's entry in the scene list, rather than onto the storyboard layout. Like its parent, create autolayout constraints pin its size to 280×280 and horizontally and vertically align it in its containers.

Time to fix our connections. Select the view controller from the scene members list and open the Connections Inspector (⌥⌘6). The userImageView is no longer connected, because we deleted the object it was connected to. Drag from that connection's circle to the new image view to make a new connection.

The gesture recognizers also have no incoming connections anymore, so they won't be called. To fix that, we're going to connect them to the 280×280 plain view, rather than directly to the image view. Select the subview, and repeat-edly drag from its gestureRecognizers entry in the Connections Inspector to each of the gesture recognizers, ultimately creating three connections.

Try running the app and drill down to the image detail view. When we drag around, any part of the image that goes beyond the bounds of the 280×280 view is simply cut off, as shown in the figure on page 234. We can also perform our gestures anywhere in the view, not just on the image view, and have them recognized. That means we can push the image entirely outside the bounds of the container view, but we can also bring it back with a double-tap anywhere in that view.

What We've Learned

In this chapter, we took hold—literally—of the touch gestures that are the hallmark of iOS user interfaces. By giving the user the ability to manipulate an image by dragging it around with one finger and pinch-zooming it with two, we immediately create a sense of close contact with the image. Gesture recognizers make it easy to pick up the most common touch gestures and have them call back to our code when gestures are detected. And because both the recognizers and the onscreen views are concerned with how much movement or scaling is indicated by a gesture, it works well to connect the two by means of affine transforms, which cleanly represent translation, rotation, scaling, and combinations thereof.

Armed with this knowledge, we can bring new touch handling features to scenes throughout our app. It will also be useful if we ever need to create our

own custom views, since a view is basically a combination of appearance and interactivity, meaning that a custom view just needs to handle custom drawing and custom event-handling. And we just saw how to do the second of those things.

3D Touch on iPhone 6s and 6s Plus

The new iPhone 6s and 6s Plus introduce a new kind of gesture, *3D Touch*, which is a touch that is sensitive to how much force the user is applying. In other words, it can tell the difference between "soft" and "hard" presses.

Apple suggests developers use 3D Touch for "peek" and "pop" gestures, which preview an item's contents without fully opening it. For example, we could add a hard-press gesture to user icons on the table of tweets, so we could pop up a little preview of a user's info without having to drill through two scenes to the user's detail scene.

We've chosen not to create an example for 3D Touch, because the support in iOS 9 is pretty limited so far. In particular, it is not supported in the iOS Simulator, so the only way to try it out is to actually get one of the new iPhone models. Still, it's worth looking at how it works.

None of the gesture recognizers know anything about 3D Touch. Instead, the only access we have is through the UITouch objects delivered to touchesBegan(), touchesMoved(), and touchesEnded(), the low-level methods we dismissed at the beginning of the chapter as "a pain in the butt."

To detect these touches, we would need to subclass UIView, and check its traitCollection for a trait called forceTouchCapabililty (notice that the APIs use the term "force touch" rather than the marketing name "3D Touch"). If force touch is available, an override of touchesBegan() could go over the Set of UITouches it receives and measure their force property. This value indicates how hard the touch was, from 1.0 for a "normal" touch up to a predefined maximumPossibleForce.

If the code determines the force is strong enough, it should then take some appropriate action, like showing a menu. However, good MVC says that kind of application logic doesn't go in the view, but rather in a controller. So we'd need a way to have a view controller handle the force touch event, like by having the view call back to the controller (the familiar delegate pattern), or having the controller give the view a closure to run whenever it gets a force touch.

Maybe iOS 10 will have gesture recognizers that provide the force of their touches. For now, handling 3D Touch is possible but kind of a hassle.

CHAPTER 14

Viewing and Editing Photos

People use mobile devices to take pictures and share them with their friends. A lot. No good Twitter app would be complete without this functionality.

Fortunately for us, the iOS SDK offers access to the user's photo library, meaning we can get pictures taken with the Camera application, as well as add new photos to the library. In addition, the Core Image framework gives us powerful tools to edit the contents of images, so we can improve photos long after they've been taken.

PhotoKit is a pair of frameworks introduced in iOS 8: *Photos* and *Photos UI*. Photos is the framework that allows us to access photos and videos from the photo library. Photos UI is a paired framework that allows us to create photo-editing app extensions (something we'll talk about in the next chapter). This allows you to store all of your neat photo-editing effects on your photos in your photo library instead of having them trapped in the application you created them with. If you create a really cool photo in one application, you can now access it with another. This wasn't possible before.

It is now possible to do anything from simply sharing a photo in a tweet—which is what we will be doing in this chapter—to creating a fully comprehensive photo-editing application on the level of Adobe Photoshop.

It has never been easier to customize your photos on the iPhone. We are just going to scratch the surface of all the awesome things that Apple gives you to express yourself and capture life's moments.

Photo Assets and PHAsset Class

Photos and videos are, at their base level, model objects. Think back to our old friend, the Model-View-Controller, introduced back in *Model-View-Controller,* on page 121. A well-designed model object should be a reusable piece of information that can be accessed from many different controller objects without any dependencies tying it to one specific application or project.

Model objects contain data, and they provide access to and implement logic on data. Photos and videos are just sets of data that we store on our phone that can be accessed and modified by many different applications. Our photo model objects are also read-only and thread-safe, so no worrying about another application coming in and changing our photos out from under us.

Every photo and video we use is also considered an asset. Individual assets belong to collections. These are the building blocks of how our photographs are organized; it's important to remember this structure when working with PhotoKit.

The *PHAsset* class is the foundation of everything we will be doing this chapter. PHAsset encompasses not just photos but videos as well. This class stores the asset's media type, creation date, location, and whether it has been tagged as a favorite. All of these properties give you a tremendous amount of control over filtering out which specific photos you would like to use.

For example, say you take a family vacation to Disney World every year. You want to find a specific picture in your photo library, but you aren't sure which trip it was that you took the picture on. You can filter the photos by location and whether they're tagged as a favorite to narrow down which photo it might be. If you know which trip it was on, you can filter them down further by creation date.

Fetching Our Assets

We know that we want to find a photo from our library and bring it into our project. Like similar functions in iOS, this is referred to as "fetching." The class we use to do this is *PHFetchResult*, which has a suite of class methods to fetch our photos from the photo library.

Adding a Camera Button

First we set up our project to allow our user to access this functionality. We have some room in the top-left corner of our root view controller, so let's set up our functionality there.

Go to the Object library and choose a new Bar Button item to add to the storyboard. Locate the Tweets scene, the one with the table view, and add the button to the top left. Over in the Attributes Inspector, you will have the option from the drop-down menu to set the button to a camera icon.

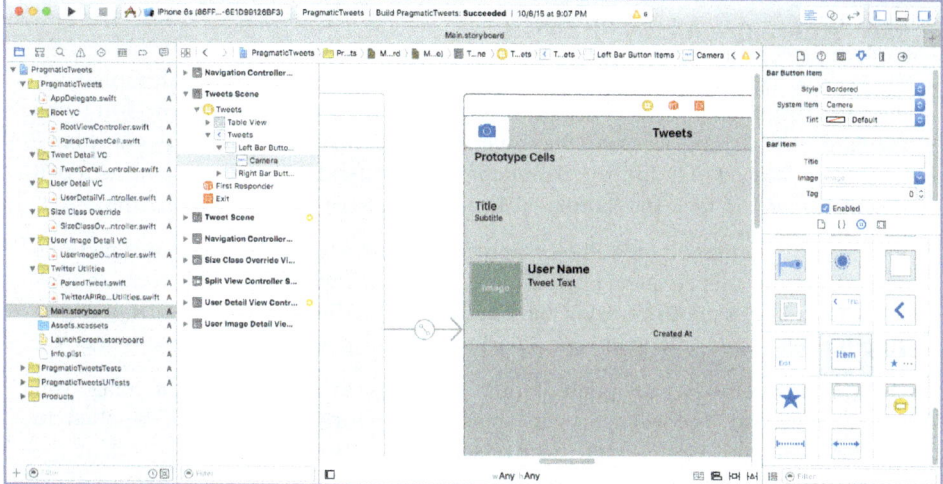

Open the Assistant Editor and connect the button to an IBAction in the RootViewController.swift to create a method that handles the button click.

photos/PragmaticTweets-14-1/PragmaticTweets/RootViewController.swift

```
@IBAction func handlePhotoButtonTapped(sender: UIBarButtonItem) {
}
```

One last thing we need to do in the root view controller before we move on is import the Photos framework. Scroll to the top of the file and add the following:

photos/PragmaticTweets-14-1/PragmaticTweets/RootViewController.swift

```
import Photos
```

Finding and Filtering Our Photos

As we mentioned earlier, there are many options for how we want to fetch our assets. We can filter them by type, collection, and whatever other filters/predicates we choose.

We just want to share photos with our Twitter followers, so let's go ahead and set up our fetch request to go and get access to our photos.

Think back to our Model-View-Controller. Our PHAsset fulfills our Model requirement. The View Controller will fulfill the "C" in "MVC."

Now we need a photo. Unfortunately, the Photos framework doesn't provide any sort of a user interface to display and choose photos from the library. We could do that ourselves by building something like a table view with thumbnail images and metadata fetched from the Photos framework. But let's keep it simple for now. In this example project, we are only going to retrieve the most

Hey, Where Are All My Photos?!

The iPhone Simulator in Xcode is a wonderful piece of software, but unfortunately it does have a few limitations. There are certain functions you can only perform using the hardware. Getting access to the camera is one of them. Your computer may have a camera attached to it, but the Simulator won't pretend that it's the same as a real iPhone camera. In fact, the Simulator doesn't even have the iOS Camera app.

Fortunately, the Simulator's Photos app comes with some built-in nature pictures you can use for this chapter. Furthermore, there are ways to add your own pictures to the Simulator's photo library. One functionality the Simulator has is the ability to surf the web. When you open your Safari app, you can search the web for images.

To save the photos to your photo library, simply press and hold on the image you wish to download. You will see a pop-up asking you if you want to save the photo to your photo library. Piece of cake, which is a lie.

And if you already have image files on your Mac, it's even easier: just drag and drop them to the iOS Simulator app while it's running, and they'll be added to the Simulator's photo library automatically.

recent photo taken. That will let us get our feet wet with the Photos framework without having to write a bunch of UI code that's not relevant to photos.

Navigate back to the handlePhotoButtonTapped method, and implement it like this:

photos/PragmaticTweets-14-1/PragmaticTweets/RootViewController.swift

```
Line 1  @IBAction func handlePhotoButtonTapped(sender: UIBarButtonItem) {
   -      let fetchOptions = PHFetchOptions()
   -      PHPhotoLibrary.requestAuthorization {
   -        (authorized: PHAuthorizationStatus) -> Void in
   5        if authorized == .Authorized {
   -          fetchOptions.sortDescriptors =
   -            [NSSortDescriptor (key:"creationDate", ascending:false)]
   -          let fetchResult = PHAsset.fetchAssetsWithMediaType(.Image,
   -            options: fetchOptions)
  10          if let firstPhoto = fetchResult.firstObject as? PHAsset {
   -            self.createTweetForAsset(firstPhoto)
   -          }
   -        }
   -      }
  15  }
```

Let's step through this code piece by piece:

1. On line 2 we need to create an instance of PHFetchOptions. We want to narrow down our search to only our most recent photo; therefore, we must figure out a way to tell the method exactly which photo we want it to return.

2. Lines 3–14 request access to the photo library from the user. The photo library requires that the user specifically authorize our Pragmatic Tweets app to access the photo library. If the user does not authorize this, the photos functionality will not work. Users can go to their Settings to authorize it later if they accidentally denied access.

"PragmaticTweets" Would Like to Access Your Photos

Don't Allow   OK

This is a naturally asynchronous action; like requesting access to the Twitter account, we don't know how long it will take the user to respond to our request. So requestAuthorization() takes a closure that will be called when the PHAuthorizationStatus is determined. Our closure runs from lines 4–14.

3. When we're ready to fetch the assets—and assuming we are authorized to do so—we will be able to request results be sorted in a given order. The fetchAssetsWithMediaType() method takes an array of NSSortDescriptors, which we prepare on lines 6–7. Since we want to retrieve our most recent photo, we need to make sure our photos are ordered chronologically. The creationDate descriptor starts with the earliest date first, so we need to specify that we want descending order. We found the creationDate descriptor in the documentation for PHFetchOptions. You can explore there to see how else you can sort your photos.

4. We make our call to fetchAssetsWithMediaType() on lines 8–9, passing in the PHAssetMediaType to look for (Images in our case), and the fetchOptions, which include our sort descriptors.

5. Finally, we check the result on lines 10–11 to make sure that there is, in fact, a most recent photo in the library. If there is, we are going to create a tweet from that photo. This calls a createTweetForAsset() method that we will be creating next.

Up next, we will need to implement our createTweetForAsset() convenience method to generate a tweet that includes our photo. Add the following code underneath our handlePhotoButtonTapped() method:

photos/PragmaticTweets-14-1/PragmaticTweets/RootViewController.swift

```
Line 1  func createTweetForAsset(asset: PHAsset) {
   -      let requestOptions = PHImageRequestOptions()
   -      requestOptions.synchronous = true
   -      PHImageManager.defaultManager().requestImageForAsset(asset,
   5        targetSize: CGSize(width: 640.0, height: 480.0),
   -        contentMode: .AspectFit,
   -        options: requestOptions,
```

```
-        resultHandler: {(image: UIImage?,
-          info: [NSObject : AnyObject]?) -> Void in
10        if let image = image
-          where SLComposeViewController.isAvailableForServiceType(
-            SLServiceTypeTwitter) {
-              let tweetVC = SLComposeViewController(forServiceType:
-                SLServiceTypeTwitter)
15              tweetVC.setInitialText("Here's a photo I tweeted. #pragsios9")
-              tweetVC.addImage(image)
-              dispatch_async(dispatch_get_main_queue(), { () -> Void in
-                self.presentViewController(tweetVC, animated: true,
-                  completion: nil)
20            })
-          }
-        })
-      }
```

1. We start on line 2 by creating a PHImageRequestOptions instance. This will be used in a few lines by requestImageForAsset(), which takes this options object as a parameter. On line 3, we set the synchronous option to true. We want to make sure that our tweet does not get sent without its photo attached, so we are specifically telling the application to wait until it has the photo.

2. The requestImageForAsset() method will give us a UIImage for our photo library PHAsset, and takes a few parameters to specify the image we get back. On line 5, we set the size of our photo to tweet. We could just say we want the photo to be the base size of the photo in our library, but the image might be 4,000 pixels wide, which would take a really long time to upload and probably be overkill for a simple tweet.

3. The contentMode parameter lets us tell the Photos framework what to do if the photo's aspect ratio doesn't match the size we just provided. On line 6, we use AspectFit to specify that we want to scale our photo to stay proportional and fit its largest dimension into the returned image. If we specified AspectFill, it would fit the entire size but possibly sacrifice pixels to do so.

4. requestImageForAsset() is another asynchronous method, so it lets us use a closure (lines 8–22) to provide the code that will run when the image is done being prepared. We start with an if let where to see that we got a non-nil image (line 10) and that tweeting is available (lines 11–12).

After these checks, we prepare an SLComposeViewController and autopopulate its default text. This is just like what we did so many chapters ago when we prepared our first tweet!

5. An SLComposeViewController can also take an image argument, and that's what we've done all this work to prepare. On line 16, we finally get to set the image on the compose view controller.

6. Finally, we can present the SLComposeViewController, so the user can review the photo and the default text, and send the tweet. Lines 17–20 wrap this with a dispatch_async() that puts it on main queue, since we have no idea what queue is running the closure that is providing us with the image.

7. We are now calling our tweet view controller. We are passing our customized tweet into the method and sending it out into the world.

Run the app, tap the photo button, and see the most recent photo attached to the tweet composer. Send the tweet and after a reload, you'll be able to see it in your timeline.

Core Image

Now that we have our photos posting properly to Twitter, wouldn't it be fun to jazz them up a little? There are all kinds of apps out on the market to apply filters to your photos, and it would be really cool if we could do that, too. Well, guess what, we can!

Core Image is a framework that was introduced in iOS 5, but it existed in Mac OS X before that. Core Image contains over a hundred photo filters —objects that can manipulate image data—for you to use and incorporate into your projects. For iOS 9, Apple has rewritten both the iOS and OS X version of Core Image to share a common code base, so nearly all the Apple-provided filters are now available for both platforms. And, if that's not enough, it's also possible to write your own image filters.

Important Core Image Classes

Core Image is made up of a small number of classes that create the basis of the functionality of the framework. These classes are like the Lego blocks you use to build your Core Image applications.

The first class we are going to explore is *CIImage.* CIImage does not contain any image data. Rather, it contains a set of instructions to be sent to the CIContext about how you plan to modify the components you are applying to an image. If we took a source image and applied two filters to it, the CIImage would basically just contain pointers to the source image data and the filters to be applied.

The next class you need to know about for Core Image is the *CIFilter* class. Filters, as we've discussed, are objects that operate on images and produce a changed version of their contents. A CIFilter contains a dictionary that holds all of the attributes for performing its work. For example, if you had a filter that adjusted RGBA color values, your CIFilter instance would hold the values for each of these attributes.

The final class we are going to talk about is the *CIContext* class. Most of the frameworks in iOS that do drawing utilize contexts. If you were to move on from here and work with Core Animation or OpenGL, you would encounter their own flavors of context. A context is basically just the thing that the drawing is being performed on. Since we want to draw the photo as altered by the filter, we need a place to do that, and that place is the context.

Any time we want to add a filter to an image, we will go through the following steps:

1. Create a CIImage object. We can do this several different ways. We can instantiate our CIImage by URL reference, by loading image data directly, or receiving our image data from a Core Video pixel buffer.

2. Create a CIContext to output your CIImage to. CIContext objects are buffers and should be reused, so you don't need to create a context for every single thing you are doing.

3. Create a CIFilter instance to apply to your image. This is the step where you will set all of the properties, the number of which will vary based on which filter you are using.

4. Receive the filter output. This is the end of the processing pipeline where you will take possession of your shiny new filtered image.

Spiffy! We have a brand-new image. Wait, what do we do with it? An image isn't like a car coming off the assembly line. We can't touch, hold, or feel it. How do we retain this image after it pops off the conveyor belt?

There are several ways of doing this, but since we already know that we are not working on a video or exporting this to an OpenGL project, the best way for us to take possession of our filtered image is to use CIContext's createCGImage(fromRect:). We could also use UIImage's imageWithCIImage(), which is slightly easier, but it performs badly. It's important to consider the most efficient way of doing something, not just the easiest way.

Filters and Filter Documentation

So far we have been talking about all of these awesome filters that exist on iOS, but we haven't actually seen any of them yet. It's time to dig into what some of these filters are and what they do.

There are well over a hundred filters, but they are broken down into a few categories. Here are some of the more useful ones:

- Blurs: These are the famous (or infamous, depending which way you look at it) effects that were utilized in the iOS 7 design aesthetic but were not implemented easily until iOS 8. Oops.

- Color Adjustments and Effects: These filters allow you to adjust your colors in a controlled way to either correct your projects or let you do complex effects with color.

- Compositing: If you have not played with compositing blend modes in either programming or in Photoshop, you are in for some fun. These are powerful filters that allow you to do some complex effects. One of the authors used these blend modes to add color and complex shading to a black-and-white manga scan by adding a layer to hold the color and having an underlying layer contain the black-and-white drawings, which was really cool.

A complete list of these filters is available in the Core Image Filter Reference in the Xcode documentation. If you are interested in seeing the kind of code associated with how these effects were created, check out *GPUImage*.[1] GPUImage is an open source framework for image processing that contains many similar filters to the ones used in Core Image. The difference is that you can look at how the shaders were written to get an idea of how that awesome effect you are using was put together so that you can learn how to modify it and roll

---

1.   https://github.com/BradLarson/GPUImage/

your own. Writing shaders is beyond the scope of this book, but if you are interested in writing shaders, this is an invaluable resource.

Adding a Filter to Our Photos

All right, enough talk. Let's go ahead and add our filter to our project.

We need to import the framework we are using. Go to the top of the root view controller and import the Core Image framework:

photos/PragmaticTweets-14-2/PragmaticTweets/RootViewController.swift
```
import CoreImage
```

We need to modify our closure within createTweetForAsset(). Replace the resultHandler closure with the following:

photos/PragmaticTweets-14-2/PragmaticTweets/RootViewController.swift
```
Line 1    if let image = image, var ciImage = CIImage (image: image)
   -         where SLComposeViewController.isAvailableForServiceType(
   -           SLServiceTypeTwitter) {
   -             ciImage = ciImage.imageByApplyingFilter("CIPixellate",
   5               withInputParameters: ["inputScale" : 25.0])
   -             let ciContext = CIContext(options: nil)
   -             let cgImage = ciContext.createCGImage(ciImage,
   -               fromRect: ciImage.extent)
   -             let tweetImage = UIImage(CGImage: cgImage)
  10             let tweetVC = SLComposeViewController(forServiceType:
   -               SLServiceTypeTwitter)
   -             tweetVC.setInitialText("Here's a photo I tweeted. #pragsios9")
   -             tweetVC.addImage(tweetImage)
   -             dispatch_async(dispatch_get_main_queue(), { () -> Void in
  15               self.presentViewController(tweetVC, animated: true,
   -                 completion: nil)
   -             })
   -         }
   - })
```

1. We need to start with a CIImage that's based on the UIImage we received from the Photos framework before. The CIImage initializer that takes a UIImage is failable, meaning it could give us back nil, so we'll add it to the if let on line 1. We'll be using this to gather the pieces to apply our filter to our photo.

2. Lines 4–5 create and apply our filter. For this example, we chose the easy-to-use (and easy-to-see!) CIPixellate, but there are over a hundred filters to choose from. If you want to apply a different filter, feel free to do so; just look it up in the Core Image Programming Guide, and replace its string name and its required parameters in the imageByApplyingFilter() call.

3. On line 6, we need to create a CIContext. Without a context, we won't be able to draw anything to our screen because our CIImage doesn't actually contain any pixels. It is a set of instructions to be passed to our CIContext, and if we don't have one, our work will go nowhere.

4. A CIContext can't create a UIImage directly, but it can provide its lower-level bitmap equivalent, the CGImage, on lines 7–8. From that, line 9 can easily create a UIImage, tweetImage.

Finally, we mustn't forget to have the SLComposeViewController use our new tweet-Image. Update the call to addImage() like this:

```
tweetVC.addImage(tweetImage)
```

Run your application and try posting another photo. The photo you see should have the pixelation filter applied to it.

What We've Learned

With the combined power of PhotoKit and Core Image, we have the ability to access the user's entire photo library in our app and manipulate each photo with more than a hundred powerful techniques. We don't have time to write our own mobile Photoshop replacement, but don't think the idea hasn't occurred to us. With powerful frameworks like these, it's entirely doable.

Next, we're going to move beyond the confines of our app and see how we can share our capabilities with other apps and the system as a whole.

Part IV

Beyond the App

CHAPTER 15

Interacting with iOS and Other Apps

We've been working to make our Twitter app better and better, gradually building out its capabilities and learning new skills along the way. Our users are going to be happy with how they can see their timeline, drill down into details, and send new tweets.

However, ours is just one of many apps on the user's device. It will come and go as needed, with the typical user spending only a minute or less in our app, or any other. That's the nature of apps on mobile devices: App A does Thing A, App B does Thing B, and never the twain shall meet. But as iOS has evolved over the years, it has accumulated more and more ways in which apps can work together to increase their mutual usefulness. Apps have gained the ability to launch one another and exchange data and documents, albeit under significant restrictions. It's even possible to offer part of our application for direct use inside other applications.

In this chapter, we're going to take advantage of these opportunities, and extend the functionality of our app into other apps the user might be using. In the process, we'll also get a feel for the life cycle by which apps are launched, killed, and launched anew.

The App Life Cycle

If someone asked us to point to the first line of our app, what would we say? Unlike old C programs—or even the Objective-C that we used prior to iOS 8—there's no command-line friendly main() function that kicks off our execution. If we think back to where started, we had just two classes: AppDelegate and ViewController, along with Main.storyboard. Clearly, we're not driving this car; we're a passenger. So let's start by getting a sense of where iOS is taking us when our app starts up and when we get an opportunity to tell the driver where we're going.

For a Swift app, iOS creates a UIApplication object to set up the app's runtime environment: its use of the display, its ability to handle touches and rotation events, and so forth. This object is also how we can interact with the rest of the iOS system, as we'll see shortly. The UIApplication has a windows array, typically one per screen, and there's only one screen unless we're hooked up with a video output cable or AirPlay. Each window has a rootViewController. And that's where the storyboard comes in: the application creates an instance of the view controller in the storyboard's initial scene, and puts its view into the window.

UIApplication can also have a UIApplicationDelegate object, which is informed of major life-cycle events that affect the app. This is the AppDelegate class that Xcode gave us to start with. When all the app setup is done, the application(didFinish-LaunchingWithOptions:) method gets called. From our point of view, this is where the app "starts," although a bunch of stuff has already been done for us by this point. Some apps will use this callback to set up stuff that needs to be working immediately, or objects that will live for the entire life of the app, like data stores.

Of course, at some point, users will leave our app by pressing the home button, taking a phone call, accepting a notification from another app, and so on. That's not the end for us; they might come back. UIApplicationDelegate tells us about these actions, with methods like applicationDidEnterBackground(), applicationWil-lEnterForeground(), and so on. We used applicationWillEnterForeground() on a lark back in *Trying Out Our Function*, on page 174, when we made a quick Twitter call every time our app was foregrounded. There are also the related methods applicationWillResignActive() and applicationDidBecomeActive() that tell us we've been suspended so users can deal with an interruption like an alert from an incoming phone call or SMS message. If they take the call or switch to the Messages app, we'll be backgrounded, but if they choose to ignore it, we'll become active again.

If our app is backgrounded long enough, it will eventually be terminated, so if our app needed to save data for the next time it's launched, going to the background is the right time to do that work. If the user force-quits us in the foreground, the app delegate finds out by way of a different method: application-WillTerminate().

Opening via URLs

The application and its delegate also have methods that relate to how our app interacts with the rest of the system. For example, if we receive a *push notification* from Apple's push notification service—something we'd have to set up on a server, and which is beyond the scope of this book—we would get it in the app delegate callback application(didReceiveRemoteNotification:fetchCompletion-Handler:).

One way we can work directly with other applications on the device is found in a rather unusual place: URLs. UIApplication offers the method openURL:(), which will launch other applications and have them deal with the NSURL. Most web page URLs, with schemes http or https, will open Safari. For example, we can background ourselves and send Safari to this book's home page with a one-line call:

```
UIApplication.sharedApplication().openURL(
  NSURL(string: "https://pragprog.com/book/adios3/ios-9-sdk-development"))
```

Not all URLs go to Safari. If the host is www.youtube.com, the YouTube app will open instead, if present. phobos.apple.com iTunes Store URLs will open the iTunes app. And other URL schemes can be used to launch default system apps—for example, mailto:, facetime:, and tel: open the Mail, FaceTime, and Phone apps, respectively. Check out the Apple URL Scheme Reference in the Xcode documentation for the exact syntax and more information.

What's really cool is that third-party applications can also participate in this system. Any app can create a new URL scheme that it handles, and then other apps that open this URL will launch that app. Since our app does so much with Twitter, let's offer up our services to other apps.

Declaring a URL Scheme

We start our URL support by just picking a name. It needs to be plausibly unique, since Apple does *nothing* to police URL schemes. If every Twitter app declares that it will open URLs with the scheme twitter:, who knows which one will launch? Instead, let's go with pragtweets:.

Let's think about what service makes sense to offer other applications. We will receive a full URL from the caller, so we could design an API kind of like REST endpoints, with different URL paths leading to different features within our app. We'll only implement one for now, but we could keep adding to it later by just looking for different strings in the URL.

The user may already have an app to show recent tweets (or see them in Notification Center), so let's choose something unique that we offer. For this example, we'll let a URL take us straight to the user detail screen. If we get a URL of the form pragtweets://host/user?screenname=name, we'll go right to the UserDetailViewController, as if we had drilled down on one of name's tweets.

At the very top of the File Navigator, click on the top-level PragmaticTweets project icon, and when the project settings come up in the Content View, make sure the selected target is the PragmaticTweets app (as opposed to the PragmaticTweetsTests target). This editor lets us configure how the build process and the resulting app work: what versions of iOS we deploy to, whether we have capabilities like iCloud or in-app purchase, which source files get built and how, and so on.

The Info tab has metadata for our app such as its display name, what features must be present on a device for it to work, and what kinds of documents it accepts or produces. At the bottom of this view, there's a URL Types section. Expand the disclosure triangle, and then press the plus (+) button to show the settings for a new URL type, seen in the following figure.

The important entry here is the URL Schemes text field, which takes a comma-separated list of schemes we accept. Enter pragtweets here, without the trailing colon character (:). The identifier should be a reverse-DNS style unique identifier, like com.pragprog.yourhandle.pragmatictweets, and the Role should be None, so that we aren't making any promises about what we do with the URL (the Viewer and Editor values are more appropriate for dealing with documents passed between apps).

After we run this app once, the system will know to send any URL with the scheme pragtweets: to our app. Now we need to actually do something with this URL when it arrives.

Creating a New Scene

When our app gets opened via a properly formatted URL, we want to go directly to the UserDetailViewController scene, bypassing the two scenes before it (the list of tweets and the tweet detail). This is possible because all we have to give the user detail scene is the screenName we want to view; it will get everything else it needs via its own TwitterAPIRequest.

We *could* create a new segue from the split view directly to the user detail scene. This would be totally legal. But there's a problem: the Done button is

Universal Links in iOS 9

iOS 9 introduces a much more advanced form of linking into apps, called *universal links*. These links offer a particularly nice user experience, since they will go directly into an app if the app is installed and to a specified website if not. If tapped in an app other than Safari, like the case where a link is in an email message, they can open the target app without going through Safari as an intermediate step.

Universal links are well beyond the scope of this book, as they require uploading a custom JSON file to your website at a specific https: path, and making a number of declarations in your app's metadata prior to submitting to the App Store. But all this work does have another nice benefit: since the links are to your website instead of being just arbitrarily chosen strings, there's no risk of multiple apps claiming the same link.

set to unwind to the tweet detail scene, but in the case where we come straight from the split view scene, there won't be a previous tweet detail scene, and that will produce an error.

We have a couple of options. We could nuke the exit segue and instead set up a button handler that calls UIViewController's dismissModalViewController() method. This would work for both cases, but it assumes we always come in via a modal segue.

The option we'll use is to just create another user detail scene, reachable only from the first scene and used only for this URL handler. It makes our storyboard a little bigger, but it lets us customize too—an acceptable trade-off.

In Main.storyboard, select the yellow ball icon for the User scene and do a copy-and-paste (⌘C, then ⌘V). The newly pasted instance will be placed exactly atop the old one. In the layout area, drag this scene by its title bar and notice that it doesn't have any segues associated with it. Move it closer to the beginning of the storyboard (perhaps under the initial view controller), and then use the name field next to its view controller icon in the scene list to give it a unique name to keep things straight (like User Detail from URL Scene).

Control-click on the Size Class Override View Controller at the beginning of the storyboard to see its connections. Under Triggered Segues, drag from the Manual connection ball down to the new user detail scene. Upon dropping, choose the Present Modally segue type. This is shown in the figure on page 256.

We're going to need to run this segue manually when the URL comes in, which means we'll need an identifier string. Select the segue, bring up the Attributes Inspector, and set the identifier to ShowUserFromURLSegue.

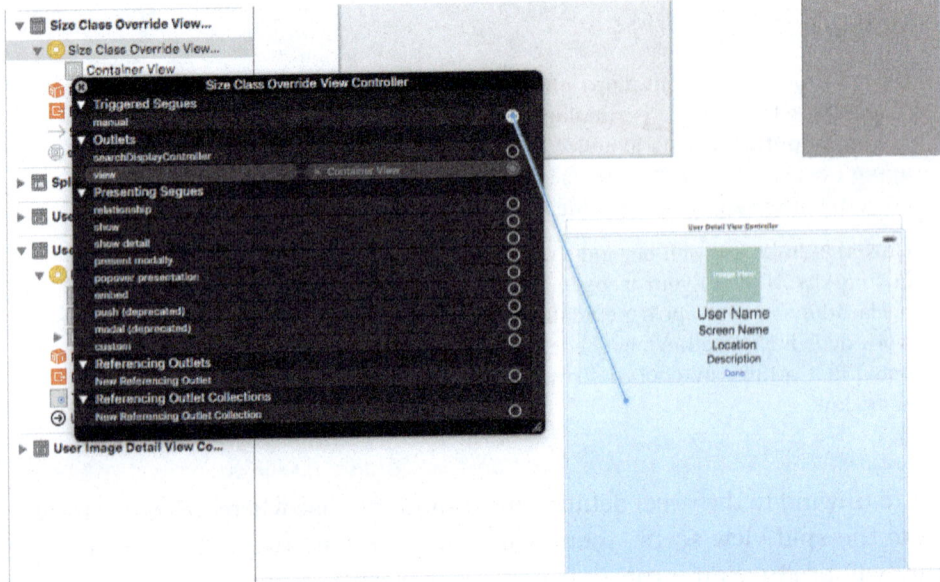

Handling the Open URL Callback

Now we're ready to call this segue when our app is launched from a URL. When that happens, our AppDelegate will receive a callback to the method application(openURL:options:). This method returns a Bool indicating whether it handled the URL successfully, so we should only return true if we can success-fully pick out a screenname.

To do that, we're going to rely on the NSURL class. It has several methods that break down a URL into its various parts: scheme(), path(), query(), and so on. We'll take the segue if the path is /user and the query is of the form screen-name=foo.

```
system/PragmaticTweets-15-1/PragmaticTweets/AppDelegate.swift
```

```
Line 1  func application(application : UIApplication, openURL url: NSURL,
   -      options: [String : AnyObject]) -> Bool {
   -        var showedUserDetail = false
   -        guard let query = url.query where url.path == "/user" else {
   5          return false
   -        }
   -        let components = query.componentsSeparatedByString("=")
   -        if components.count > 1 &&
   -          components[0] == "screenname" {
  10          if let sizeClassVC = self.window?.rootViewController
   -            as? SizeClassOverrideViewController {
   -              sizeClassVC.performSegueWithIdentifier("ShowUserFromURLSegue",
   -                sender: self)
```

```
                      showedUserDetail = true
15          }
       }
       return showedUserDetail
 - }
```

We start on line 3 with a showedUserDetail Boolean that will become true only if we kick off the segue (way inside the ifs, on line 14). Then on line 4, we use a guard let where to make sure url.query is non-nil and that the URL's path is user.

Once we have the query part of the URL, we can split apart the name and value on line 7 with componentsSeparatedByString(). That lets lines 8–9 verify that there are two components, and the first is screenname. Note that we're kind of cheating because there is only one key-value pair; the more general case of *?key1=value1&key2=value2&...* would take a lot more work to pick apart.

If we made it this far, then our URL is good. Lines 10–11 ask for our window's rootViewController as our SizeClassOverrideViewController class, the first scene in the storyboard. If that cast works, then we can tell the view controller to manually perform the ShowUserFromURLSegue segue, on lines 12–13.

At the very end, on line 17 we return a Bool to indicate whether we set showe-dUserDetail to true. This is to uphold the contract established in the docs for the application(openURL:options:), which expects us to return true or false to indicate whether we handled the URL. For us, that's determined by whether we made it all the way to performing the segue.

We now have enough done to try it out. Run the app, and then in the Simulator, use Hardware > Home (⇧⌘H) to background our app. Open up Safari and enter a URL like pragtweets://localhost/user?screenname=pragprog (the hostname is ignored, so anything will work there). Press Return or click Go and it should show an alert as shown in the figure, asking if you want to open the page in PragmaticTweets. Click Open.

This opens our app and goes immediately to the user detail scene. None of the fields are filled in yet because we haven't sent the values to that view controller. Let's take care of that.

Our AppDelegate can't see the UserDetailViewController when it kicks off the segue. But the first scene will get a look at it, in prepareForSegue(). That scene will need to know about the screen name to show, so switch to SizeClassOverrideViewController.swift and add a screenNameForOpenURL property:

```
system/PragmaticTweets-15-1/PragmaticTweets/SizeClassOverrideViewController.swift
var screenNameForOpenURL: String?
```

This class already has a prepareForSegue() method, to deal with the embed-SplitViewSegue at startup, so just add an else if to handle the ShowUserFromURLSegue:

```
system/PragmaticTweets-15-1/PragmaticTweets/SizeClassOverrideViewController.swift
override func prepareForSegue(segue: UIStoryboardSegue, sender: AnyObject?) {
  if segue.identifier == "embedSplitViewSegue" {
    embeddedSplitVC = segue.destinationViewController
      as! UISplitViewController
  } else if segue.identifier == "ShowUserFromURLSegue" {
    if let userDetailVC = segue.destinationViewController
      as? UserDetailViewController {
        userDetailVC.screenName = screenNameForOpenURL
    }
  }
}
```

Now that this view controller is ready for the segue, go back to AppDelegate.swift and, on a new line right before we performSegueWithIdentifier(), send the screen name to the view controller that needs it.

```
system/PragmaticTweets-15-1/PragmaticTweets/AppDelegate.swift
sizeClassVC.screenNameForOpenURL = components[1]
```

Run again, switch to Safari, open the pragtweets: URL, and this will show the user detail scene with the real name, description, and avatar image.

The last thing we have to do is to fix the Done button, which still thinks it can unwind to the tweet detail scene (since that's what was in the scene we copied over). First, in SizeClassOverrideViewController.swift, create an unwind method that we can go back to:

```
system/PragmaticTweets-15-1/PragmaticTweets/SizeClassOverrideViewController.swift
@IBAction func unwindToSizeClassOverrideVC (segue: UIStoryboardSegue) {
}
```

Then, back in the storyboard, go to the new User Detail From URL scene and Control-click or right-click the Done button to show its connections (or bring up the Connections Inspector, ⌥⌘6). Use the x-button to delete any existing unwind segue, close the connections pop-up, and then Control-drag from the button to the orange Exit icon in the title bar atop the scene; when the list of unwind methods appears, choose unwindToSizeClassOverridingVC().

Run again, and open the user detail URL from Safari. Now, not only can we view the user details, but we can also use the Done button to return to the first scene of the app. Now not only is our app useful to our users, but it also offers other apps (or web pages in Safari) the ability to send users over to us with just a simple URL.

App Extensions

Using URLs to bring users into our app, and even to a specific feature, is a very handy feature. But it does mean leaving the app the user was in and coming over to ours. Throughout the history of iOS, each app has lived in its own *sandbox*, prohibited from directly interacting with other apps. Each app has its own section of the filesystem and can't see anything outside its folders. Each app runs in its own process and cannot share resources like frameworks or dynamic libraries. This can lead to a lot of duplication of effort across apps.

Recent versions of iOS have poked some holes in the walls between applications by allowing apps to create *app extensions*. From the user's point of view, extensions are packaged with an app and allow it to extend some of its functionality into other apps. From the developer's point of view, the extension is another target in the Xcode project, one that can share code and certain runtime resources.

iOS defines several *extension points*, which are different kinds of functionality that an app extension can provide, and a hook into that functionality via an API or some aspect of the user interface. In iOS 9, the following extension points are provided:

Extension Point	Description
Action	Manipulate content from the host app, such as translating text or grabbing contents from a web page
Audio Unit	Process audio in real time
Content Blocker	Block web content (such as ads) from being viewed in Safari
Custom Keyboard	Provide text input with custom keyboard input method
Document Provider	Access and manage a shared filesystem
Photo Editing	Edit a photo or video within the Photos app
Share	Share text, photos, or other content with others, like via a social network
Shared Links	Expose app content in Safari's "shared links" list
Spotlight Index	Expose app content to Spotlight, the system-wide search tool
Today	Provide "glanceable" content in Notification Center

In addition, Apple Watch apps use app extensions: a watchOS app target is just a storyboard for the user interface, and all the work of populating the UI (including "glances" and "complications") and communication back to the host iPhone app is done with extensions. To learn more about developing for Apple Watch, check out *Developing for Apple Watch, Second Edition.*[1]

In most cases, we develop an app extension as a view controller, which allows us to customize the view for our extension as well as put the control logic behind it. Extensions have a shorter life cycle than full apps; they're expected to be small and short-lived, since they come up only briefly in order to provide services to another app that's already running. They're also more limited in what they can do; extensions can't access the camera or microphone, and some have to ask permission to do things like access the network.

The idea of an extension is to offer something that our app can do, that would be useful to other applications. Our app knows a lot about getting data from Twitter, so maybe there's something we can do related to that.

Creating a Keyboard Extension

Have you ever wanted to type an email and use someone's Twitter handle but could not remember it exactly? Maybe you were on a forum and you wanted to praise that book by @RedQueenCoder and...wait, was it really @invalidname? (That can't be right, can it?)

Well, with our extension, we're going to offer a custom keyboard that is a table of all our user's Twitter friends. That way, when users are in this scenario, they can just switch to our keyboard, tap the name of their friend, and have that text inserted directly into the host application.

Start a keyboard extension by clicking on the project icon at the top of the file and choosing File > New > Target. This opens the Target Template sheet shown in the figure on page 261. From the list on the left, choose Application Extension, and on the right, choose the Custom Keyboard template and click Next. On the following page, name the product PragmaticTweepsKeyboard, and ensure the language is Swift.

Once the new target is created, Xcode will ask if we want to "activate" the PragmaticTweepsKeyboard scheme. This means that the Build (⌘B) and Run (⌘R) commands will build and run the keyboard code, not the main app. That's what we want to do for now. Later, when we're done with the extension and ready to turn our attention back to coding and debugging the main app,

---

1.   https://pragprog.com/book/jkwatch2/developing-for-apple-watch-second-edition

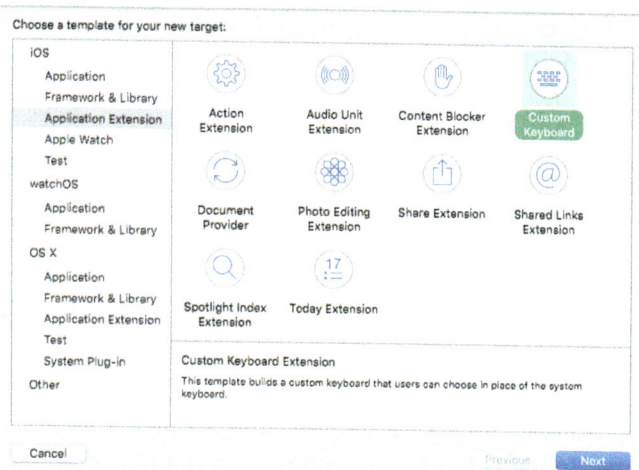

we can do that by choosing PragmaticTweets in the scheme selector, next to the stop button on the toolbar.

The template creates a group called PragmaticTweepsKeyboard that contains a single KeyboardViewController.swift file, and a Supporting Files group that has a file called Info.plist. This target is actually runnable as is. Try it. A sheet will slide down asking which app we want to run, listing the default apps on the Simulator, as well as our own Pragmatic Tweets. Safari is a good choice, since it has a text field that's easy to get to.

Once Safari runs, the custom keyboard will now be available, but we have to explicitly ask for it. Switch to the Settings app in the Simulator and navigate to General > Keyboards > Add New Keyboard. PragmaticTweets will now be listed as one of our choices, as you can see in the figure.

Click on PragmaticTweets to add its keyboard. Switch back to Safari, and click in the address bar to show the default keyboard (if the keyboard doesn't show at all, check the Hardware > Keyboard menu, and select Toggle Software Keyboard if necessary). Next to the spacebar, there will be a globe icon; this is the button that switches between keyboards when more than one is available, either through internationalization settings or custom keyboards like ours. Click the globe to cycle through keyboards. Eventually, one of them will be a gray space that just says Next Keyboard. This is our keyboard, and it's providing the one thing all keyboards *must* offer: a button to advance to the next keyboard. It may not be very interesting, but it's a start!

Creating an App Extension Storyboard

In Xcode, click Stop and switch over to KeyboardViewController.swift. Curiously, Xcode's template for keyboard extensions builds the user interface with code, in viewDidLoad(). It adds the Next Keyboard button, and connects it to a method called advanceToNextInputMode(). That's something it inherits from its superclass, UIInputViewController, and we'll have to remember to implement that ourselves.

Building our UI in code isn't something we've done before, and isn't necessarily a good idea in most cases, so let's give ourselves the ability to lay out our keyboard with a storyboard instead.

We don't add our UI as a scene to Main.storyboard, since that's part of the main app and won't be available to our extension. Instead, we need a new storyboard. Select the PragmaticTweepsKeyboard group, and choose File > New > File. When the template chooser comes up, select the iOS User Interface group and the Storyboard template, as shown in the following figure. Name the file PragmaticTweepsKeyboard.storyboard, and in the list of targets in this dialog, make sure that the PragmaticTweepsKeyboard is checked and PragmaticTweeps is not; this will include the storyboard in the keyboard extension, but not in the main app (which doesn't know anything about it).

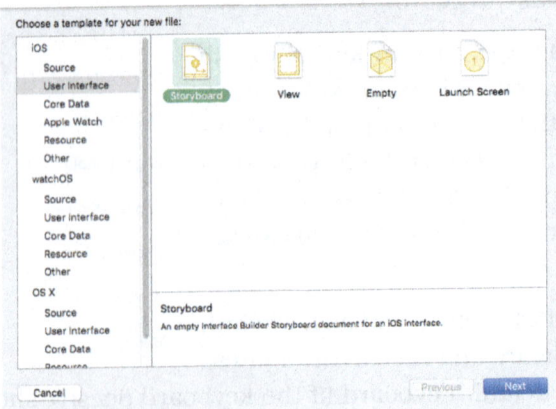

The new storyboard is completely empty. Drag in a view controller to create a new scene, and in its Attributes Inspector (⌥⌘4), choose Is Initial View Controller.

This scene looks like any other scene, and that's actually a problem. Our usual storyboard scenes take up a whole screen, but a keyboard should only fill part of the screen. We're going to do some custom sizing to make things fit. At the top of the view controller's Attributes Inspector, change Size to Freeform, and in the Size Inspector (⌥⌘5), change the height to 204. This doesn't lock us into that height; we'll have to set that with our views' autolayout constraints. What this setting does give us is a more realistic sense of our custom keyboard's size.

We'll keep the UI simple but still distinct so users know it's a custom keyboard. Drag a Navigation bar from the Object library (^⌥⌘3) to the top of the view, and use the Pin button to set its height to 44, its top constraint to 0 and its left and right to 0, with the Margins check box deselected; this lets us stretch all the way to the side of the screen. Edit the title to say Pragmatic Tweeps, and add a bar button item on the right. The button will be our Next Keyboard button; you can change the text to Next, or paste in a globe emoji if you want to get fancy (Xcode makes this easy with the menu command Edit > Emoji and Symbols).

Immediately below the Navigation bar, drop in a table, pinning its top constraint to 0 points from the navigation bar, and its leading and trailing constraints to 0 points from the superview with margins off. That leaves 160 points vertically in our current simulated size for the table, although the system will decide how much space to give the table, so it may need to grow or shrink as needed. Good thing that tables are good at that.

Finally, custom keyboards usually use different color schemes to set themselves off from the app content. A simple way to do this is to play with the tint and the title color of the Navigation bar in its Attributes Inspector. In the following figure, we've used the slate gray color scheme of the http://pragprog.com home page banner.

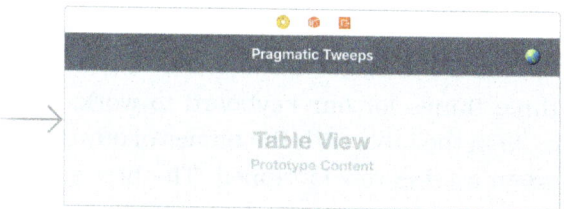

Now we have to get the keyboard extension to use the storyboard instead of building the UI in code. Under PragmaticTweepsKeyboard > Supporting Files, open Info.plist, which is a special kind of XML file called a *property list*. This file opens with the custom editor seen in the following figure. Use the disclosure triangle to expand the NSExtension group, select it, and use the minus (-) button to remove the NSExtensionPrincipalClass line. This entry described which class provided the keyboard, and implied we would build our UI in code.

Instead of a main class, we need an approach to let us supply a storyboard, so the extension will know to load the keyboard from the storyboard's initial scene. We do that by using the plus (+) button to add a new node called NSExtensionMainStoryboard (making sure it's a child of NSExtension), setting its type to String, and providing the value PragmaticTweepsKeyboard, which is the name of the .storyboard file we created earlier.

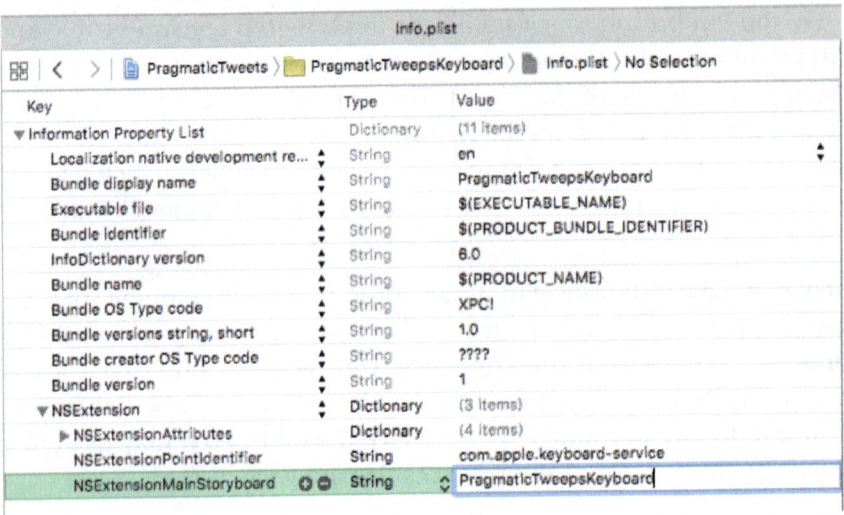

Once we've added the keyboard, go back to Safari and cycle through keyboards with the globe key. We'll be able to see our keyboard from its customized Navigation bar. It doesn't do anything yet...in fact, we're trapped because the Next Keyboard button doesn't do anything. Still, we're getting close!

Implementing the Custom Keyboard

We have to do three things for our keyboard to work: implement the Next Keyboard button, fill in the table with the names of our user's Twitter friends, and insert text when a table row is tapped. The first step is the easiest, so we'll do that first.

Implementing the Next Keyboard Button

We might as well make all our storyboard connections at once, since there aren't many to do. Switch to KeyboardViewControllerStoryboard.storyboard, and select the view controller. In its Identity Inspector (⌥⌘3), set its Custom Class to KeyboardViewController. Now we can use the Assistant Editor (⌥⌘↩) to bring up KeyboardViewController.swift in the right pane. Control-drag to create outlets to the tableView and nextKeyboardBarButton. The properties at the top of the class should look like the following (in addition to a nextKeyboardButton hanging around from the original template):

system/PragmaticTweets-15-2/PragmaticTweepsKeyboard/KeyboardViewController.swift
```
@IBOutlet weak var nextKeyboardBarButton: UIBarButtonItem!
@IBOutlet weak var tableView: UITableView!
```

Also, Control-drag from the bar button item to create an action (not another outlet!) called nextKeyboardBarButtonTapped(). We'll write this in a bit to handle switching keyboards.

Let's code! In KeyboardViewController.swift, we'll start by clearing out junk we don't want. Delete the methods textWillChange(), textDidChange(), updateViewConstraints(), and all the contents of viewDidLoad() except for the first line, super.viewDidLoad. Also, delete the nextKeyboardButton property that the template gave us (but not the nextKeyboardBarButton property that we just created with the Assistant Editor).

Advancing to the next keyboard turns out to be easy. Our superclass gives us a method for it: advanceToNextInputMode(). So we just call that in our nextKeyboardBarButtonTapped():

system/PragmaticTweets-15-2/PragmaticTweepsKeyboard/KeyboardViewController.swift
```
@IBAction func nextKeyboardBarButtonTapped(sender: UIBarButtonItem) {
  advanceToNextInputMode()
}
```

Run the keyboard target, and, once we bring up the keyboard, we should now be able to cycle through all the keyboards, including our own, now that its Next Keyboard button works. Yay, integration!

Implementing the Table View

Next we implement the table view that shows our user's Twitter friends. For this, we need the "Twitter Utility" files that we developed for the app a while back. Select TwitterAPIRequestUtilities.swift and ParsedTweet.swift in the File Navigator and bring up the File Inspector (⌥⌘1). In the Target Membership section, click the check box to add each of them to the PragmaticTweepsKeyboard target. This means these files will be built for and deployed with each project.

Our strategy is going to be that viewDidLoad() will call the Twitter API and request the list of friends, which we'll put in an array that will serve as a table model. This means our class needs to implement the usual table protocols, UITableViewDataSource and UITableViewDelegate. Add these protocols to the class declaration:

```
system/PragmaticTweets-15-2/PragmaticTweepsKeyboard/KeyboardViewController.swift
class KeyboardViewController: UIInputViewController,
UITableViewDataSource, UITableViewDelegate {
```

We said we'd keep our list of tweeps in an array for the table methods to use, so add that as a property near the top of the class.

```
system/PragmaticTweets-15-2/PragmaticTweepsKeyboard/KeyboardViewController.swift
var tweepNames: [String] = []
```

Now we're ready to implement the UITableDataSource methods based on this array. There will be one section, it will have as many rows as the array has members, and each cell will be a default cell whose text is the array member string, prepended with an @ character. So here are the methods to do that:

```
system/PragmaticTweets-15-2/PragmaticTweepsKeyboard/KeyboardViewController.swift
func numberOfSectionsInTableView(tableView: UITableView) -> Int {
  return 1
}

func tableView(tableView: UITableView,
  numberOfRowsInSection section: Int) -> Int {
  return tweepNames.count
}

func tableView(tableView: UITableView,
  cellForRowAtIndexPath indexPath: NSIndexPath) -> UITableViewCell {
  let cell = tableView.dequeueReusableCellWithIdentifier("DefaultCell")
    as UITableViewCell!
  cell.textLabel?.text = "@\(tweepNames[indexPath.row])"
  return cell
}
```

For that to work, we need to do a few things in the storyboard. First, select the table, and in its Attributes Inspector, change the number of Prototype Cells to 1. This creates a table cell in the storyboard. Select it and change its identifier to DefaultCell, since that's what the tableView(rowForCellAtIndexPath:) method we just wrote expects. Next, right-click or Control-click the table (or show its Connections Inspector), and connect the delegate and dataSource properties back to the Keyboard View Controller icon, so our methods actually get called.

Our last task for now is to get the friend names from Twitter. There's an API for that, https://api.twitter.com/1.1/friends/list.json, which returns a richly detailed dictionary for each of our user's friends.

system/PragmaticTweets-15-2/PragmaticTweepsKeyboard/KeyboardViewController.swift
```swift
override func viewDidLoad() {
  super.viewDidLoad()
  let twitterParams = ["count" : "100"]
  guard let twitterAPIURL = NSURL(string:
    "https://api.twitter.com/1.1/friends/list.json") else {
      return
  }
  sendTwitterRequest(twitterAPIURL,
    params: twitterParams,
    completion: { (data, urlResponse, error) -> Void in
      dispatch_async(dispatch_get_main_queue(), {
        self.handleTwitterData(data, urlResponse: urlResponse, error: error)
      })
  })
}
```

This makes a call to sendTwitterRequest(), just like our others throughout the book, asking for up to 100 responses, with a completion-handler closure that calls a yet-to-be-written handleTwitterData() method to deal with the response.

handleTwitterData() gets the JSON back from Twitter, from which it needs to pull out screen names and populate the tweepNames array that the table uses. Let's go ahead and write that.

system/PragmaticTweets-15-2/PragmaticTweepsKeyboard/KeyboardViewController.swift
```swift
Line 1  func handleTwitterData (data: NSData!,
   -      urlResponse: NSHTTPURLResponse!,
   -      error: NSError!) {
   -        guard let data = data else {
   5          NSLog ("handleTwitterData() received no data")
   -          return
   -        }
   -        NSLog ("handleTwitterData(), \(data.length) bytes")
   -        do {
  10          let jsonObject = try NSJSONSerialization.JSONObjectWithData(data,
   -            options: NSJSONReadingOptions([]))
   -          guard let jsonDict = jsonObject as? [String : AnyObject],
   -            usersArray = jsonDict ["users"] as? [ [String : AnyObject] ] else {
   -              NSLog ("handleTwitterData() can't parse data")
  15              return
   -          }
   -          tweepNames.removeAll()
   -          for userDict in usersArray {
   -            if let tweepName = userDict["screen_name"] as? String {
  20              tweepNames.append(tweepName)
```

```
          }
        }
        dispatch_async(dispatch_get_main_queue()) {
          self.tableView.reloadData()
25      }
      } catch let error as NSError {
        NSLog ("JSON error: \(error)")
      }
    }
```

The top of this method is like most of our other JSON parsing in the book. What's different is the contents, which the authors puzzled out from logging the raw response: it's a top-level dictionary, with a key users that contains an array of dictionaries, each with the details of one friend. So we start parsing with a guard let that tries to get the top-level dictionary (line 12) and to get its users child as an array of dictionaries (line 13). We then clear out the current tweepNames on line 17, in preparation for repopulating it.

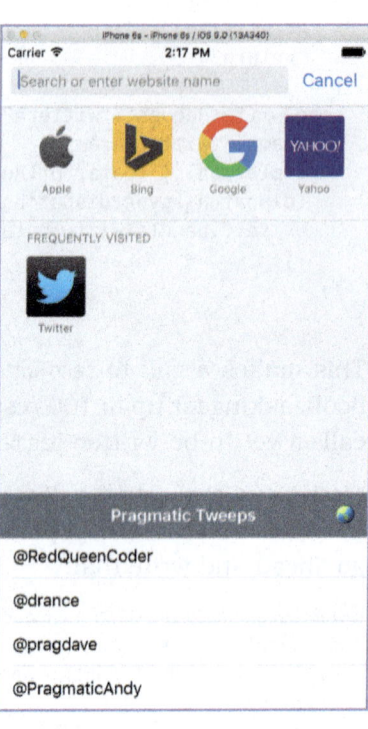

For each dictionary in the users array (line 18), we try to get the screen_name from the dictionary on line 19, and append it to the tweepNames array on line 20. Finally, lines 23–25 put a closure back on the main queue to do a reloadData() on the table.

That was a fair amount of work, but now we have live data in our keyboard. Run the keyboard target again and check out the results. Our keyboard should show a table of our friends' screen name, as seen in the figure. Awesome!

Inserting Text into the Host App

We're almost there! We can bring up our keyboard and see all our tweeps; we just need a tableView(didSelectRowAtIndexPath:) method to insert the text of a given cell into the host app.

The extension classes provided by the Xcode templates provide objects that give us a hook into our host application. These vary by the type of extension. For custom keyboards, the UIInputViewController we subclass has a textDocumentProxy object that is our gateway to the text component that we're typing into. This object conforms to a hierarchy of three protocols, which together give us everything we need to insert text into the document:

- UITextDocumentProxy—Provides the text before and after the insertion point and lets us move the insertion point

- UIKeyInput—Lets us determine if the document is empty and insert text into it

- UITextInputTraits—Indicates traits like what kind of input is needed (plain text, URL, phone number, and so on), whether autocorrection is on and what kinds of corrections it wants to make, and so forth

The one that will help us the most here is UIKeyInput. We can use that to insert the text of the selected row directly into the text component. So add the following tableView(didSelectRowAtIndexPath:) method:

```
system/PragmaticTweets-15-2/PragmaticTweepsKeyboard/KeyboardViewController.swift
func tableView(tableView: UITableView,
  didSelectRowAtIndexPath indexPath: NSIndexPath) {
    let atName = "@\(tweepNames[indexPath.row])"
    textDocumentProxy.insertText(atName)
    tableView.deselectRowAtIndexPath(indexPath, animated: true)
}
```

This just calls the textDocumentProxy's insertText() method (from the UIKeyInput protocol) to insert the selected row's text, prepended with the customary Twitter @ character, and deselects the row.

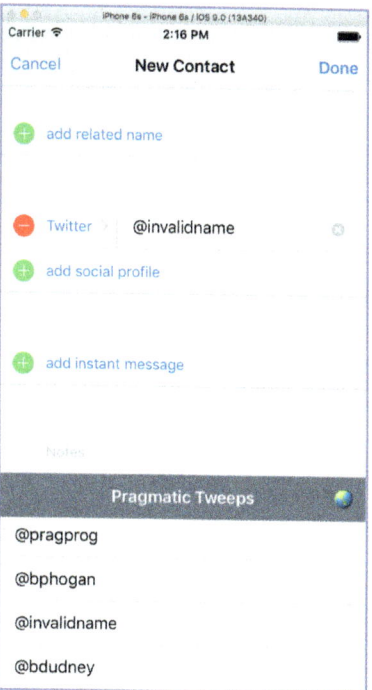

Try it out. A great place to use it is in the Contacts app, as seen in the following figure, where we've scrolled down to the Twitter field to directly insert Chris's Twitter handle (yes, he really is @invalidname).

Bundling Shared Code in Frameworks

Now we have a working custom keyboard that reuses the code from our app and extends our features into other apps on the system. However, there's one shortcut we took that's a little ugly, and cleaning it up will show us an important technique for sharing code on iOS.

"What shortcut?" you might be asking. It's back where we added our Twitter utility code, ParsedTweet.swift and TwitterAPIRequestUtilities.swift, to both the PragmaticTweets app target and the PragmaticTweepsKeyboard extension target. That means this code is built twice, and two copies of it exist in memory at runtime. Sure, it's small, so it's not a big deal for now. But as our app grows, we can do better.

When we share code between an app and one or more extensions, the right thing to do is to put that code into a *framework*, which can be called by the app and the extensions. On iOS, a framework is a shared code library and any resources it needs, such as graphics, localized strings, and documentation.

Creating a Framework

To finish this chapter, we'll move that code into a framework, and then have both the app and the keyboard extension call it. To create the framework, select the top-level project icon in the File Navigator. The content view shows properties for the main project, as well as the four current targets (the app, its unit tests, its UI tests, and the keyboard extension). Use the plus (+) button again to create a new target. From the Framework & Librar group, select Cocoa Touch Framework. When asked, call it PragmaticTweetsFramework, and accept the various defaults, making sure the Embed in Application pop-up is set to the PragmaticTweets app target.

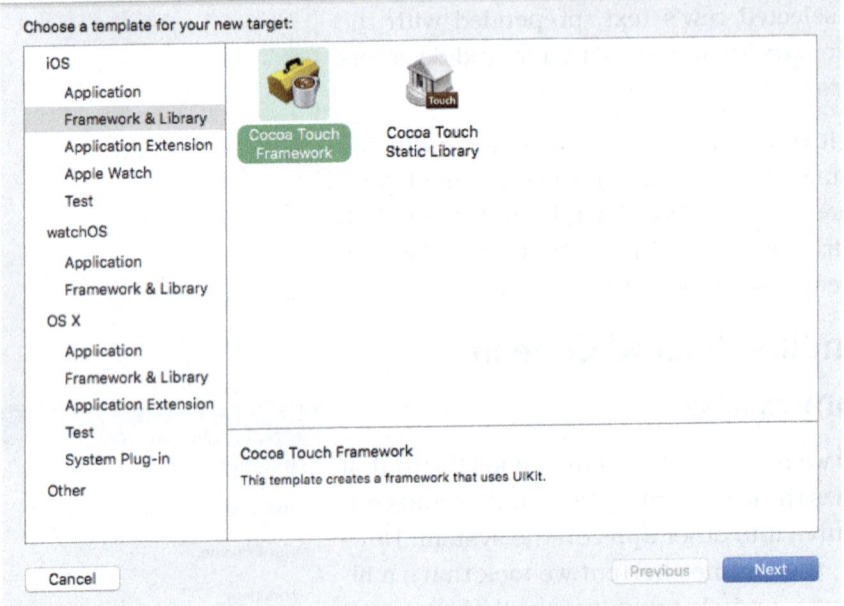

This creates a new group after the test and extension groups that contains an Info.plist metadata file and a PragmaticTweetsFramework.h C header. We won't need to work with either of these. Instead, drag ParsedTweet.swift and TwitterAPIRequestUtilities.swift into the new group, and delete the now-empty Twitter Utilities group.

To really make these files part of the framework, we need to tell Xcode to build them as part of the framework target. For each, bring up the File Inspector (⌥⌘1) and uncheck all the boxes except for PragmaticTweetsFramework.

Target Membership

- ☐ PragmaticTweets
- ☐ PragmaticTweetsTests
- ☐ PragmaticTweetsUITests
- ☐ PragmaticTweepsKeyboard
- ☑ PragmaticTweetsFramework

Once we've done this, our app and our custom keyboard targets will no longer build, since they no longer know about the ParsedTweet structure or the sendTwitterRequest() function. We need to fix that!

Importing and Using Frameworks

The way we're going to get our app and our keyboard extension to work again is to do what we always do with frameworks: we import them.

Start in the source files for the app and the extension. Every file that uses our utilities needs to import the framework. So, in RootViewController.swift, TweetDetailViewController.swift, UserDetailViewController.swift, and KeyboardViewController.swift add the following line:

```
system/PragmaticTweets-15-3/PragmaticTweets/RootViewController.swift
import PragmaticTweetsFramework
```

Earlier, when we imported frameworks like Social or Accounts, this has been all we needed to get our code running, but neither the app nor the extension builds yet. Apparently, we have more work to do.

Even though we've imported the framework, building the app still indicates it can't find ParsedTweet or the sendTwitterRequest() function. The reason for that can be found way back in *Creating Tests*, on page 104 when we talked about access modifiers. The struct and the function both default to internal accessibility, making them visible only within their own module. Now that they're in the PragmaticTweetsFramework module, they're no longer visible to the app or extension targets.

To fix this, we need to declare anything we want our callers to see as public. Start by putting the public modifier on the sendTwitterRequest() function in TwitterAPIRequestUtilities.swift:

```
system/PragmaticTweets-15-3/PragmaticTweets/TwitterAPIRequestUtilities.swift
public func sendTwitterRequest (requestURL: NSURL,
```

Now we also have to make everything in the ParsedTweet structure public (well, anything we want callers to see; we could still have private helper properties or methods). So add the public modifier to all the properties in ParsedTweet, and make the struct itself public.

```
system/PragmaticTweets-15-3/PragmaticTweets/ParsedTweet.swift
public struct ParsedTweet {
  public var tweetText: String?
  public var userName: String?
  public var createdAt: String?
  public var userAvatarURL: NSURL?
  public var tweetIdString: String?
}
```

It turns out the no-argument initializer for ParsedTweet that we got for free won't be visible outside the framework module, so we need to explicitly provide a public version of that, too, just before ParsedTweet's closing curly brace:

```
system/PragmaticTweets-15-3/PragmaticTweets/ParsedTweet.swift
public init() {
}
```

This eliminates nearly all our build problems, but there's one last error: the keyboard extension still doesn't seem to know about the framework. To fix this, select the top-level project, and let's go back to the target's properties. Select the PragmaticTweets app target and look under the Build Phases tab. In the Target Dependencies section, there are two entries: one for the extension and one for the framework. This means that the app will build those *first*, before even attempting to build the app.

Now look at the PragmaticTweepsKeyboard target's build phases. It has no target dependencies, so Xcode doesn't realize that it needs to build the framework first in order to build the keyboard extension.

To fix this, click the plus button at the bottom of the build phases section, and in the sheet that slides out, select the PragmaticTweetsFramework target.

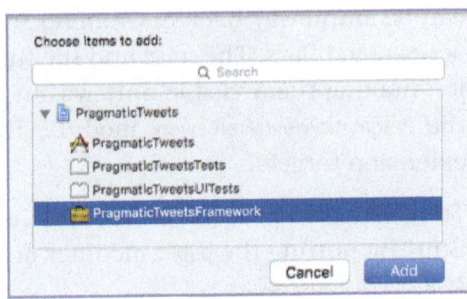

Now we should be able to build and run both the app and the keyboard extension. And our project is cleaner because we're not building the utility code twice and storing it in memory twice.

As our codebase grows, properly factoring out reusable code like this is an important consideration. In fact, we might eventually create a project just for the framework, and then add that project itself to other app projects that need it as a dependency.

iOS has a robust ecosystem of third parties developing reusable frameworks, and as you work on bigger apps, it's likely you'll end up incorporating such frameworks into your own apps and extensions. You might download a framework from a site like GitHub, or use a dependency-manager application like CocoaPods (http://cocoapods.org) to both download framework project code and keep it up-to-date.

What We've Learned

In this chapter, we've gone beyond the bounds of our original application and opened up our functionality to other apps on the user's device. By defining a custom URL scheme and implementing openURL() in the app delegate, we made it possible for other apps to open our app programmatically, and even pass in data for us to work with, like the screen name of a user for our app to fetch and display details about.

Thanks to iOS extensions, we now have the ability to go the other way: users can stay in another application but use functionality we provide through extension points like custom keyboards. We've also seen how frameworks let us share our code between app and extension, and how frameworks can also be used to share reusable code with other projects entirely.

Now that we've got a pretty complete application, our next task is going to be learning how to take a step back to figure out what to do when things go wrong.

CHAPTER 16

Fixing the App When It Breaks

Congratulations! We have completed all the code for our app. Now we can get started on the real work we will be doing as a developer: debugging.

Bugs happen. Even the most awesome rock-star programmer writes bugs. In truth, developers spend only a fraction of their time writing code. A lot more time is taken up by debugging that code. So one of the single biggest favors we can do for ourselves is to become fast and efficient debuggers.

In this chapter you'll learn about several methods for debugging, starting with the most basic one, NSLog(). We'll cover the various kinds of breakpoints, and then we'll take a nickel tour of LLDB, Xcode's default debugger. You will learn how to print to the console using a breakpoint and how to monitor a variable for changes. Finally, you'll find out how to make your app crash in the place that the problem exists and not several steps afterward.

By the end of this chapter you'll have the skills for dispatching bugs fast so you can move on to bigger and better things.

NSLog(): The First Line of Defense Against Bugs

If you've spent time among other iOS developers or gone on Stack Overflow, you've probably heard someone mention the NSLog() method, or perhaps println(), a more primitive Swift logging function. This is the first—and often the last, unfortunately—piece of debugging advice new developers receive. We first saw it way back in *for Loops*, on page 28, and have used it occasionally throughout the book, usually as a placeholder to make sure our app reached the new code we were writing.

The gist of NSLog() is that it will print a time-stamped message to the console that only we will see. It might seem counterintuitive to create output that only we will see, but it is vitally important to have some means of verifying what is happening in our program. NSLog() output also goes to a system log file, so we can collect it from beta testers to illuminate problems with our app.

Let's put ourselves in a situation where we might want to use NSLog() to find our way out. In RootViewController.swift, find the reloadTweets() method, and change the URL it uses, like this:

```
debugging/PragmaticTweets-16-1/PragmaticTweets/RootViewController.swift
guard let twitterAPIURL = NSURL(string:
  "https://api.twitter.com/1.1/statuses/foo_bar.json") else {
    return
}
```

Of course, there is no Twitter API call at the endpoint https://api.twitter.com/1.1/statuses/foo_bar.json, but this isn't a completely unrealistic scenario either. We might have mistyped the URL, or the web service API might change and remove something we were counting on. At any rate, when we run the app, we come upon an empty table. Pull to refresh, and it's still empty.

If we didn't know the root cause was the bad URL, we'd have to think of reasons this might be happening. We might be parsing the JSON incorrectly. It's possible the table is not connected to the view controller, causing self.tableView.reloadData() to do nothing. Or the delegate might not be connected, so we'd never get callbacks to tableView(rowForCellAtIndexPath:). We can mentally walk along the path our code takes from the refresh to the updated table, as shown in the following figure, in order to figure out where the problem might be, but we can't verify it without running some kind of test.

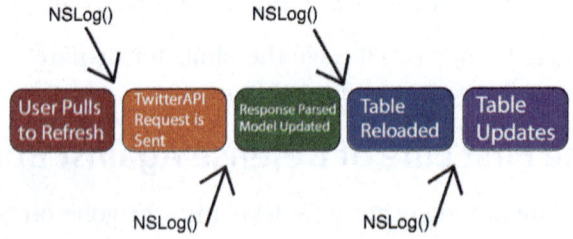

As you can see from the figure, there are at least four points in the operation where something could have gone wrong—maybe more, when we consider that some of these steps have multiple steps within them. We don't need to add an NSLog after the last operation because we already have observed that the table did not update.

By setting up feedback for every step in the process, we can now observe at what point in this chain the message breaks down: the request is sent, and the response is parsed (to some degree), but we never update the table. By throwing down a bunch of NSLog()s, we can at least focus our search on han-dleTwitterData(), since we reach that method but it fails to update the table.

Breakpoints

At this point, you might be looking at this and thinking, "There is something wrong with this. My Spidey sense detects Code Smell." Trust your Spidey sense. This solution is fraught with potential problems for your project.

Look at all those nasty NSLog statements all over our project. Ideally, we should never include an NSLog command in code that we send to Apple. Although they may help for debugging, NSLog statements are inefficient and slow our app for absolutely no reason. Additionally, any code we add to our project opens up the possibility of breaking something. What's the point of using something that might break our code in order to figure out how to fix it?

Wouldn't it be great if we could still print all our commands to the console without having to sift through all our code looking for those sneaky NSLog statements?

Breakpointing Bad

The answer to our conundrum are *breakpoints*. You have probably inadvertently already created a breakpoint when you clicked on an error icon to try to see what it said. Now we are going to create breakpoints on purpose.

Breakpoints are a feature in the Xcode development environment that lets us freeze our app at a specific point and figure out what our code is doing. They are like a photograph of all the functions that are happening, what threads are running, and what all our variables are set to at a given moment in time. Understanding breakpoints is the key to many of the debugging techniques available to us in Xcode.

Breakpoints are part of the *Low-Level Debugger*. LLDB is the debugger for Xcode. Many of its functionalities have been built into the user interface, such as the ability to create and edit breakpoints, as we'll see shortly. It also has many other commands that are not included in the user interface and need to be entered via the Xcode console. By learning these, we can become efficient debuggers...plus, we can do things that look like magic and we can impress our friends and family.

We have already seen the easiest and most common way people create breakpoints in Xcode. Click in the gutter to the left of our

```
122        do {
123            let jsonO
124                options
125            guard let
```

code to create a breakpoint on any line. Create a breakpoint in the first few lines of handleTwitterData(), inside the do catch block.

Right now when we create a breakpoint, it is kind of limited. It will just signal the code to pause on this line. That's helpful enough, as it will let us know the app got that far, which is what we were tempted to use NSLog()s for. Fortunately for us, breakpoints can do so much more than that.

Right-click (or Control-click) on the breakpoint to reveal the breakpoint menu, as seen in the figure. As you will see, one of our options is Edit Breakpoint. Let's go ahead and select that and see what we can do with it.

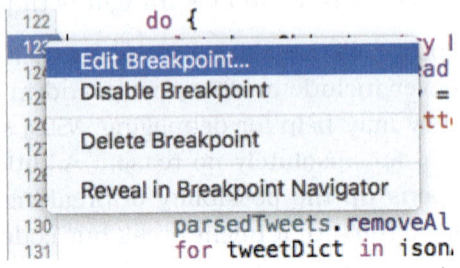

Take a look at the default options for editing breakpoints (as seen in the next figure). Notice that we have the following options:

- Add a condition.
- Ignore the breakpoint a variable number of times.
- Add an action.
- Determine if we want the program to pause or not after the program hits the breakpoint.

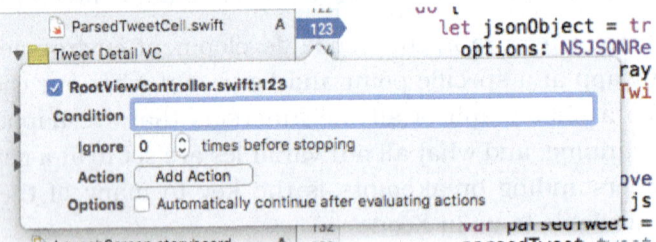

The ability to ignore a breakpoint is particularly useful if we are dealing with a large collection of items. If we were analyzing a collection of ten million keys and values but we only wanted to know what the forty-second value was, we could tell the compiler to ignore the first forty-one values and analyze the one we want to make sure it is "Life, the Universe, and Everything."

Breakpoint Logging

Rather than burdening our code with lots of NSLog() statements, breakpoints offer something easier to remove when we have finished debugging our code.

Click the Add Action button. Notice that one of our options is Log Message, as seen in the following figure.

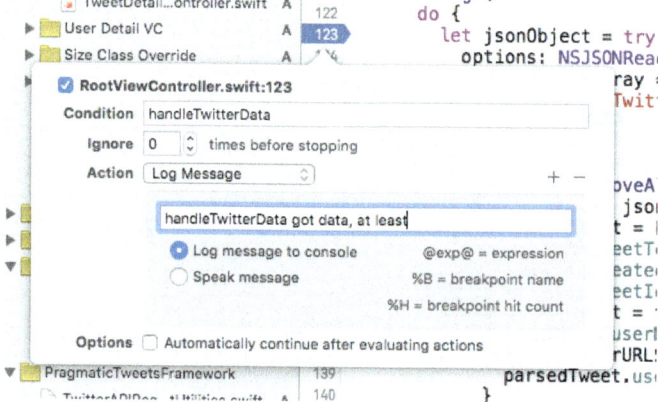

Log Message lets you do exactly that: log a message to Xcode's debug console. Since we are attaching this behavior to a breakpoint, it is easier to go back later and filter out all of our debugging tools. Instead of a lot of messy code, we have some nice, neat breakpoints, as seen in the following diagram. In fact, it gets better: breakpoints are saved only in the local user's Xcode configuration. So, if we send this project to our colleagues, there will be nothing for them to clean up.

The Debugging User Interface

So far, what we've accomplished is pretty much what we got from using a bunch of NSLog()s: we can tell how far our code got before something went wrong. But handleTwitterData() is a long method; are we seriously going to have to put breakpoints all over it and edit each to add a unique log message?

At this level of debugging detail, we can do better. Go ahead and run the app. The usual startup routine will call reloadTweets(), eventually resulting in a callback to handleTwitterData(), which is where it hits our breakpoint and the Mac automatically switches the foreground application from the iOS Simulator to Xcode. By default, stopping on a breakpoint also causes two debugging-related panes (shown in the following figure) to appear automatically.

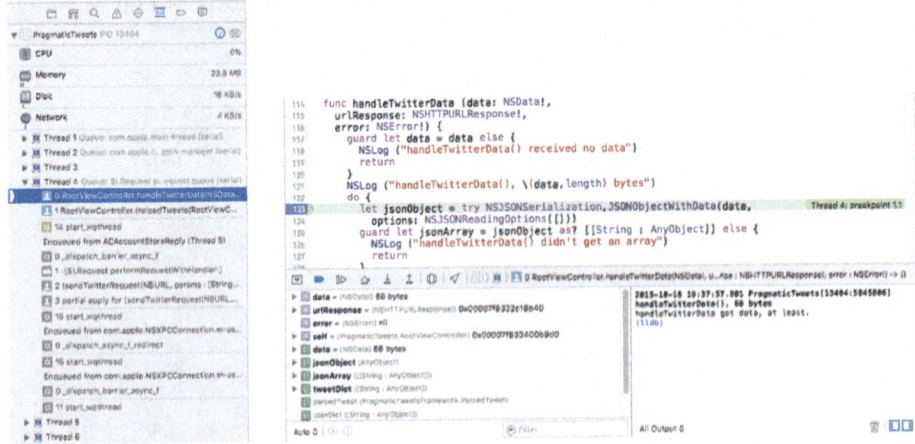

- Debug Navigator (⌘6)—Shows the app's usage of CPU time, memory, and other resources. When the app is stopped on a breakpoint, it also shows the state of active threads.

- Debug Area (⇧⌘Y)—As first mentioned in *The Xcode Window*, on page 62, this space at the bottom of the window can show output from NSLog(). When stopped on a breakpoint, it also lets us look at variables and their values. In this figure, the Debug Navigator is on the left and the Debug area is on the right.

In the bottom right of the Debug area are three important icons: a trashcan and two little boxes. The trashcan clears logged text from println() or breakpoints that log messages. The two boxes show or hide the two panes of the Debug area: the left shows a variables view, and the right shows the log messages.

At the top of the Debug area, there's a toolbar that includes a blue breakpoint icon, along with  several other tiny buttons. The breakpoint button turns all breakpoints on or off. The next button to the right is a play/pause button, which allows us to continue after hitting a breakpoint.

The next three buttons are the *step buttons*. The first, *Step Over*, allows the app to continue to the next statement in the current method and then stops again. Further right, the down and up arrow icons represent *Step In* and *Step Out*, respectively. Step In means that we will enter the statement on this line of code and stop on its first line. Usually, this is only useful if the statement is in code we've written, as the debugger can't show us the source for Apple's framework code (or third parties'). Step Out does the opposite: it lets the app

Debugging Grand Central Dispatch Issues

Back in *Putting Work on the Main Queue*, on page 156, we noted that there isn't an easy way in code to tell what queue is running our code, but breakpoints make it easy. In the figure on page 280, notice that the Debug Navigator's list of threads and queues shows us the breakpoint is stopped in Thread 4, whose GCD queue is called "SLRequest perform request queue (serial)" (it's truncated in the figure, but while you're stopped on the breakpoint, enlarge the left pane to see for yourself).

Right above that, notice that the first thread we're *not* on is called com.apple.main-thread (serial). That's obviously the main thread, meaning that the code we're currently executing is not main, so it cannot touch UIKit methods or properties, unless it puts its work back on the main queue...and we've surely learned by now that the way to do that is via dispatch_async().

continue until the current method returns, and stops on the first line in the calling method after returning.

Stepping Through Breakpoints

We are going to use the step buttons to solve our problem. Use the Step Over button to advance one line at a time after the breakpoint. A green arrow in the source will show us where we are after each step.

Our progress may go back and forth on the call to JSONObjectWithData() a few times, but it will eventually reach guard let jsonArray = jsonObject as? [[String:AnyObject]], and then enter the else block. Here, it logs the message handleTwitterData() didn't get an array, and it does an early return out of the method.

Progress! We now know we are failing because our JSON response isn't an array of dictionaries like we expect. That, of course, begs the question "what the heck is it then?"

To figure that out, we need to make another trip through this method. Press the Continue button (between the Breakpoints and Step Over buttons) to let the app continue normally. It finishes its work and fails to update the table. In the Simulator, do a pull-to-refresh on the table, which will make a new Twitter request and hit our breakpoint again. Press Step Over until we're sitting on the guard statement again.

Use the pane buttons next to the trashcan icon to make sure that both the variables and console panes are showing. The variables view shows us all the variables currently in scope: the parameters that were passed in to handleTwitterData(), local variables we've created, and self. Variables that have public properties have disclosure triangles that we can use to inspect those variables; we could look at the self.parsedTweets array this way.

Since we know we aren't getting past the guard on this line, we know that jsonObject isn't an array of [String : AnyObject] dictionaries. But why not? We can see in the variables view that there is an error that was passed into us, but it's nil, so that's probably not the problem. Also, if the try had failed on NSJSON-Serialization.JSONObjectWithData, we would have been thrown to the catch block, so parsing the JSON isn't the problem either.

We need details! Fortunately, LLDB is here to help us out. Any of these variables can be inspected in multiple ways. Let's hypothesize that the Twitter API has used its response to tell us about an error. That would be in the url-Response. Right-click (or Control-click) urlResponse, and from the pop-up menu, choose Print Description Of "urlResponse", as shown in the following figure.

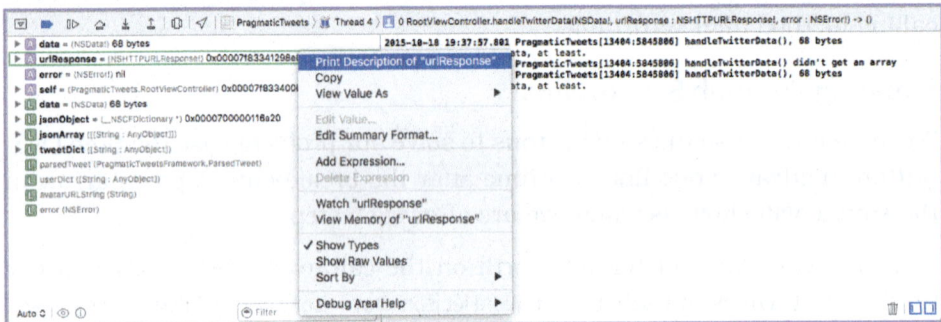

The Debug area will fill in with a log of the object, in this case formatted like a dictionary (only the first few lines are shown here, reformatted to fit the book's layout):

```
Printing description of urlResponse:
<NSHTTPURLResponse: 0x7f83341298e0> { URL:
  https://api.twitter.com/1.1/statuses/foo_bar.json?adc=phone&count=100 }
  { status code: 404, headers {
    "Content-Encoding" = deflate;
    "Content-Length" = 80;
    "Content-Type" = "application/json;charset=utf-8";
```

Clear as a bell, we can pick out status code: 404. We asked for an endpoint that doesn't exist, and that leads us back to the underlying problem.

Sometimes, we don't even have to print the description. When possible—which usually means for simple things like numeric values and strings—the variables view will show a simple description in the list itself, and we can mouse over a variable in the source while we're stopped on a breakpoint to see its value.

For images, an "eye" icon on the debugging toolbar sometimes lets us even see a popover of an image variable selected in the variables list.

Exception Breakpoints

Another class of breakpoints happens when dealing with uncaught exceptions. Certain problems, instead of failing or crashing immediately—which would at least let Xcode show us which line of code blew up—will throw an NSException object. The exception bubbles up through calling methods until someone deals with it. If nobody does, we usually end up seeing it on a page of scary-looking machine code with a message like libsystem_kernel.dylib`_pthread_kill:. Lot of good *that* does us.

Pretend that Xcode is a dinosaur. Xcode goes about its merry way grazing on a bunch of leaves until it accidentally eats some poisoned berries. Xcode starts feeling kind of sick but decides to keep walking and consuming leaves, even though it knows it is sick. It finally succumbs to the poison and falls over dead a mile away from the poisoned berries.

As the caretakers of the Xcode dinosaur, we want to make sure we don't keep poisoning it, and it would be helpful to us if the Xcode dinosaur knew not to wander away from the berries so that we can figure out where they are and clear them out.

That is what *exception breakpoints* are for. When we set an exception in the code, we are telling Xcode that if it encounters something that is going to eventually kill it, we want it to stop going and show us where the bad stuff is. In more concrete terms, we want a breakpoint when the exception is raised, not 20 returns later after it hasn't been caught.

Creating an exception breakpoint is easy. We start in the left pane with the Breakpoint Navigator (⌘7), which shows all breakpoints currently set for our project, organized by class and method. Down at the bottom of the screen we have a plus 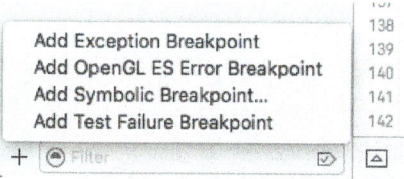 sign. Clicking on the plus button will open a dialog allowing you to create a few new types of breakpoint.

Choose the Add Exception Breakpoint option. This will create a breakpoint that will automatically stop the program at the exact location where an error will occur. It is a good idea to set the exception breakpoint at the beginning of our program to deal with any issues we might encounter while we are coding. We only need one exception breakpoint.

Fortunately, we need exception breakpoints a lot less in Swift than we did in Objective-C and earlier versions of iOS and Xcode. For example, an array index out of bounds mistake—like asking for the eleventh member of a ten-member array—would be an exception in Objective-C and would dump us into the main() method that launched the app. In Swift, array index out of bounds shows up as fatal error: Array index out of range, with Xcode pointing to the offending line.

Still, other classes in Foundation sometimes throw NSExceptions, and exception breakpoints are the key to making sense of them.

Symbolic Breakpoints

If we look at the list of breakpoints we can create with the plus button in the Breakpoint Navigator, we observe that there is an option called Add Symbolic Breakpoint.

A *symbolic breakpoint* is a breakpoint programmed to pause the app whenever a specified method is called. The thing that makes this interesting is that we can set a symbolic breakpoint on *any* method in *any* class, not just the classes we wrote. So we could set a symbolic breakpoint to pause the app whenever viewDidLoad is called. Since viewDidLoad exists in all our UIViewController subclasses, this could be a good way of monitoring behaviors that span the scope of our project.

The following figure updates our hypothetical control flow to use a symbolic breakpoint. If we put a breakpoint on UITableView's reloadData() method, we'd stop on any call to it, whether directly from our code or as a side effect (for example, from navigating between scenes).

Unfortunately, in Xcode 7, the symbol in the Breakpoint Editor pop-up needs to be written in Objective-C syntax, not Swift. So, setting the symbol to UITableView.reloadData() won't do anything, but -[UITableView reloadData] will pause as we expect. It's been this way since Xcode 6, so we're kind of resigned to it staying this way.

We have covered a lot of different ways that we can use breakpoints in our program. At this point, you might be wondering which is the best way. The best way is the one that works for you. We have debugged our program using several kinds of breakpoints, so it is possible to do the same task many different ways. Pick which one you like best or what works best for your specific issues.

Setting Up Your Debugging Environment

When we're in serious debugging mode, it can sometimes help to make sure our debugging tools are ready to deploy immediately. With that in mind, we are going to set up a special debugging tab with an immersive debugging environment. In programming, being organized is vitally important. It will help our efficiency to have a dedicated space where all of our debugging tools are laid out consistently.

Think of your debugging tab like you would your kitchen. When you go to your kitchen to cook, you can get a recipe started right away because you know where all your tools are. If you didn't know where to find your measuring cups and the food processor, it would take a lot longer to get something started.

First thing we'll do is to create a dedicated debugging tab. You can create a new tab by pressing ⌘T, just as you would in a web browser, but there is a better way to create a dedicated debugging tab.

Choose Xcode > Preferences or press ⌘ to access the Preferences window. The third tab from the left is Behaviors. This panel controls all of the behaviors an app will have at each and every stage of its life, along with controlling behaviors present in both automated testing and using OpenGL. Since these skills are a little beyond the scope of a beginner book, we won't be going over them, but we just wanted you to know they are there for when you want to take your next steps.

We want to make sure that we can see all of our testing tools while we are running and debugging our application. Find the Running section of the list. Instead of just waiting to hit a breakpoint, we want to see the debugger when the app starts, when it pauses, and when it generates output.

Joe asks:
How Do You Get Line Numbers in the Editor?

Maybe you've noticed that our screenshots of the breakpoint gutter on the left side of the code editor show line numbers and wondered why your Xcode isn't showing line numbers. We are big fans of showing line numbers. It's a nice reminder that once one of our files hits 1,000 lines, it's clearly time to refactor that code. Also, it makes the breakpoint gutter a little wider.

To turn on line numbers, go to Xcode's preferences and select the Text Editing section. The first check box under the Editing tab is Line numbers, and that's where you can turn them on.

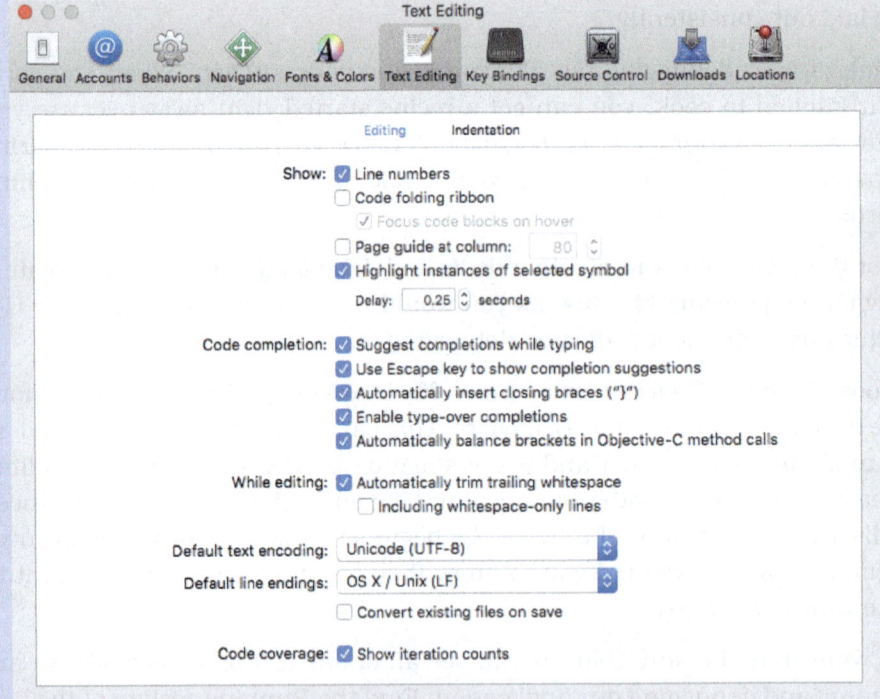

While here, there are a number of other preferences you can set, and the Indentation tab lets you stake out your position in the never-ending tabs-versus-spaces war (although this is also available as a setting on your project as a whole, and the project setting takes precedence over your local preference).

Another useful Xcode preference group is the "Fonts and Colors" group, which features various themes for styling your editor's color scheme and font sizes.

Click Starts and look at the options available to us. You will see an option that says "Show tab named *empty text box* in *drop-down menu*." Click on the check box to ensure that it is selected. In the text box, name it something appropriate, like Debugging. Lastly, go into the drop-down menu and select Active Window.

The last thing we need to do before moving on to other parts of the run cycle is to make sure our debugger is showing. If we look at the option two below the Show Tab option, we will see one that says "Show debugger with *drop-down menu*." Again, click on the check box to ensure this option is selected and choose Variables & Console View from the options. Our Behaviors for the Starts menu should look the way it does in the following figure.

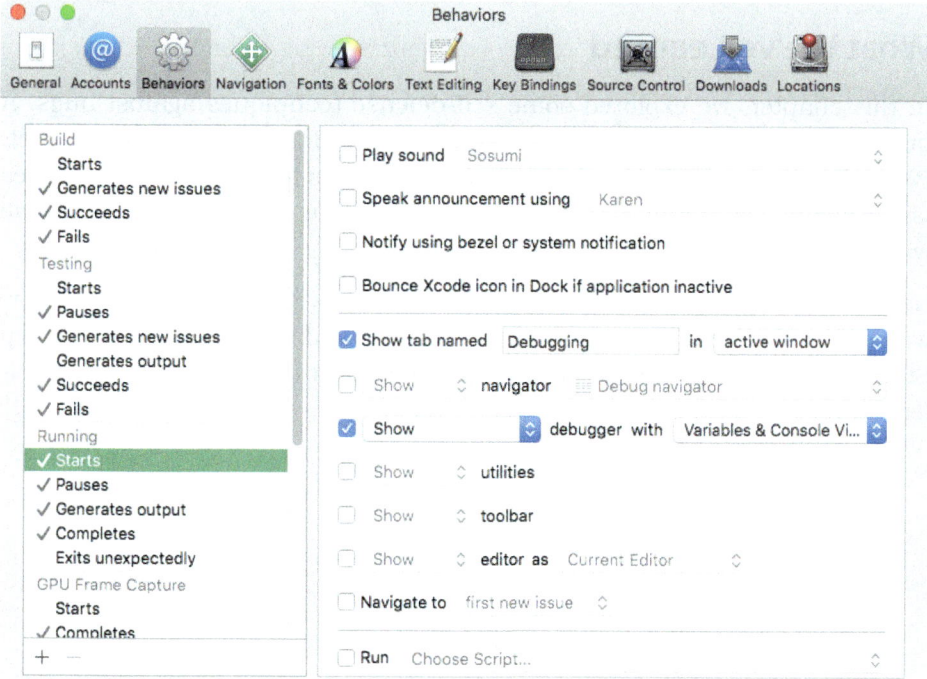

Next, let's move on in the left column to the behaviors we want when we pause our program. We want to show the debugger with Variables & Console View, but now we also want to select the option above that one, which selects a navigator window to show, and we want the Debug Navigator. Make sure your options look the way they do in the following figure.

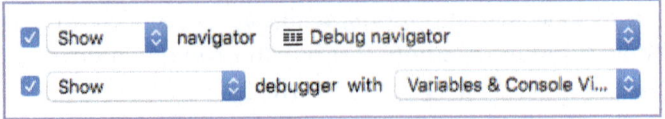

Lastly, in Generates Output make sure that you have it set to show the debugger with Variables & Console View.

There! Now we have a handy debugging environment that will always be there for us when we need it. Since this is your debugging environment, make sure you go through and look at all the options you think you might want or need. There is nothing that says everyone must have the same options, so feel free to customize this to suit you.

What We've Learned

In this chapter, we explored some self-defense techniques against bugs. A bug we wrote in five seconds might take five hours to track down and correct. Being able to effectively use the tools provided to us to track down our issues faster means we free up more of our time for doing the fun coding stuff we want to be doing.

Next, we tackle our final challenge. We have our awesome bug-free app. Now we need to do the most important thing of all: publish the app on the App Store so that we can rake in the dough, or at least the accolades of our colleagues!

CHAPTER 17

Publishing and Maintaining the App

Look how far we've come! We started from nothing, learned our way around in playgrounds, and then started on our Twitter app. By learning new things and adding new features, we've been able to build a genuinely useful app. So far, though, we're the only ones who've seen it.

In this chapter, we're going to get our app out of the Xcode build-and-run cycle and into the world where people can actually see and use it. We'll start by packaging the app for submission to the App Store and letting testers try it out before we release it to the world. We'll finish up by talking about what's next, both for our app and for our journey through iOS development.

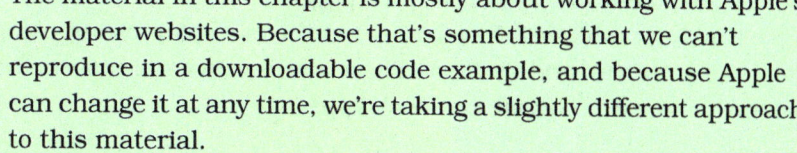

A Change of Pace

The material in this chapter is mostly about working with Apple's developer websites. Because that's something that we can't reproduce in a downloadable code example, and because Apple can change it at any time, we're taking a slightly different approach to this material.

In this chapter, we'll walk through the steps of submitting apps for testing or publishing in general terms, but we won't expect you to necessarily run through the process of actually publishing your copy of PragmaticTweets to the public.

Getting with the Program

To publish an app on the App Store, we need to have a paid account with Apple's developer program. The free level of membership lets us run apps on our own device, but to use the publishing resources of the App Store, we need to pay up. When you're ready to take this step, sign up at https://developer.apple.com/programs/.

You can join the program as either an individual or an organization. Joining as an individual means your own name is shown on App Store listings, which means the authors' apps literally show up as being by "Chris Adamson" or "Janie Clayton." To join as an organization like a company or nonprofit, there are many more requirements, such as being legally incorporated and having a D-U-N-S Number that Apple can use to verify your organization's legal status. You can't just make up a cool doing-business-as (DBA) name and expect Apple to roll with it.

As of February 2016, membership costs US$99 per year, and covers development for all Apple platforms: iOS (including iPhone, iPad, Apple Watch, and Apple TV), Mac OS X, and Safari extensions. Along with the ability to publish apps through the App Store, membership benefits include TestFlight testing services (which we'll cover shortly), and access to pre-release versions of iOS, OS X, and Xcode. Members also get two *technical support incidents* per year, which provide answers from Apple support engineers to problems in your code. These are great for really tough problems that aren't easily fixed by searching Stack Overflow or Apple's own developer forums.[1]

Once you've joined the program, there are two sites you'll use to handle your development and publishing needs.

Member Center

The Apple Developer *Member Center*[2] is where you manage assets specific to your development process. The front page has links to helper sites like the Apple Bug Reporter[3] and the forums, but the essential resource here is "Certificates, Identifiers, and Profiles." These are the electronic assets that identify and authenticate both you and your apps.

Certificates authenticate your identity to Apple and Apple's identity to you. When you first used "Fix Problem" to run the app on your device, Apple set up these certificates in the OS X keychain on your Mac. Anytime we run on the device or submit to Apple, these certificates need to be found, which is important to remember when upgrading to a new computer. Fortunately, Xcode's preferences allow us to import and export developer accounts in a format that includes this data.

Profiles are used for two distinct purposes. A *development profile* allows an app to be run on one or more specific devices. Combined with a matching

---

1. https://forums.developer.apple.com
2. https://developer.apple.com/membercenter
3. https://bugreport.apple.com

certificate, it tells the iPhone "it's OK for this developer to install this app on this device." On the other hand, a *distribution profile* asserts your identity to Apple itself; it's used in the distribution process to prove to Apple that "we know this person, and it's OK for them to submit apps for review."

Finally, *identifiers* are just unique strings to identify a given application in the store, or to work with some advanced iOS features like iCloud and Passbook (now called "Wallet" in iOS 9) that need globally unique identifiers.

iTunes Connect

If the Developer Center is the heart of development for the App Store, iTunes Connect[4] is all about distribution.

As a new member, your first task in iTunes Connect will likely be agreeing to multiple legal agreements for Apple to distribute your apps for you, and setting up banking information (so you can get paid!). Later, you can come back here to check out sales reports on published apps, and see how the app is being rated and reviewed on the App Store.

The most important section of iTunes Connect is "My Apps," where we assemble everything we need to get our app on the store: artwork, pricing data, descriptions and other metadata, and so on.

In fact, we haven't done any of those things yet, so let's go back to Xcode and get our app ready for the store.

Preparing the App for Submission

Currently, our app lacks the polish that we'd expect to see on the App Store. There's more to address than we can really do in a book of this size—entire books are devoted to iOS app design, after all—but at an absolute minimum, we really need a proper app icon. Since we haven't created one, what we see in our Simulator home screens is the iOS "generic" icon.

App Icons

By default, our app has no icon, and it has the name we gave it when we created the project. It looks like the figure—not pretty.

Let's get to work on that. We'll start with the name being cut off. Click on the project icon at the top of the File Navigator, select the Pragmatic Tweets target, and click the Info tab. We can set some of the app's metadata here, including

---

4. https://itunesconnect.apple.com

the Bundle Name, which defaults to the internal PRODUCT_NAME. Instead, just change the bundle name to Prag Tweets.

Now about that generic icon. The first step here is to bring in a real designer. "Why?" you might ask. Why slow things down by bringing in someone else?

Deadlines are a fact of life. We have all been forced by one deadline or another to do something we didn't want to do. But when that happens, skip features; don't skip design. The biggest mistake developers make is not having a designer in the loop from the beginning. The design of your app is the way that users will perceive it. After spending countless hours thinking about the internal workings of your app, you don't want to leave the users' interaction to chance. Just as classes need to be designed, user experiences need to be designed.

Interfaces designed by programmers tend to look like programming languages: specific and detailed but tedious. Users don't want tedious; they want it to *just work.* If you expose the switch to toggle the 20 percent feature, that leaves 80 percent to wonder at the complexity of the app.

Programmers fight for control; designers fight for the user. Make sure your app has someone fighting for the users. Don't ship an app that has not been designed from start to finish. If the idea is worth your time and energy, then it's worth getting a designer involved.

So, eating our own dog food, we had Scott Ruth of BraveBit App Studio[5] design a proper icon for Pragmatic Tweets.

One advantage of bringing in a designer who is specifically experienced with iOS design is the dizzying number of app icon sizes that are now required for app store submission. In previous editions of this book, we've tried to list all of these, but between iPhones at single, double, and triple resolution, different app icons for iPhone and iPad, additional icons for the settings app and Spotlight, it is now far too much for us to cover. Take a look at Icon and Image Sizes in the iOS Human Interface Guidelines if you're interested. But we're very much of the opinion that it can and should be your designer's problem.

Scott delivered our icons in the form of an Assets.xcassets file, as seen in the figure on page 293. This file has been present, albeit empty, since we started our app. By default, it has a single entry called AppIcon, with blank spots for all the known image sizes and pixel depths. Aside from providing app icons, this file can also be used for any images shown by the app (such as those

---

5. http://bravebit.com

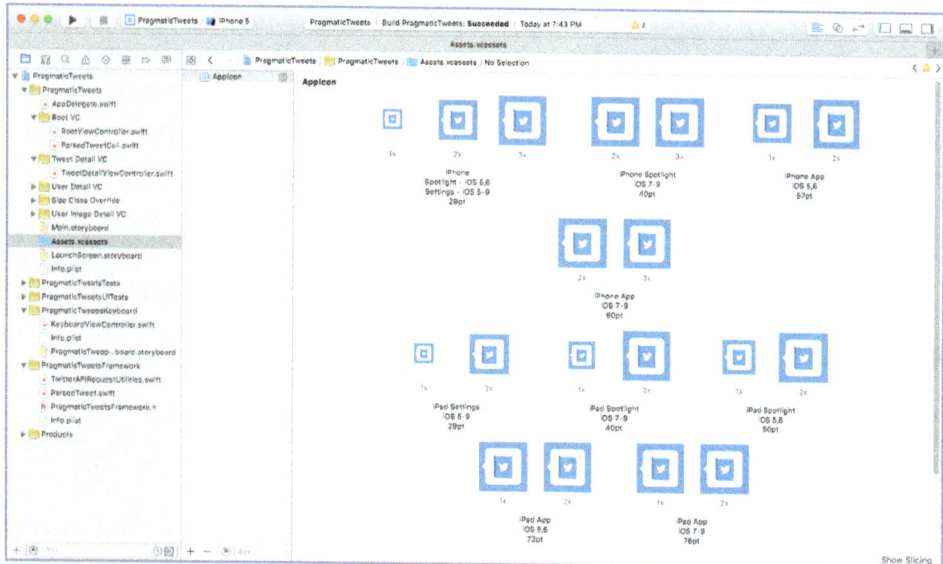

used in UIImageViews). Simply add a file at 1x and 2x resolutions to the collection, and they become available to use for image views in storyboards. They can also be read by code by using the initializer UIImage (named:), passing in the filename without an extension.

With a proper name and icon, our app looks a lot more polished on the home screen, ready for our users to open it.

Launch Images

Another bit of visual polish we can attend to is what users see at the instant the app is launched. When they tap the app icon, iOS presents a *launch image* until the app is fully initialized and showing its first view.

Prior to iOS 8, the launch image was a static .png file. Initially, Apple's guidance was that the launch image should look exactly like the app's first screen so that the user wouldn't notice the time it took to create and populate the first view. In practice, though, many apps used the static image as a "splash screen," displaying a logo for the app or perhaps its developer or publisher.

The problem with this scheme is that designers had to create static launch images for every combination of screen size and portrait-versus-landscape orientation, meaning they potentially needed a dozen or more different, yet related, launch screen designs. And that was *before* iPhones came in four different sets of screen resolutions and iPads in two.

Clearly, there needed to be an approach that wasn't tied to explicit screen dimensions. The LaunchScreen.storyboard offers a launch image that will work at any combination of size, resolution, and orientation. The trick is that this file is a genuine iOS view, in a genuine iOS storyboard, just like our app's Main.storyboard.

By default, LaunchScreen.storyboard has only a title and a copyright statement on a white background. But these labels are set with autolayout constraints, so they will work at any combination of device shape, orientation, and pixel depth. All we need to do to have a fancy launch image is to customize this view with colors, images, fonts and styling, and so on.

We'll leave that as an exercise...for your designer.

Setting the App ID

Our next step requires a little thinking ahead. We submit apps to the App Store via Xcode, but that won't actually work if Apple doesn't know what we're sending them. It turns out we need to do a little work on the Developer Center to prepare for our upload.

To upload an app to the store, we'll need a distribution profile. For that, we usually need an *App ID*. We say "usually" because there are certain edge cases where this isn't necessary. The trade-off is that while certain features like iCloud require a unique identifier for each app that uses the feature, there are a few scenarios where multiple apps can share a "wildcard" identifier and work together. The latter case is rare and hard to do, so it's best to just always create App IDs for our apps.

With your browser, log in to the Developer Center and visit the Certificates, Identifiers, and Profiles section. In the Identifiers section, choose App IDs, and press the + button to create a new App ID. We just need two entries here: a name (which cannot have spaces or special characters), and the app's bundle ID. We created the bundle ID way back in *Our First Project*, on page 59, when we combined a reverse-DNS style unique string with the name of the app. You can check the bundle ID in Xcode by going to the ..xcodeproj in the File Navigator and looking at the App target; it should be something like com.pragprog.yourhandle.PragmaticTweets.

So, in the form, enter a memorable string for the App ID (we used PRAGMAT-ICTWEETSIOS9), and under Explicit App ID enter the bundle identifier. We don't need any of the listed App Services for Pragmatic Tweets, but keep in mind this is how you would signal to Apple that your app uses features like Apple Pay or Push Notifications.

App IDs Are Forever

You might notice that the App IDs and bundle identifiers in the screenshots all have a gratuitous ios9 in them. This is because we screwed up by using com.pragprog.yourhandle.PragmaticTweets for a previous iOS SDK book. App IDs are globally unique, so once we claimed that bundle identifier for the previous book's app, it became unavailable to us for this book. So we had to come up with a new bundle identifier for this chapter to get our app submitted.

Two takeaways here: App IDs are universal, and they're pretty much forever.

Creating a Distribution Profile

Next, we use the App ID to create a Distribution Profile. This is what Xcode's uploader will send to Apple to prove that we're a legitimate member of the developer program, authorized to upload apps for testing, review, and sale.

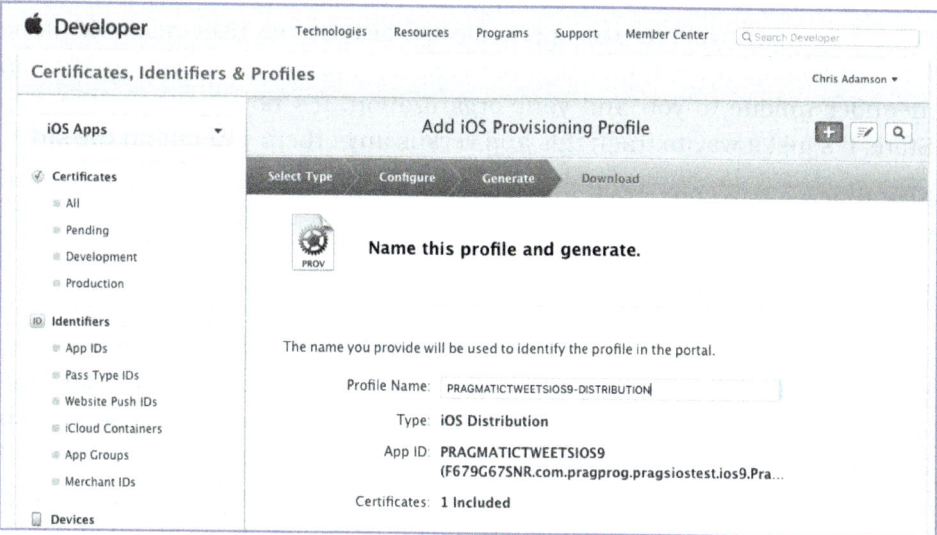

Still in the Certificates, Identifiers, and Profiles section, under Provisioning Profiles choose Distribution. Click + to create a new distribution profile. This lets us choose which kind of profile we want: whether we're sending an app to the iOS or tvOS App Store, or whether we're doing *ad hoc distribution*, which lets us send the app to a limited number of registered devices, usually for testing. We just want the regular iOS App Store, so choose that and click Continue.

Next, we choose which of our App IDs we're creating the profile for (the one we created in the previous section, of course), and on the following screen, which of our signing certificates will be used to prove our identity as registered iOS developers (there should only be one certificate, so choose that). After these screens, the profile file is created and can be downloaded to your computer. Click the button to download it, and then drag the downloaded .mobileprovision file onto the Xcode app icon to install it into Xcode.

By doing these steps, we've prepared Xcode to send our app to Apple. Now we need to tell the App Store what we're sending it.

Creating an App Store Entry

For App Store distribution, we also need to prepare at least a minimal entry in iTunes Connect to tell them what we're going to upload. Log in to iTunes Connect and visit the My Apps section. The main page here is a list of all apps ever uploaded from your account. It will initially be empty. Click the + button to create a new iOS app.

There are only four fields that need to be set to create a basic iOS app in iTunes Connect: whether the app is for iOS or tvOS, its user-readable name (like "Pragmatic Tweets"), its bundle identifier, and a *SKU*. The SKU is an identifier unique to you and your organization. It's not visible on the App Store; it's just a way to track this app versus any others you put on the store.

Now that we have prepared a distribution profile and an App Store record, we're finally ready to upload our app!

Uploading the App

Our first step to upload the app is to do a *release build*. So far, Xcode has been giving us *debug builds*, telling the compiler to insert symbols into the executable code that makes it easier to debug. That's what lets us stop on breakpoints and figure out what's going on. But at this point, our code should be fully debugged, so we can eliminate the cost and size of these debugging aids, and instead tell Xcode to build the fastest-running file it can. In practice, a release build will often run 10% or more faster than an equivalent debug build.

Archiving

It's possible to use the scheme selector to create a release build for the device —and this is a good practice for a final round of pre-submission testingem- dash;but let's cut to the chase. Select a connected iOS device or the Generic iOS Device from the scheme selector, then choose File > Archive. The Archive command does two things for us: performs a release build, and packages it in a format that's suited for distribution.

When the Archive operation completes, a new Organizer window opens. It has two tabs: Archives and Crashes, with the Archives tab showing a list of apps on the left, and for each of them, every build of that app that's ever been created on this machine.

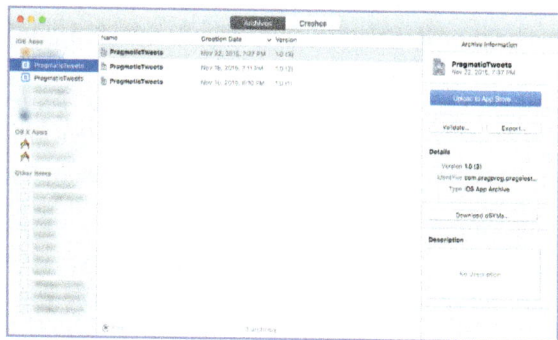

Each archive is listed by its build and version number. These are set in the build target's General info pane, and have different uses. The version number is meant for the users and expresses the recency of the app and its features. The build is for internal use, and tracks different revisions of a given version. In other words, a given version may have many builds. We need to update the build every time we want to make a new archive, and update the version when we want to do a new release to users.

With an archive selected, click the Validate button on the right. This does an up-front validation of the code and our signing credentials prior to uploading to Apple. It reports which signing identity will be used to identify the binary to Apple, and which distribution profile is associated with the submission (which it gets by matching the App ID to the app's bundle identifier).

Extensions Are Like Separate Apps

If you try these steps yourself, you will get hung up on the keyboard extension we wrote back in *App Extensions*, on page 259. That's because the extension has a different bundle identifier (com.pragprog.yourhandle.PragmaticTweets.PragmaticTweetsKeyboard), and

Extensions Are Like Separate Apps

therefore requires its own App ID and distribution profile to match it.

It's straightforward to create those assets on the Member Center, but in writing this chapter, we also discovered that keyboard extensions have another requirement imposed by iTunes Connect: because of the privacy implications of our code seeing everything the user types, keyboard extensions require a URL for a publicly visible privacy policy.

In the interests of simplicity, we've removed the keyboard extension from our App Store submission screenshots.

Uploading

Now we're ready to upload our app to the App Store. For this to work, we need to have at least a minimal record entered into iTunes Connect that matches our app's bundle identifier, something we did back in *Creating an App Store Entry*, on page 296.

Click the Upload to App Store button to begin the transfer. It will take a while to get started, but eventually you'll see the progress bar as the upload begins.

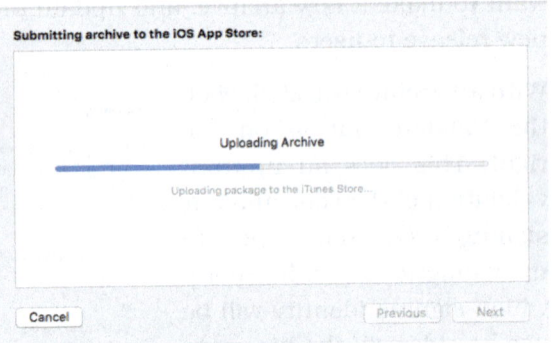

Eventually, the upload finishes and, well, we're not on the App Store yet, but we've made a big step forward by getting the app off of our own machine. That's critical, because there's one big thing we should do before we release: *make sure our app actually works.*

Testing with TestFlight

Of course, we've been testing our app all along; we had a whole chapter about testing our code early on. But developers never see their apps the same way users do; we come in with biases and assumptions, and with insider knowledge of how the app works. A typical user has none of these things.

We need some typical users!

Lucky for us, uploading our app gets us a lot closer to typical users. Previously, we could only run the app on a device directly connected via USB cable to our Mac running Xcode. But now, from iTunes Connect, we can send the app to testers all around the world and have them try it out.

To do that, we're going to use a testing platform called *TestFlight*. This service allows us to send our app to testers of our choosing, lets them install it prior to its release on the app store, and lets them send us their feedback. All they need is their own iOS devices.

Testing with Internal Testers

Let's try it out. On the iTunes Connect page, go to My Apps and visit the Pragmatic Tweets app. Among the tabs at the top of the page is TestFlight, so let's go there.

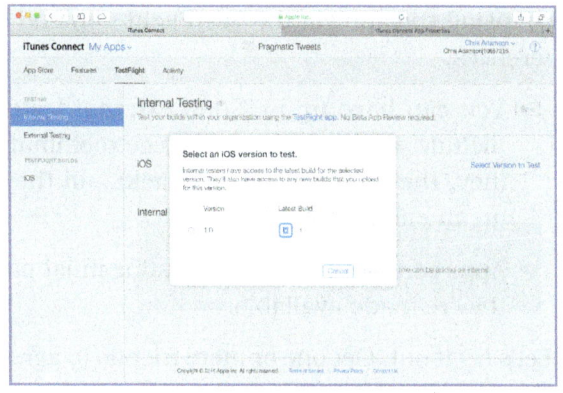

On the left side of the page, there are two menu items at the top, Internal Testing and External Testing, followed by a list of platforms under the heading TestFlight Builds.

Let's start with Internal Testing. These are builds that go to trusted members of your own development team. We can have up to 25 internal testers, including ourselves. In the Internal Testers area, click the + to add yourself as a tester.

To send a build to yourself or other team members, click Select Version to Test and choose the version/build you just uploaded. Then click Begin Testing.

Beginning a test cycle sends out invitation emails to all members of your team. The invitation includes two important links: a download link to your app, and a link to the TestFlight iOS app. Once you receive the email, open it on your device, and download TestFlight from the App Store. When you run it, you'll also have to install a special profile; this is like the provisioning profiles that let Xcode put apps on your device, but in this case it lets the TestFlight app install apps.

Once the TestFlight app is set up, return to the email and click the Start Testing link. This will download the app and install it on your device. Run the app as usual, and look for any bugs you missed. Back on the Mac, the internal testing page will show that you've installed and run the app.

This is all well and good, but our own developers and colleagues aren't always going to be the most rigorous critics. For that, we need to go outside our organization.

Testing with External Testers

The opposite of internal testers is, of course, external testers. These are people who aren't your fellow team members in iTunes Connect. In fact, you might never know them by anything more than an email and their feedback on your app.

External testing works like internal testing in a lot of ways: you choose a version and build to test, and an email is sent to all the testers, allowing them to install the app via the TestFlight app and try it out. There are two big differences:

- You can have up to 2,000 external testers of your choosing. These can include your mom, your college roommate, your lover, your worst enemy (hey, they'll give good feedback)...all they have to have is an iOS device an an email address.

- Apps sent out for external testing must pass a brief review by Apple before they're made available.

Let's try it out. Get one or more friends to agree to help test the app and collect their emails. Click External Testing from the left-side menu; this brings up a page showing which version/build combination we're testing, and who our testers are. For our screenshots, Janie isn't on Chris's team in iTunes Connect, so she's the external tester. Click the + next to External Testers to add testers by name and email.

In the iOS section, click the Add Build to Test link to choose any build we've uploaded (after a brief processing delay immediately following the upload). When we pick one, we go to a screen in which we describe what the app is (mostly for the benefit of Apple's TestFlight reviewers), and what we want our testers to focus on. Also, provide an email where testers can contact you.

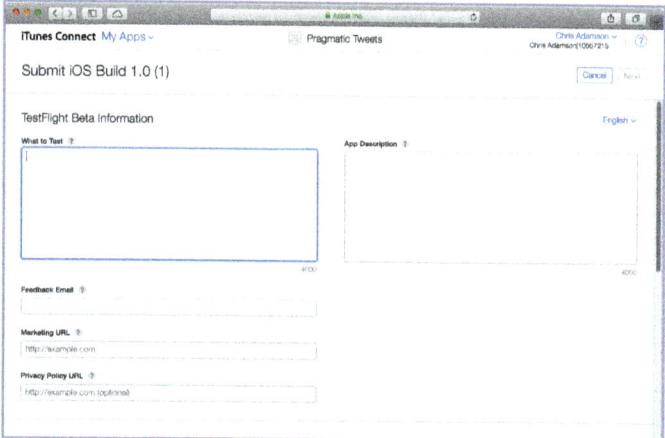

Approval can take as little as 30 minutes, though when we tried it, we added the build on a Sunday and didn't get approval until the next day. At any rate, once approved, your external testers all receive an email linking them to the TestFlight app and our app to test, just as we saw with the internal testing.

Fixing Problems

And now we wait. Our testers will be notified by email that a new build is available, and by installing the TestFlight app, they can install our app. If they find bugs, they can return to the TestFlight app and click the Send Feedback button.

And chances are they will find bugs. It's just a matter of time, so we wait and...oh look, there's an email from Janie, with an attachment that gives us the specs of the device she was testing on. Let's see what her feedback says.

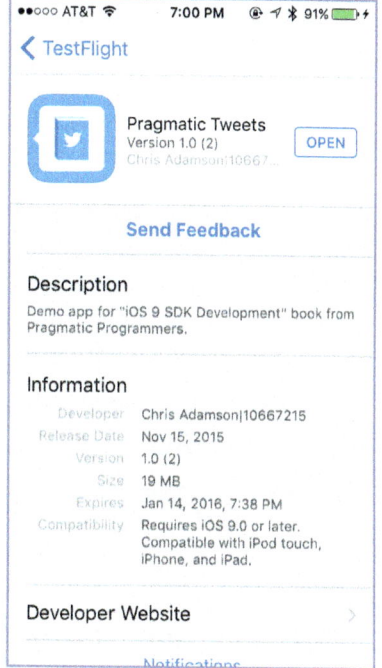

The app does nothing at startup? Oh darn, that's right. Way back when we started parsing tweets, we just wrote out errors to the console, and left ourselves a mental to-do to fix that.

Let's take a moment to fix that, because we said we would pop up an error alert or something, and we've never seen how to do that. If we clear out our Twitter accounts in the Settings app and run again, we see that the message no twitter accounts configured is written to the console. We can search and find that this message is sent from sendTwitterRequest() in TwitterAPIRequestUtilities.swift.

We can't really put up an error alert in that part of the code, because that utility function has no references to any part of the user interface, and because it's a general-purpose function that's called from many places in our code. We should give this general-purpose method a way to the send the error to the UI part of our codebase if there's a problem.

If we look at the signature of the sendTwitterRequest() that we created, it has a completion handler of type SLRequestHandler, which is a type that receives an NSData, NSURLResponse, and NSError. So we could provide our own NSError and call the completion handler ourselves when we can't continue because there are no Twitter accounts configured.

Let's do that. In sendTwitterRequest(), replace the guard that checks our Twitter accounts as follows:

publishing/PragmaticTweets-17-3/PragmaticTweets/TwitterAPIRequestUtilities.swift

```
guard twitterAccounts.count > 0 else {
  NSLog ("no Twitter accounts configured")
  completion(nil,
    nil,
    NSError (domain: "PragmaticTweets",
      code: 1000,
      userInfo: [NSLocalizedDescriptionKey :
        "no Twitter accounts configured"]))
  return
}
```

This calls the completion closure with no data, no response, and an NSError of our own devising. The error takes a string that indicates the module or framework that spawned the problem, an arbitrary error code as an Int, and a dictionary with further details. As we create many different errors, we would do well do formally collect the error codes, perhaps in an enum. As for the dictionary, the most useful key to provide is NSLocalizedDescriptionKey, as this provides a human-readable error message.

There are other places we should employ similar techniques to pass errors back to callers, but for now, let's show this error in the UI. Back in RootView-Controller, go to the beginning of the handleTwitterData() method and handle the NSError if there is one.

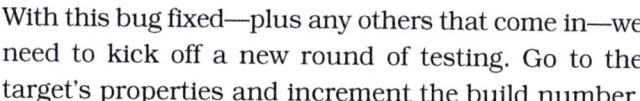
publishing/PragmaticTweets-17-3/PragmaticTweets/RootViewController.swift

```swift
if let error = error {
  dispatch_async(dispatch_get_main_queue()) {
    let alert = UIAlertController(title: "Error",
      message: "An error occurred: \(error.localizedDescription)",
      preferredStyle: .Alert)
    let ok = UIAlertAction(title: "OK", style: .Cancel, handler: nil)
    alert.addAction(ok)
    self.presentViewController(alert, animated: true, completion: nil)
  }
  return
}
```

This creates a new kind of view controller, a UIAlertController, which gives us the modal error dialog we see throughout iOS. Its initializer takes a title, a message string, and a style, for which UIAlertControllerStyle.Alert shows the typical middle-of-the-screen modal error dialog. The alert controller also lets us specify multiple buttons to be shown with the alert, each as a UIAlertAction. Each action takes a title for the button, a style, and a closure to be run when that button is tapped. We add the actions to the alert controller, and then our view controller shows the alert controller with presentViewController().

With this bug fixed—plus any others that come in—we need to kick off a new round of testing. Go to the target's properties and increment the build number, since we will want to track this build separately. Then, as before, we archive, upload to Apple, go to TestFlight in iTunes Connect, mark this new build as the one to test, and click Start Testing to send the new and better build to our testers. Testers will get an email telling them about the new build, and the TestFlight app will let them install it over the old one and continue testing.

Publishing and Beyond

After some give-and-take with our testers, we'll eventually reach a point where we're ready to release our app publicly. To do this, we need to provide the materials that will appear on the App Store page. This metadata is prepared in iTunes Connect, under the App Store tab.

There is a *lot* of material that needs to be provided for an App Store submission. The App Information section contains the basics of the app that we already provided, like its name, bundle identifier, and SKU. We can also assign one or two categories here, set a rating, and provide a custom license agreement (if we don't, a standard Apple license is used).

In Pricing and Availability, we set a price for the app. Prices are arranged in "tiers" that are similar across different regions and currencies. Tiers are shown in your local currency; once you select a non-free price, click Other Currencies to see how the app will be priced around the world.

Preparing for Submission

Most of the metadata that users see on the App Store is in the section titled Prepare for Submission. Filling out this section takes a while, and in companies or organizations, may be the responsibility of a project manager or release manager rather than individual developers.

Screenshots

Depending on whether the app is built for iPhone, iPad, or both, we have to provide screenshots showing the app running on those devices, at various sizes. For an iPhone app, we need to provide at least one screenshot on a 3.5-inch device (iPhone 4 series), and a 4-inch device (iPhone 5). If we support larger screens, there are tabs for 4.7-inch (iPhone 6 and 6s) and 5.5-inch (iPhone 6 Plus and 6s Plus). For iPads, we have a tab for the regular iPad screen size, and another for iPad Pro.

There are two easy ways to get screenshots. From the Simulator, we can choose File > Save Screen Shot (⌘S) at any time to save a screenshot to the desktop. So by just switching devices in the Xcode scheme selector, we can collect screenshots at the needed sizes. If we want to get a screenshot from a device instead of the Simulator, we can use the Organizer window, which has a Save Screenshot button that grabs the device's current screen and saves it to the desktop.

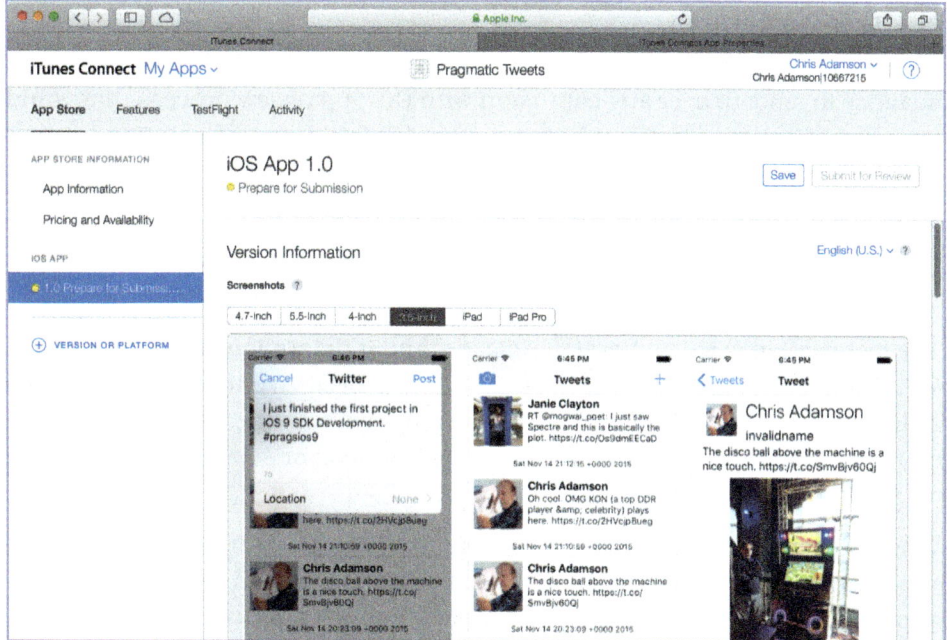

Descriptive Metadata

The Description is where we get to make the case for our app to shoppers on the App Store. The challenge is that although we can enter up to 4,000 characters of text, only the first line or two is visible by default, and only intrepid readers will click the More button that shows the rest. So it's critical to make our case with a catchy first line, like a witty slogan that captures the essence of the app, or a quote from a rave review.

We can also provide keywords that will assist with searching, along with support and marketing URLs. Because of the way the App Store works, this is our users' only way to contact us, so developing a page that greets users, helps them out, and gives them a way to provide feedback is a good defense against one-star reviews, which unfortunately are the easiest and most common way for users to communicate with developers.

For presentation in the App Store UI and web page, Apple also requires a 1024×1024 app icon (which hopefully our designer has provided us with!), a publicly visible version number, and content information for assigning an age rating based on the possible inclusion of elements like profanity, violence, and simulated gambling.

App Review and Release

A section called App Review Information allows us to provide information in advance to smooth over any confusion with the app review process that could lead to a rejection. There's a Notes section for free-form information to send to the reviewers, and contact information for Apple to call or email us if they have questions.

If our app provided access to a service we hosted online, we would want to include a username and password in the Demo Account section.

The last section is called Version Release, and it determines how the app will be released to the public if and when it is approved. We have three options: automatically release it to the App Store immediately once it's approved; hold on for us to manually release it via iTunes Connect; or schedule it for release on a given date and time.

When all our metadata and screenshots are uploaded and entered, we can send it to Apple by clicking the Submit For Review button. At this point, the app goes into a queue for review by Apple. The review process typically takes about a week, during which time the app will appear in iTunes Connect as Waiting for Review. Once a reviewer gets to the app, it will show as Under Review. If it's rejected, the status will be Rejected, and we'll get an email explaining the reasons for the rejection. At this point, we'll have to address the problem in our code, upload a new build, and submit for review again.

Once the app is approved, it will briefly appear as Processing for App Store, and then Pending Developer Release if we chose a manual release, Pending Apple Release if we chose a scheduled release, or Ready for Sale if we chose for it to be made available immediately upon approval.

Success!

Our app is on the store and we are done!

Kidding! We're just getting started.

Once version 1.0 is out the door, inevitably our attention will turn to version 1.1. We'll include features that didn't make the cut for 1.0, and incorporate feedback from users and reviewers. By visiting the Activity tab in iTunes Connect, we can see ratings and reviews from the App Store. There's also an App Analytics section that shows us sales data.

It's also possible that our app has bugs bad enough to crash the app. Hopefully not, but maybe we force-unwrapped an optional somewhere that we shouldn't have. When users allow their diagnostic data to be sent back to

Apple, that actually shows up on our end in the Organizer. For any of the builds we've archived, the Crashes tab shows us where the app crashed. However, this only works if we keep the archive for that build on this machine. The internally stored archive allows the crash report to be *symbolicated*, meaning that the crash report's data about memory addresses where crashes occurred can be compared against the archive to figure out what line of code caused the crash. Without the archive, crashlogs are almost impossible to make heads or tails of.

Next Steps

You've learned so much to get to this point, but there's a lot more you can master in the iOS SDK. Where to go from here depends in part where you want to focus your interests. The platform is so large, it's possible to be a generalist with an interest in many different iOS technologies, but also very rewarding to focus on a few specific areas. We'll finish up with a look ahead to some directions you might want to go from here.

Networking

Our Twitter example was made much easier with the Social framework, though we did get to make pretty much raw web-service calls to Twitter REST end-points with the SLRequest class. Of course, many iOS apps call web APIs as their basic functionality and aren't using the Social framework. For general-purpose networking, the first place to look is in Foundation, specifically at the NSURLSession class and its various helper classes. NSURLSession offers performant, asynchronous networking that lets you work pretty much the way we did with Twitter: compose a request, send it off, parse the response in a closure, and pull out the returned NSData.

Networking is an area where third-party frameworks have won over a lot of iOS developers. One of the most popular is AFNetworking,[6] and its more Swift-friendly equivalent, Alamofire. [7]

Productivity

Many iOS apps help users get the most value out of their data: finances; appointments; and various kinds of personal records, from contacts to comic book collections. For these productivity applications, you may want to learn Foundation's UIDocument class, which is the cornerstone of saving documents

---

6.   https://github.com/AFNetworking/AFNetworking

7.   https://github.com/Alamofire/Alamofire

to the local filesystem or iCloud. Another option is *Core Data*, a data persistence framework that provides object-relational mapping: the power and speed of a database with the simplicity and elegance of an object model.

Some of the user's data is also exposed to apps via iOS frameworks. You already saw how the Photos framework lets us work with the user's photo library. The *Contacts* framework lets you work with the Address Book entries, while the *MessageUI* framework allows apps to compose email or SMS/iMessage posts. This way, your app has the ability to provide access to the user's personal data and organizational features, without leaving your app in favor of built-in Apple apps like Contacts, Mail, and Messages.

Games

Games are among the most popular apps on the iOS platform, and there are lots of ways to get started. For 2D games, *Sprite Kit* offers a great place to get started, by letting you focus on the design, physics, and gameplay, while handling the drawing, animation, and collision detection for you.

2D graphics can also be created with *Core Graphics*, the system framework for vector-based drawing.

3D games are a stiff challenge, but frameworks exist here to help as well. For cross-platform code, the *OpenGL ES* library is a good place to start, with lots of resources and sample code for drawing 3D graphics. The newer *Metal* framework offers higher performance, at the price of being limited to Apple platforms, because it gets its performance gains by cutting out cross-platform abstractions and working directly and explicitly with the graphics chipsets found on iOS devices.

Media

iOS devices are popular for watching video and listening to audio: music, podcasts, movies, TV shows, livestreams...it's hard to find an iOS user who doesn't enjoy at least one of these. Most media developers should start with *AV Foundation*, which offers capture, editing, export, and playback of both audio and video. Playback support includes local files, remote URLs, and streams using the HTTP Live Streaming protocol. Media developers can also use the *Media Player* framework to access the music library on the device.

For more advanced media processing needs, you can drop down to the lower-level media processing frameworks, *Core Video* and *Core Audio*, which offer more power but also much more complexity.

For a bigger challenge and a bigger screen, tvOS is an iOS-based platform for writing apps for Apple TV. While the interaction model with a remote is different than the touch-based gestures of iPhone and iPad screens, many of the APIs will be familiar.

Device-Specific Features

Finally, there are a number of frameworks that exist specifically to provide access to the unique hardware on iOS devices. *HealthKit* is the first stop for developers interested in physical data collected by sensors like the step sensor in the iPhone or the heart-rate sensor in the Apple Watch. *Core Motion* provides access to the accelerometer and gyroscope data, allowing developers to react to the motion and orientation of the device as the user handles it.

And it's not just the iOS devices themselves anymore. *HomeKit* allows your app to interact with Internet-of-things devices that support Apple's HomeKit standards. And *Core Location*, which helps your app figure out where in the world it is, can work with *iBeacons*, which are used in indoor positioning systems, like helping customers find their way around a store.

What We've Learned

In this final chapter, we put our app in the hands of users. We learned how to package up the app in an archive, both for uploading to Apple and for use in handling crash reports sent to us by end users. Before publishing, we used TestFlight to have testers other than the developers try out the app on their own devices and give us feedback. After that, we saw all the steps involved with submitting the app to Apple for approval and publishing on the App Store.

We finished up with a look at what's next. The iOS SDK is much too big to fit in one book, so it's up to you to figure out what kind of app you want to write next, and where you can find the features in the iOS frameworks to create it. With the foundations learned in the preceding chapters, you're ready to build on your knowledge and create great new things.

Index

Core Data

For databases on iOS, you need Core Data. Find out how to leverage it best from your choice of Objective-C or Swift versions.

Core Data in Objective-C, Third Edition

Core Data is intricate, powerful, and necessary, and this book is your guide to harnessing its power. Core Data is Apple's recommended way to persist data: it's easy to use, built-in, and can integrate with iCloud.

Learn fundamental Core Data principles such as thread and memory management. Discover the powerful capabilities integrated into Core Data, and how to use Core Data in your iOS and OS X projects. All examples are updated for OS X El Capitan, iOS 9, and for the latest release of Core Data. In this third edition, the focus remains on Objective-C.

Marcus S. Zarra
(250 pages) ISBN: 9781680501230. $38
https://pragprog.com/book/mzcd3

Core Data in Swift

Core Data is intricate, powerful, and necessary. Discover the powerful capabilities integrated into Core Data, and how to use Core Data in your iOS and OS X projects. All examples are current for OS X El Capitan, iOS 9, and the latest release of Core Data. All the code is written in Swift, including numerous examples of how best to integrate Core Data with Apple's newest programming language.

Marcus S. Zarra
(250 pages) ISBN: 9781680501704. $38
https://pragprog.com/book/mzswift

More for iOS

Learn how to do full-stack testing of your iOS apps and get up to speed with the latest version of WatchKit.

Test iOS Apps with UI Automation

If you're an iOS developer or QA professional tapping through an app to reproduce bugs or performance issues you thought were solved two releases ago, then this is your book. Learn how to script the user interface, assert correct behavior, stub external dependencies, reproduce performance problems, organize test code for the long haul, and automate the whole process so the machine does the work. You'll walk through a comprehensive strategy with techniques using Apple's tools that you can apply to your own apps.

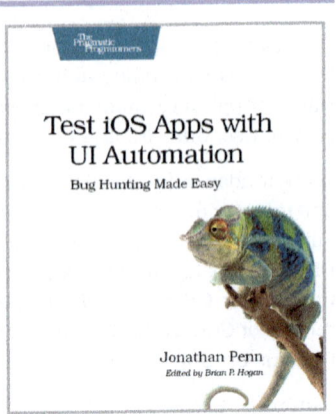

Jonathan Penn
(224 pages) ISBN: 9781937785529. $36
https://pragprog.com/book/jptios

Developing for Apple Watch, Second Edition

You've got a great idea for an Apple Watch app. But how do you get your app from idea to wrist? This book shows you how to make native watchOS apps for Apple's most personal device yet. You'll learn how to display beautiful interfaces to the user, how to use the watch's heart rate monitor and other hardware features, and the best way to keep everything in sync across your users' devices. New in this edition is coverage of native apps for watchOS 2. With the new version of the WatchKit SDK in Xcode 7, your apps run directly on the watch.

Jeff Kelley
(200 pages) ISBN: 9781680501339. $36
https://pragprog.com/book/jkwatch2

Pragmatic Programming

We'll show you how to be more pragmatic and effective, for new code and old.

Your Code as a Crime Scene

Jack the Ripper and legacy codebases have more in common than you'd think. Inspired by forensic psychology methods, this book teaches you strategies to predict the future of your codebase, assess refactoring direction, and understand how your team influences the design. With its unique blend of forensic psychology and code analysis, this book arms you with the strategies you need, no matter what programming language you use.

Adam Tornhill
(218 pages) ISBN: 9781680500387. $36
https://pragprog.com/book/atcrime

The Nature of Software Development

You need to get value from your software project. You need it "free, now, and perfect." We can't get you there, but we can help you get to "cheaper, sooner, and better." This book leads you from the desire for value down to the specific activities that help good Agile projects deliver better software sooner, and at a lower cost. Using simple sketches and a few words, the author invites you to follow his path of learning and understanding from a half century of software development and from his engagement with Agile methods from their very beginning.

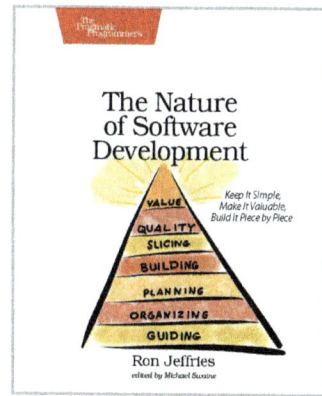

Ron Jeffries
(178 pages) ISBN: 9781941222379. $24
https://pragprog.com/book/rjnsd

The Pragmatic Bookshelf

The Pragmatic Bookshelf features books written by developers for developers. The titles continue the well-known Pragmatic Programmer style and continue to garner awards and rave reviews. As development gets more and more difficult, the Pragmatic Programmers will be there with more titles and products to help you stay on top of your game.

Visit Us Online

This Book's Home Page
https://pragprog.com/book/adios3
Source code from this book, errata, and other resources. Come give us feedback, too!

Register for Updates
https://pragprog.com/updates
Be notified when updates and new books become available.

Join the Community
https://pragprog.com/community
Read our weblogs, join our online discussions, participate in our mailing list, interact with our wiki, and benefit from the experience of other Pragmatic Programmers.

New and Noteworthy
https://pragprog.com/news
Check out the latest pragmatic developments, new titles and other offerings.

Save on the eBook

Save on the eBook versions of this title. Owning the paper version of this book entitles you to purchase the electronic versions at a terrific discount.

PDFs are great for carrying around on your laptop—they are hyperlinked, have color, and are fully searchable. Most titles are also available for the iPhone and iPod touch, Amazon Kindle, and other popular e-book readers.

Buy now at *https://pragprog.com/coupon*

Contact Us

Online Orders:	*https://pragprog.com/catalog*
Customer Service:	*support@pragprog.com*
International Rights:	*translations@pragprog.com*
Academic Use:	*academic@pragprog.com*
Write for Us:	*http://write-for-us.pragprog.com*
Or Call:	+1 800-699-7764